PRAISE FOR *MY MOTHER. BARACK OBAMA. DONALD TRUMP. AND THE LAST STAND OF THE ANGRY WHITE MAN.*

———————

"Kevin Powell's writing never fails to be both profoundly insightful and brilliantly inciting. His words are unassuming daggers, piercing the skin of racism in America, gender inequality, misogyny, and the sociopolitical impact of our greatest icons while expertly avoiding clichés and pretension. His work provides a compassionate examination of our contemporary ethos and inspires us to move beyond apathy into full social accountability."

—DOMINIQUE MORISSEAU, OBIE AWARD–WINNING PLAYWRIGHT

"Hip-hop has been the most influential cultural force of the last fifty years, and no writer has understood its power quite like Kevin Powell. It's not just music. It's a lens to understand the world, and Kevin Powell wields it to further our understanding of racism, manhood, and our troubled political times. Make no mistake about it: whether writing about Harvey Weinstein, his mother, or American football, this book is hip-hop in the best sense of the phrase, in that it challenges the readers to step outside of themselves. Powell takes us to a place beyond the beats. It's a place most fear to tread, but if we hope to salvage this country, it's a place we all need to understand."

—DAVE ZIRIN, WRITER AND EDITOR FOR *THE NATION*

"Kevin Powell thoughtfully weaves together the connective tissue between gender, race, sexuality, pop culture, and sports through a series of raw, incredibly personal essays. He masterfully uses his own life experiences to force us to take an uncomfortable look at how we've been conditioned to adopt, accept, and extend the unfortunate American traditions of hate and violence."

—JEMELE HILL, ESPN ANCHOR, COMMENTATOR, WRITER

MY
MOTHER.
BARACK
OBAMA.
DONALD
TRUMP.

And the Last Stand of
THE ANGRY WHITE MAN.

KEVIN POWELL

ATRIA BOOKS
New York London Toronto Sydney New Delhi

ATRIA
BOOKS

An Imprint of Simon & Schuster, Inc.
1230 Avenue of the Americas
New York, NY 10020

First Atria Books hardcover edition September 2018

ATRIA BOOKS and colophon are trademarks of Simon & Schuster, Inc.

For information about special discounts for bulk purchases, please contact Simon & Schuster
Special Sales at 1-866-506-1949 or business@simonandschuster.com.

The Simon & Schuster Speakers Bureau can bring authors to your live event.
For more information or to book an event, contact the Simon & Schuster
Speakers Bureau at 1-866-248-3049 or visit our website at www.simonspeakers.com.

Manufactured in the United States of America

10 9 8 7 6 5 4 3 2 1

Library of Congress Cataloging-in-Publication Data is available.

ISBN 978-1-5011-9880-9
ISBN 978-1-5011-9881-6 (ebook)

For the rainbow children—today, tomorrow, in the future. . . .

The tragedy of life is not death but what we let die inside of us while we live.
—NATIVE AMERICAN PROVERB

For a long time, I was scared I'd find out I was like my mother.
—MARILYN MONROE

The answer, my friend, is blowin' in the wind.
—BOB DYLAN

Well it's like cranes in the sky
Sometimes I don't wanna feel those metal clouds.
—SOLANGE

We are all part of one another.
—YURI KOCHIYAMA

The only way to deal with an unfree world is to become so absolutely free
that your very existence is an act of rebellion.
—ALBERT CAMUS

CONTENTS

Allow me to re-introduce myself. . . . xiii

Letter to a Young Man 1

Will Racism Ever End? Will I Ever Stop Being a _____? 13

The Day Our Prince Died 35

A Letter to Tupac Shakur 41

Why Is Baltimore Burning? 65

Cam Newton, and the Killing of a Mockingbird 73

The Liner Notes for the A Tribe Called Quest Greatest
Hits Album That Never Happened 123

JAY-Z and the Remaking of His Manhood. Or, The Crumpled
and Forgotten Freedom Papers of Mr. Shawn Carter. 129

Me and Muhammad Ali 163

Hamilton, O.J. Simpson, Orlando, Gun Violence, and What
the Fourth of July, Alton Sterling, Philando Castile, and the
Dallas and Baton Rouge Police Shootings Mean to Me 169

Prodigy and the America That Raised Him 205

Re-defining Manhood: Harvey Weinstein and how his
toxic manhood is our toxic manhood, too 211

My Mother. Barack Obama. Donald Trump. And the Last
Stand of the Angry White Man. 225

Acknowledgments 283

MY
MOTHER.

BARACK
OBAMA.

DONALD
TRUMP.

And the Last Stand of
THE ANGRY WHITE MAN.

Allow me to re-introduce myself. . . .

M y name is Kevin Powell and I am a writer, I am an artist. I say this with great pride, today, because I have not felt this sort of thing for many years, until the middle of this decade, to be mad honest. You see, I have known I wanted to be a writer since I was a child, kept it to myself because in the world in which I was born, given my name, and told, almost immediately, what I could and could not do, who I could and could not be, there were no examples for poor people like me to be an artist, to be a writer. Or at least it was never told, not to me. So: I buried my dream of being a writer and guarded my imagination closely, except for those days in our Jersey City, New Jersey, tenement where I would speak aloud, as my mother went about her business, of my "friends" who were not there, of the countless characters I imitated from our broken-down television set. From where did I get that imagination and that love of storytelling? Why, my ma, of course, she of the American South, the Low Country of South Carolina: folks who are and speak in a beautiful, tongue-twisting dialect they call Geechee. My mother's stories captivated me, then, now, regardless of how many times I heard them, because they were a story of people, of a people who had done nothing that bad to be so black and blue, yet they were. And it was my ma who took me, when I was eight years old, to the Greenville Public Library on John F. Kennedy Boulevard in Jersey City, and allowed me to roam free, to find myself, my imagination, my voice, amongst those dusty books with the strange titles. As my voice changed and my height grew I would come to inhale the words of Ernest Hemingway, Edgar Allan Poe, William Shakespeare, Charles Dickens, S. E. Hinton—writers who fed me, fed my American hunger for adventure, for escape, for a better life than what I had. And thus a writer I became, eventually, like for real, at Henry Snyder High School when my twelfth-grade English teacher, Mrs. Lillian Williams, spotted something in the way I wrote and encouraged me to enter a city-wide essay contest. I won, at age seventeen, the only thing I had ever won in my life, except for a few medals as a track runner. I was shocked, proud, felt alive in a way I could not express, in those innocent days, as a woefully shy teenager with a bad temper and dangerously low self-esteem. By age twenty, while a full-time student on a financial aid package at Rutgers, the State University of New Jersey, as they call it, I was not only writing for various campus newspapers but also commuting from Central Jersey to New York City collecting my first paychecks as a professional writer. That young Kevin said as he raced to the top of the world: *I am on a mission and in a hurry.* In my early twenties I enlisted in the army of fearless and idealistic poets in New York spitting our hastily scribbled words here there everywhere; by my mid-twenties I was writing cover stories for Quincy Jones's *Vibe* magazine, and at that publication I would also document the life and times of Tupac Shakur; and on behalf of *Rolling Stone* magazine I was there in Las Vegas when

'Pac tragically died at twenty-five. As for me, by age thirty I was burnt out, a has-been, a drunk, suicidal, dazed and confused about what to do with myself as a writer, contemplating on many a night how my rites of passage had swung so wildly between great success and embarrassing failure—

No one said the walk of a writer would ever be easy. . . .

All these years later I present to you this, my thirteenth book, a collection of thirteen essays—*blogs*—written over the past couple of years, yes, but really reflecting much of what I have experienced and learned since I was that puny kid-writer so many chapters ago. It is called *My Mother. Barack Obama. Donald Trump. And the Last Stand of the Angry White Man.* because my mother has been very sick for the past two years (and because we have a very complicated relationship); because Barack Obama changed history, but, then again, he did not; and because Donald Trump has ushered in a wave of hatred and venom and violence that is new but is also not new. These things have been deeply etched in my mind, and I've had a flurry of writing gush like a volcano from my spirit in a way I have not since the 1990s. And I have digested the reactions to what I have penned the past few months, via email, via social media, after my speeches, in random spaces. I feel I have found my voice again, one that was lost for long stretches, save my autobiography—*The Education of Kevin Powell: A Boy's Journey into Manhood*—which was a monumental struggle to produce before this collection. Indeed, that autobiography, so stressful to relive, so traumatic in getting it out of me, took up seven years of my life. But then I was free, because I told the truth, my truths, without fear, and without care of who would read it or what they might say.

So here I stand, today, an utterly grateful man married to an amazing woman; I am a skateboarder and a hiker, a two-time New York City Marathon runner, and I am also a vegan and a yogi long ago done with alcohol and those other things far too many of us writers absorb and do, as if sabotaging or destroying ourselves will somehow make us better writers, greater artists. *No*. . . . I am not interested in what I call slow suicide, nor do I feel one has to be miserable or in constant rage or pain or chaos to create one's art. Been there, done that, I am good. These days I am a very different human being, in what I hope are merely the middle years of my life, writing with a great sense of urgency, about race, about manhood and gender and gender identity, about class, about mental health, about politics and social issues, about popular culture, about sports, about violence and hate, about love and peace, about our America, which is precisely why the context of this book is that it is an autobiography of America. If I can turn the mirror on myself, then we all must make an effort to do the same. I remain a woefully imperfect, hypersensitive, and battered human being, but I am not afraid to say that about myself, or about us, or this country, or this planet. What I said many years ago, I say again this moment: *I am on a mission and in a hurry.* What I said many years ago, I say again this moment: I only wanted to see my name, my byline, in a magazine or newspaper or on the cover of a book one time. Anything beyond that is more than I could have ever imagined, or expected, given where I come from. What I said many years ago, I say again this moment: Writing is as important to me as breathing. What I said many years ago, I say again this moment: I just want to be a good man, a good writer, a good helper, and a good servant to others. And I just want us all to be free, truly free. That is my prayer, that is my dream, and that will never change. . . .

Letter to a Young Man

Dear Sam:

I have read the very open and very fearless email you sent to me several times since it first arrived a few months ago. I know we have met in person and had a good talk about life, about manhood; but something of your words on my computer has been shadowing me, whispering to me time and again that you deserve a greater response, that I need to give you the sort of exchange I wish an older man had had with me when I was in my very early twenties, as you are now.

I am humbled by your words, by your thoughts that I have somehow figured out this thing called manhood, that I am leading a movement to redefine how we men and boys see ourselves, this world, how we relate to women and girls on this earth. No, Sam, I do not have it figured out, not even close, nor am I leading any movement. I remain a very imperfect human being, a very imperfect man.

As I creep toward my fifth decade of life, I do know now more than ever that how we in America, and across the globe, have come to define manhood is absolutely destructive to us, to women and girls, and to our planet. There is no other way to say it, Sam. I did not know any of this when I was growing up as a boy in New Jersey where I was born and raised. My father and mother never married, I had no father figure or role model to speak of my first eighteen years, so I sought out male images wherever I could find them: on television, in movies, in books, at church, while playing sports formally and informally, and on the streets of Jersey City, my hometown. In each and every single one of those spaces I was taught, as a child, as a teenager, as a young man where you are now, Sam, that manhood was about competition, survival of the fittest, domination, winning at all costs, and, yes, violence. Women and girls, well, they were reduced to a few basic roles: mother and caretaker, sex object and girlfriend and wife. Some men, Sam, will say I am making these things up, that I am exaggerating, but I am not. Just think of what you, I, we, all of us, have been taught from the moment we had thoughts, about what a boy is, about what a man is, and how those ideas were amplified and spread, over and over, in pretty much every area I've named.

I wish I could say I was not affected by any of this, but I was, Sam. My father, the original male figure in my life, was mostly ghost, but I did see him a few times until I was eight years old. He grudgingly came around on three separate occasions, because of my mother's pleas, to buy me a watch, a bicycle, and to take me on a ride in his tractor-trailer truck. In that vehicle, my jaw dropped when I saw endless pictures of nude women taped everywhere. My father laughed heartily, thought it funny that I was so red-faced, and said I would understand one day.

Yes, Sam, I was learning sexism very early on, that women are there for our pleasure, any time we want them to be, including when I became a teenager and imagined myself making it with a girl who the

MY MOTHER. BARACK OBAMA. DONALD TRUMP.
AND THE LAST STAND OF THE ANGRY WHITE MAN.

3

boys in the 'hood called "Whorey Dorey" because she, allegedly, had had sex with most of us homies. No one ever questioned if this was true or not. The boys said it, so it must be so.

Same with how we ran through grade school and high school grabbing, uninvited, the blossoming body parts of our girl classmates. Combine this with the fact that my education about women and girls, kindergarten through high school graduation, might have totaled two or three pages. Little wonder, Sam, that I, that we, become men who disrespect women and girls, who have a reckless scorn for women and girls, who do not view women and girls as our equals, who molest, assault, hit, beat, stab, shoot, rape, and kill women and girls, just because. Most of us know so very little about the lives of women and girls, including our own family members. That gross miseducation is gross ignorance. Ignorance can easily become hatred, and fear, and we know that hatred and fear can become violence and destruction in multiple ways.

Like you, Sam, college was both a very enlightening and highly confusing period for me. It was there that I began to find my voice, as a leader, as a writer, and where I began to think earnestly about my identity. But it was also during my college years when my sexual life, first time ever, was rampant and irresponsible. I claimed to respect women leaders on campus but undermined them whenever I felt my manhood and my authority threatened; and it was there at Rutgers University where I was violent, on a couple of occasions, toward a woman student, including getting kicked out of college, short of graduation, for flashing a knife on a female campus leader.

Truth be told, Sam, every bit of my behavior was inevitable. I come from violence, experienced it as a child, so it's not surprising that I would become violent as an adult. But deeper still is the reality that I had no clear idea what a man was, or was supposed to be. So, I just imitated what was around me—in my community, on that college campus, in popular culture. My single mother did the best she could, in her own way, and whatever kind of man I am today I owe to my mom. But I was also terribly puzzled whenever she would say, in one breath, "Don't be like your father!" and declare in another, "You are just like your father!"

This is where I come from, Sam: the bottom of society, where male role models are woefully missing in action. It puts you in a sort of male prison, forever knocking your head against invisible bars as you stumble through life hoping the answers you are seeking will manifest.

You, Sam, come from privilege, from a wealthy family, you have a father and many other male relatives in your life. But something in you has rung a mighty loud alarm, just like an alarm was rung for me, a few years after college, when an argument with a live-in girlfriend led me to push her, in a state of rage, into our bathroom door. My alarm went off instantly, the moment that girlfriend darted from our apartment in fear for her safety. For I had become what my mother had warned me not to be: a no-good man, just like my father . . .

Your life of privilege, allegedly, means your life should be different, Sam, that you would be exposed to new and expansive ideas, that you would not be typical, that men like you would not be the same as me. But, alas, I have learned, since that fateful day with the bathroom door, that destructive manhood in America, or globally, does not care about your race or color or culture; nor does it care about your money or class or status. I have learned that manhood, the twisted and debilitating definition of manhood most of us have been given, links us as closely as the wild branches of a poplar tree.

This is because much of the history we've been taught is about violent men that we label "explorers" and "settlers" and "pioneers" and "warriors." This is because we learned more about war than we ever learned about peace. This is because women have been conveniently left out of our educations, with a few exceptions like Betsy Ross or Emily Dickinson or Marie Curie or Helen Keller or Eleanor Roosevelt or Rosa Parks. This is because we see violent and abusive men in so many forms, be it the bluster and bravado of a Donald Trump, or the shock and awe of ISIS or Boko Haram, or homegrown terrorists we call mass shooters in America. This is because sexism, patriarchy, misogyny are as natural to us as breathing; why we see, every time the Super Bowl rolls around, men engaging in sex trafficking of young girls in that game's host city, or men here there everywhere trafficking in domestic violence under the guise of enjoying the big game.

And this is why women and girls I meet and speak with and listen to in all fifty states I have visited in America, and in my trips to five of the seven continents—women and girls of every race and color and culture and class—speak louder and louder about the violence and abuse they suffer or have suffered at the hands of us men and boys. It is rampant, Sam, that violence against women and girls, that definition of manhood that says to be a man, a boy, is to be a brutal and dangerous terror to ourselves, to those women and girls.

In spite of these indisputable facts, I have heard some men take offense with the things I say, or suggest I am pandering to women and girls, or that I exaggerate greatly. Just the other day I posted something on Facebook about my lack of respect for able-bodied men who take advantage of single women, including single mothers, by preying on their money, their homes, their cars and other material items, their kindness, their loneliness, and their love. One man in particular felt the need to go on and on about how women do these things to men, too. That was not my point, and I am the first to say that no one, regardless of gender or gender identity, should ever want to be in any kind of relationship that is not healthy and loving.

But what I have noticed, Sam, is that whenever I post things about the behavior of us men and boys, it never fails that a male will jump on my Facebook page or Twitter timeline and blast women, as a knee-jerk reaction. This, Sam, is the height of sexism, of oppression. It takes great courage and great vision for us who are self-defined as men to begin to hear the voices of women and girls. The easy thing to do is say to women and girls that it is their fault. If they had watched their mouths, or their attitudes, if they had not dressed a certain way, or been in a certain place at a certain time, or had not drank that alcohol or taken that drug, then maybe what happened to them would not have happened.

What we men are essentially saying, Sam, is that it is OK to damage the lives of women and girls, because this is just how boys and men are, and because, well, girls and women helped these things to happen. That it is mad cool, OK, the norm to blame women and girls for the things men and boys do to them. This is the logic I have heard at lectures and workshops I have given on college campuses, at faith-based institutions, at community centers, in corporate America, from elected officials and other leaders, with professional and amateur male athletes, with musical artists and other entertainers, from certain public intellectuals, and in prisons.

This is the logic I even hear with far too many manhood or male-development campaigns, where grown men talk with the younger men and boys about everything—except sexism, patriarchy, misogyny, and definitions of manhood that destroy the bodies and self-esteem of women and girls. This is why, Sam, twenty-five years or so after pushing my then-girlfriend into that bathroom door—and thanks to years of therapy and spiritual healing circles—my life is not only dedicated to redefining manhood, my own, yours, all of ours, away from this mind-set, but also why I cannot support any rite-of-passage or mentorship program, or any other kind of male group, that does not take a very serious stand consistently against sexism and the violation and abuse of women and girls.

Again, I do not pretend to be a perfect man. When you have spent time, as I have through these many years, visiting battered women's shelters, or fielding one email or phone call after another from a woman or young girl seeking help because she is either trapped in an abusive situation or has just escaped one, you begin to develop a massive empathy and compassion for what it is to be a woman or girl. We will never know what women and girls experience, Sam, nor should we ever say we do. But we can listen. And we can truly hear their voices. And we can truly begin to care. And we can truly become allies to women and girls, if we have the courage to do so.

I thought of this when my assistant, a young woman about your age, Sam, said to me upon beginning her employment a year ago, that she really had no reason to trust men based on her experiences, that she had never worked with a man in this way before. It was jarring to hear, quite difficult to hear, but who am I to deny her life and her life experiences? I could either be a different kind of man, or I could be the stereotype of a sexist male employer who bullies, who insults, who sexually harasses.

This also means that I have a responsibility to be aware always; that I have duly noted how many women and young girls, for example, I have met in my life who are the survivors of some form of sexual violence or assault. One in four in America, Sam, and one in three on the planet Earth, or over one billion. Can you imagine if that many men and boys were able to say the same thing? Because of how we favor and side with men and boys in every single way, those kinds of statistics would be cause for an international effort instantly. But because it is women and girls, we drag our feet, we resist and ignore those stats, we make excuses why we cannot get involved around gender issues, and we blame the women and girls whenever we deem it appropriate.

Meanwhile, the hatred and venom so many of us feel for women and girls is everywhere: on social media, in our music, in pop culture, in our religious institutions, in politics. Whether people support Hillary Clinton or not is beside the point. Fact is, Mrs. Clinton has been subjected to a level of hatred, in spite of her background and qualifications to be president, completely unseen when it comes to men. As much as I may agree more with the politics of Bernie Sanders, there's no denying that some of the so-called progressive men who support Bernie can barely contain their sexism when attacking Hillary. We focus on her trustworthiness, her demeanor, her tone, her attitude, her language, her hair, her clothes, yet we rarely if ever say those things about male politicians. But when you are living in a male-dominated world, and dealing with male-dominated spaces, this is the result: pure animosity toward a woman for who we think she is, as opposed to regarding her as a whole human being.

A lot of men say things to me like they would never hit or beat or rape or assault or stab or shoot or set on fire or outright kill a woman. (Yes, Sam, I have heard every variation of these kinds of tales, tragically.)

My response is always the same: Violence and control and domination are not just physical, they can also be verbal or mental or spiritual or financial, too. And, even if you are not the kind of man who would ever touch women without permission, or would ever say inappropriate things to women or girls in public, on the streets, or behind closed doors; even if you are not the kind of man who would ever engage in any form of violence and control and domination against a woman or girl, but there are men who do—in your family, in your network, in your fraternity, on your sports team, at your religious institution, at your company or place of work—and if you say nothing about it, then you, we, are just as guilty of sexist behavior toward women and girls as those perpetrators. The silence of men in the face of sexism is an agreement that it is OK to oppress and abuse and attack women and girls whenever we feel like it.

On an intimate level, Sam, I think about my mother, what she has survived in her own life. We, as men, if we truly want to understand what we must do, can start by absorbing the stories of the women nearest to us. My mother is now in her early seventies, a senior citizen, a woman who has endured both the harshnesses of the American South and the American North. She is a woman who once tried to give her love to a man but was used and betrayed, tossed aside like unwanted trash, and told, by my father, when he felt he could, that she had lied to him, that I was not, in fact, his son. I listened for years, Sam, while my mother and my Aunt Cathy, at their kitchen-table summits, would talk about men, how most of us, they agreed, were no good. I was a boy absorbing those words even as I went into my young manhood seeking guidance and help. Those words came back to me as I battled with my demons, my dysfunctions, trying to figure out how to free myself of the male prison I had been stuck in, quite literally, since birth.

Speaking with you the one time we sat down, Sam, reminded me that none of us is immune to destructive definitions of manhood. You have a father and I do not. I do not know your father, but for whatever reason you sought me out to discuss this, and, again, I am honored you did, it is also not lost on me that your aunt sent a previous blog post I wrote about sexism in America to the men in your family. I now understand what she herself has been through with betrayal, in spite of her own privilege. It does not truly matter—that privilege, your lot in life—if another human being or people do not recognize you for the full person you are. My mother once was the help to a rich family. When alone with her, the husband chose to sit on a chair across from my mother, in a robe, with his penis and testicles revealed. It is a miracle my mother escaped that situation without being assaulted, or raped. I am sure your aunt and the many women in your family, Sam, can attest to what it feels like to be so blatantly disrespected by men, simply because they are women.

I will not waste a lot of time on Donald Trump here. He is too easy to criticize because he has a portfolio full of patriarchal, sexist, and misogynistic actions and words. Donald Trump is merely a symptom of the big problem of sexism in this world. He is merely the latest poster boy for its ugliness, its vileness, joining the likes of sexist men like Woody Allen and Bill Cosby and any random professional male athlete or male celebrity or male politician any given week. As for Trump, it does not matter if some women say The Donald has empowered them. What matters is the consistency of what we say and do, in public, in private, when many are looking and listening, and when no one is looking and listening at all. I think of this much, Sam, as I travel the country, as I think about my own male privilege, as a writer, as a speaker, as an activist in service to our communities. How easy it would be to bed one woman after another, to exploit my station in life. Again, I am a very imperfect man, Sam. My work does not mean I do not think certain things, or feel certain things. Most important, I think about my soul, my spirit, what kind of man I want to be for the rest of my life. And I think about what kind of commitment I have made to myself, to the people who say they trust me, who say they believe in me—

And, Sam, this is what you must think about as well. You have your entire life ahead of you, my friend. Strip away whatever wealth and privilege you might hold, and you are still a man who must find himself, on his own terms. No one can do this for you. You must struggle with every fiber of your being to be your own man, Sam, to be a very different man. The fact that you sent me that email saying you want to go a new path, that you have been questioning the definitions of manhood you have been given, is refreshing and it is revolutionary. If we can get more younger and older men like you, Sam, then there is the movement you want to see. And if more men of all backgrounds make a pledge to unlearn what we have been taught, and read and study the women I was told, by women, to read, like bell hooks, like Eve Ensler, like Ntozake Shange, like Gloria Steinem, like Pearl Cleage, like Audre Lorde, and countless others, we may one day get a body of writings and ideas, from men like you, Sam, that will transform this entire world.

I say this to say, Sam, please do not make the mistakes I made, if you have not yet. Do not hurt or sabotage or imprison yourself, Sam, and please do not hurt women and girls, or men and boys, either. Violence in any form should be absolutely unacceptable to you as a man.

What I am requesting, Sam, is please be different, please be free, please continue to be unafraid to explore manhood from all angles. Learn from men and boys of every race and culture, and have the courage, as a straight man, to learn from men who may be gay or bisexual or transgender. There are lessons everywhere, if we are willing to look, if we are willing to listen. As a straight man myself, I know what gay men like James Baldwin have given to my life, just by how they lived their lives, with no apologies. And I also know what I have gotten from straight heroes of mine, like Malcolm X and Bobby Kennedy, men who were also very imperfect, but who were also fearless and bold in the way they constantly remixed and evolved and questioned themselves, right to the very ends of their very short lives.

This is the kind of commitment we men need to make to ourselves: to live a life of peace, of love, of respect for women and girls as our equals as our equals as our equals, because they are, Sam—they really are. And if we can move in that direction, if we men and boys can, with humility, become allies to women and girls, then maybe we can rid the world of sexism once and for all. Because that sexism, that rape culture, that hatred and violence toward women and girls, Sam, will not end until we men and boys make it end—

Your brother & friend,

Kevin

Will Racism Ever End?
Will I Ever Stop Being a Nigger?

The Lord is my shepherd, I shall not want.

—Psalm 23

What happens to a dream deferred?

—Langston Hughes

What brush do you bend when dusting your shoulders from being offended?
What kind of den did they put you in when the lions start hissing?

—Kendrick Lamar

I am not a nigger, or a nigga, or a nigguh. I am not your nigger or anyone else's nigger, either. Nor do I belong to some specialized society that contains within its boundaries niggers, or niggas, or niggaz4life. No—

I am a man, a Black man, a human being, and I am your equal. After this piece goes live, I am never again going to utter that word *nigger* to describe myself, to describe Black people, to paint a picture of a certain type of mentality born of racial oppression, self-hatred, confusion, of ignorance; not publicly, not privately. No—

Yet when I look at race and racism in America in the twenty-first century, how could I not help but feel like I am nothing but that loaded and disgusting word? I often wonder if it actually matters that I came up from the ghetto; me, the product of a single mother who escaped, barely, the color-line insanity of the Jim Crow South only to confront a different kind of race and class insanity in Northern slums; me, the son of an absent father who completely and permanently abandoned my mom and me when I was eight because he was a broken Black man and did not know it; me, a Black boy who has known rivers, poverty, violence, abuse, fear, hopelessness, depression; me, who made it to college on a financial aid package, never got my degree, but still made a name for myself, against all odds; me, who has published twelve books and who has visited all fifty American states—as a writer, as a political activist, as a speaker; me, the kid who did not get on an airplane until I was age twenty-four, but who has since been to five of the seven continents, and who is interviewed virtually each week on television and radio and elsewhere for media outlets from every corner of the world. What does it matter that I, as my mother has said with her grits-and-butter South Carolina dialect, "speaks well," that I have the ability to converse with equal comfort on college campuses and on concrete street corners, that I can easily flow from exchanges on presidential campaigns and gender politics to basketball and pop culture? What does it matter, indeed, if I have produced a body of work, my writings, my speeches, my humanitarian and philanthropic efforts, in service to people, all people, and that I really do see you, me, us, as sisters and brothers, no matter who you are or what you look like, as part of the human race, the human family, if you, in the smoked-out buildings that are your mind's eyes, refuse to see me, or refuse to see me as a ghettoized. This is why a brutally violent "explorer" like Christopher Columbus is mythologized as a hero, why Thanksgiving celebrants are in denial about the horrors done to Native Americans, why things like slavery and the Civil Rights Movement are essentially skimmed over, if taught at all, to any of us, in public schools or private schools, be we wealthy or working-class. Racism in America means being so immune from it that you do not even think about being White. You just are. Does this mean that I believe every single White person in the United States is racist? No, not hardly, because I have encountered far too many brilliant, honest, big-hearted, and integrity-filled White sisters and brothers who are willing to challenge their power and their privilege, even at their own material, physical, and spiritual expense. I have far too many White sisters and brothers in my life who are dear friends, allies, supporters, confidantes, mentors, and sheroes and heroes of mine. But what I do believe, because I have lived it and because I inhale it habitually, is that racism is a toxic and deadly cancer; no one is immune from it, and even the good and well-meaning amongst us have been profoundly contaminated with it, simply by virtue of your not wanting to have this conversation, or because you are having a hard time reading my words this very moment.

Yes, I do see very clearly that we are all connected, and I truly love and acknowledge every race, every ethnic group, every identity, and every culture that exists in America, on this earth. But I, we, would be lying if we did not also admit that the longest-running drama and the single most dysfunctional racial relationship in American history is between White people and Black people. That as long as that dynamic dysfunction exists, there is no way we will ever do right by Native Americans who were the victims of genocide, or ever

whole human being, or, worse, simply see me as that word? Or what if you see me as an animal, a monster, some *thing* to be dissed, avoided, detested, labeled as angry or a thug or difficult or arrogant or a problem or a burden?

Yes, a nigger, that creature and creation born of a vicious racism seemingly as long as the nightmares of my African ancestors shocked and awed as they were bamboozled and kidnapped from the motherland centuries back; their sweaty raw bodies the infrastructure for the first global economy in this world—slavery, the trans-Atlantic slave trade. That slave trade built and enriched Europe, built and enriched America, and turned places as different as New York City and the American South and the West Indies and Latin America and the United Kingdom into real and metaphorical castles for powerful and privileged White people. Meanwhile, the bodies of my beautiful ancestors were brutalized by a diabolical scheme to bend and bomb any memory of their names, their identities, their very beings, until they became that which they were told: niggers. . . .

So there is simply no way to have what my Alpha Phi Alpha fraternity brother David Young dubs "courageous conversations" about race and racism in America if you refuse to hear me, if you refuse to read this essay to the very end, if you refuse to acknowledge that my history is your history, too. We are chained together like those slaves were chained together on those ships and those auction blocks.

I can hear my White sisters and brothers say now, as many often declare to me when this uncomfortable dialogue occurs, "But I did not own slaves, I had nothing to do with that" or "My relatives did not do that." It does not matter if you or your long-gone relatives were directly involved or not, or if you believe that "that is in the past." The past, tragically, is the present, because we've been too terrified to confront our whole history and our whole selves as Americans.

Furthermore, what matters is that a system was put in place, rooted in slavery, based on White skin privilege and White skin color, that revolved around power, land, property, status, shared values born of oppression and discrimination and marginalization, and that has never changed in America. Never. That system and its values have been passed generation to generation as effortlessly as we pass plates at the family dinner table. So it does not matter if you never openly refer to a Black person as a nigger or not. It does not matter if your college fraternity puts on Blackface and mocks Black culture on Halloween or not. It does not matter if you are a practicing racist or not. It does not matter if you call yourself a Democrat or a Republican or an independent. It does not matter if you call yourself a progressive or liberal or a centrist or conservative. It does not matter if you have Black friends or a Black wife or Black husband or Black partner or Black relatives or Black or biracial children (biologically or adopted). It does not matter if you love hip-hop or other Black music and Black art, or that you grew up in or around a Black community, or spend much time there now as an adult. It does not matter if one or a tiny handful of Black writers, or Black artists, or Black public intellectuals, or Black spokespersons, or Black entertainers and athletes, or Black media personalities, or Black anything are given major platforms and fame and awards and tons of money and status to prove racism is not what it was, or, equally tripped out, to tell you about your racism. That nutty game of the "special" Black person, handpicked to represent the rest of us, is as old and tired as racism itself. We are all your equals and all equally valuable—from the 'hood to Hollywood, from Harlem to Harvard—not just the select few anointed and celebrated by White American tastemakers.

So what ultimately matters is what you are willing to give up to sacrifice, in every aspect of your life, to speak out and push back against that which has taught you that you are superior and that I am inferior, that you are always right and I am always wrong, pretty much in every space imaginable, both consciously and subconsciously. Silence is unacceptable in the face of injustice, and being neutral is being a coward and an accomplice to the evil sides of our history.

Thus, to be mad blunt, in our America racism is race plus power and privilege; who has the favorable race or skin color, who has the power and privilege, and who does not. Yes, Black folks and other people of color sure can be prejudiced, bigoted, hateful, and mean toward our White sisters and brothers. I certainly have been in past chapters of my life, but I am no longer and never will be again. I believe in love of self, love of us all. But be that as it may, I am also clear that we Black folks do not control or own the majority of politics and the government, education, the mass media culture, social media and technology, Hollywood, corporate America, sports teams, music and other entertainment, the arts, the book industry, police departments, anything that shapes the thinking of every single American citizen and resident during our waking hours. Not even close. We do not set the standard for what is considered beautiful or attractive, what is considered courageous or intelligent, nor do we dictate what becomes popular, visible, viable. And we certainly do not say what matters in history, what does not, what stories should be told, and which ones are irrelevant, not for the multitudes—not even close. Our stories, our versions of America, of our history, are marginalized, put to the side, specialized,

look at Latinx immigrants as anything other than cheap labor and outlaws, or ever view Asians as anything other than the stereotypically quiet and often invisible "model minority." And definitely no way we will ever come to know and understand and feel the humanity of people who are Arab, Middle Eastern, Muslim while the Black-White conundrum continues, excruciatingly, uninterrupted. Stated the way they did in "the old country"—Down South—when I was a child, my momma and them said, religiously, that a liar is a thief. Well, it is way past time we stop lying to ourselves, fellow Americans, and stop stealing away the solutions that are in our very hands, and have always been there—

WE'VE HAD AT LEAST three major opportunities in American history to confront and end systematic racism directly, but we merely toyed around with the notion, then backed away.

The first was when the colonies were warring with the mother country, England, for independence. How incredible it would have been if "founding fathers" like George Washington and Thomas Jefferson had seriously and instantly freed their own slaves while declaring in their promissory note "all men are created equal." How incredible if Native Americans were treated with dignity and grace, and a part of the vision, instead of as mortal enemies. How incredible if poor Whites and women of all hues, too, were included in the concept of freedom, justice, and equality. And, my God, how incredible would it have been for those Black slaves, my ancestors, to become free women and free men and free children, to participate, from the very beginning, in the building of what we claim to be a democracy?

The second chance was during the Civil War and its aftermath known as Reconstruction. We who truly know American history know that President Abraham Lincoln was not the great emancipator he is hailed to be. Sometimes he was for slavery and sometimes he was against slavery. And unambiguously his releasing from bondage Blacks in selected states gave the North more men to fight and win the war. You think not? Then Google one of Dr. King's last speeches where he referred to Lincoln as the "great vacillator." But, regardless, Lincoln's Emancipation Proclamation was put forth; he was assassinated yet still there was a flickering hope of a better day as colored folks marched from plantations to liberty. But that long walk to freedom turned out to be fool's gold. Reconstruction lasted only a dozen years, until The Compromise of 1877 put Rutherford B. Hayes into the presidency, troops protecting the basic rights of Black folks were removed from the South, and an insidious White domestic terrorism—physically, mentally, spiritually—exploded across America for nearly a century.

Blame Black folks for every moral issue in our fair land. Make Black men and Black women the poster children for every bad behavior or crime or social misstep in America. Tell Black folks that voting is a ticket to a better society, and then deny it from them every chance you get, with poll taxes, with voter ID laws. Create a perpetual atmosphere of intimidation and fear where Black folks never know if they will be tarred, feathered, hung from trees, lynched, bombed, shot, racially profiled, or choke-holded to death . . . simply for being Black. . . .

It is a minor miracle of the gods and heavens that in the midst of that post–Civil War America Blacks were able, under harsh segregation laws, to build homes, own land, create schools of every variety, set up businesses that met each of their basic needs, and have whole communities, largely separate from White America—because they had no other choice. A minor miracle, too, that as racism reared its dreadful head and destroyed people's lives and neighborhoods that there were not more race rebellions, each and every year, across America during the Jim Crow era.

Look what happened to my great-grandfather, Benjamin Powell, who was murdered amidst this racist hysteria in the early 1900s. He had the audacity to own four hundred acres of land in the Low Country of South Carolina, right near Savannah, Georgia. He had the nerve to be an entrepreneur, a cook, and a man who did things his way on his own terms. The good White men of that community did not take too kindly to a Black man with that brand of swagger, who thought and knew he was their equal. They pressured my great-grandfather to sell the land. When he did not, one day his wife got a knock on the door and was told my great-grandfather had choked on his own food and was found dead in nearby water. No, they had killed him; my great-grandmother was forced to sell 397 acres of that land to the White men for one penny each, and scores of my relatives on the Powell side fled for their lives to other states, never to be heard from again. Years later, when she was an eight-year-old girl, my mother would pick cotton on that very same Powell property, her life reduced to being the help for the good White people, the same good White people whose relatives had a hand in killing my great-grandfather—

We got one more opportunity to correct the racial wrongs in the last century. It was called the Civil Rights Movement. We who know history know there had been energy and agitation for decades around voting and civil rights, but the height of that effort occurred roughly between 1954 and 1968—the years of the *Brown v. Board of Education*

Supreme Court decision and the ruthless murder of fourteen-year-old Emmett Till in Mississippi, and Martin Luther King's assassination on April 4, 1968.

What a majestic movement it was. People, Black people of all backgrounds, and some loyal White allies, too, peaceful, largely nonviolent, but courageous in the face of job firings, shootings, bombings, water hoses, attack dogs, not letting anyone turn them around. African Americans were not asking for much. Can we vote? Can we be full-fledged citizens? Can we move about without fear of being murdered simply for who we are?

The movement was powerful, it was diverse, it had voices as different as Fannie Lou Hamer, Ella Baker, Dr. King, Malcolm X, and the Black Panther Party. It desegregated public spaces, it appealed for voting and basic citizenship rights; it challenged police brutality and poverty and economic injustice. There were many big and small victories, and I owe the fact that I am a first-generation college student to these many unsung warriors of the Civil Rights era. But then it was over—

As soon as Dr. King's blood was scrubbed and washed from that Memphis motel balcony, America, our America, under the guise of taking the country back, began an all-out assault on those very minimal triumphs that occurred during the Civil Rights era. We have witnessed Nixon, the Reagan Revolution, the crack epidemic, the HIV/AIDS pandemic, mass incarceration and the prison-industrial complex; we have seen record numbers of poor Black folks thrown off welfare and locked in jails during the era of President Bill Clinton and First Lady Hillary Clinton; we survived the administration of George W. Bush, his infamous wars and his failed "no child left behind," and that hideous stain on America's face called Hurricane Katrina. We stand idly by as gentrification, under the pretense of urban development, destroys long-standing Black and Latino communities, from Brooklyn to Oakland, from The Bronx to Seattle, from Detroit to Atlanta, leaving the very poor people Dr. King urged us not to forget largely alone to fend for their lives, isolated and alienated by the triple evils of racism and classism and indifference. Public schools and an overemphasis on testing and zero-tolerance discipline in these poor communities are a disaster; there are few to no jobs; there is constant fear of the police and of each other; there is endless violence born of self-hatred and despair; there is little to no hope; there are racist and classist stereotypes they confront every single day of their lives; there is the looming threat of prison or an early death that has swallowed their peers and family members. If this is what integration was supposed to be coming out of the Civil Rights Movement, then it has been a complete and monumental failure for poor Black people in America. Black communities are not what they were; the multifaceted and thriving Black "businesses" of yesteryear have been reduced to barbershops and beauty salons, churches and funeral parlors, and the mom-and-pop soul food restaurants. The class divide between poor and middle-class African Americans is larger than ever, and there is a convenient and perpetual need to blame poor Black folks for everything that ails Black America—like guns and violence, like drugs—when we know, factually, that White folks—rich ones and poor ones—shoot guns, are violent, and take drugs, too. But people lie and make up convenient truths to suit their agendas, and we know that when racism and intra-racism are the order of the day, it's very easy to blame the ghetto, the 'hood, or so-called niggers.

And it is within that context, now, that we also bear witness to the meanness and venom manifested during the Obama years with a president elected by a rainbow coalition that made some believe, naïvely, that the United States was at its best: full of empathy and compassion and magically post-racial. Instead, during his term, Barack Obama has received more death threats than any other commander in chief in American history; he has been thoroughly disrespected by Congressional members and other elected officials, sometimes to his face; and the "they" we Black folks like to talk about still question Obama's nationality and ethnic origins, his religion, his loyalty to the country. It is a Fox News Channel mentality that thrives on fear, hatred, violence, and intimidation. It is a Republican Party where even Lincoln's flip-flopping politics would be welcome given the fire-breathing inhumanity spewed from its leadership in these times.

It has been in this climate that there seems to be an explosion of racial profiling cases throughout America. Say their names and you hear Trayvon Martin, Sandra Bland, Michael Brown, Rekia Boyd, Oscar Grant, Aiyana Stanley-Jones, Eric Garner, Renisha McBride, Tamir Rice . . . so many dead Black bodies that I have lost count. Some killed by police, some killed by civilian White folks, some Black adults and some Black children, some where it was clear-cut and captured on video, some where the circumstances are murky, the alleged causes feeling like the lies they told my great-grandmother after her husband was found dead in that water.

But let's be clear. These racial murders did not end with the Civil Rights Movement. They never ended. I have been an activist since I was a teenager, since the 1980s. I have worked on so many racial profiling cases that I have come to expect, weekly, news of yet another

Black woman or Black man killed. What has changed is that we have, in these times, cell phones and social media to record and share these tragedies. I do not know if that is a good thing or a bad thing. For every single time a Black person has died at the hands of a police officer, or White person, usually a White male, in their car, in their church, in their 'hood, my soul grows taut and my heart aches because I know but for the grace of the God I believe in, that can be me.

That is because to be Black in America is to live a sort of death every single day of your life. It makes for a stressful, paranoid, and schizophrenic existence: Am I an American, or am I not? You do not know how you will be assaulted, so you brace yourself for the worst and hope for the best. For me that means I am forever thinking about things my White sisters and brothers do not have to think about. Like if I carry my black iPhone in my hand will it be mistaken for a gun, and will I consequently get shot by a cop? Like if I, a marathon runner, jog my miles through certain neighborhoods at certain times of the day or night, will someone call the police on me or, worse yet, will they morph into George Zimmerman to my Trayvon Martin and be judge and jury and executioner of my life? Like if I dare to show an emotion like outward confidence, will I be deemed a menace to society, a threat to the status quo, an uppity nigger or "boy" who needs to know my place, the way some in America have been offended by Super Bowl quarterback Cam Newton, his smile, his smirk, his proclamations that he is Superman, his doing the dab dance whenever he makes a big play?

Like if I dare to challenge or question a White woman, a White man, as I have many times—the White female journalist on the New York public radio podcast, the White male editor of that national men's magazine, the White women and men both who like to come on my social media pages to criticize and challenge, randomly and disrespect-fully, my posts—will I be penalized, ostracized, deemed a problem child simply because I use the mind my God gave me?

Like if I dare to express, aloud, pride in my heritage, my culture, my people, and to acknowledge, through my art, as Beyoncé does with her song "Formation," will I be told that I am offensive and unaccept-able to Middle America, because I also reference the revolutionary el-ements of my history like the Black Panther Party?

Like if I dare to convey any anger, as I did when I was in my twen-ties as a cast member on the MTV reality show *The Real World*, will I be branded as such for the rest of my life, to the point where, two decades later, I have absolutely outraged White people, coming on my Twitter or Facebook pages, cursing me out, telling me they did not like me then and they do not like me now? Or like every single time I am on Fox News Channel, or some other network, talking about issues like violence, guns, abortion, race, gender, whatever it may be, and I inevitably get tweets, emails, you name it, threatening my life, calls for me to go back to Africa, to kill myself, to be killed, just because I happen to be a Black man in America with a voice and an opinion—

This is what the cancer of racism does to me, to people like me. We die and have to resurrect ourselves day to day. We laugh and party and praise God hard to keep from crying and dying inside, from commit-ting slow suicide. We cry and battle low self-esteem and debilitating angst and sadness simply because we wonder, aloud, what did we do to be so Black and blue? We swallow the racism until it becomes as natu-ral to us as our heartbeats, and that internalized racism becomes Black self-hatred, Black abuse, Black-on-Black violence physically, spiritu-ally, mentally; it becomes the Black elite, the Black gatekeepers, the so-called Black leaders and thinkers, the ones who have no real plan, no real vision, no real imagination when it comes down to the real challenges facing Black America, yet are quick to pimp or put down Black America, particularly poor Black America, every chance they get, but have nothing to say about American racism and its devastating effects, like ever; it becomes the Black woman writer who recently attacked me so nastily on social media because she did not like my private, off-the-record feedback on her work or her approach to Black issues; or it becomes the Black male airport worker who loudly disrespected me at the security checkpoint because his false sense of power told him I was nothing but a nigger to be bossed around and controlled; or the many times in my own life where I, too, have been so wounded by this system of oppression that I lashed out at any and all Black folks because in doing so, I was trying to smash the mirror that was myself once and for all. We are pained, we are hurt, we are distressed, we are bewildered, many of us do whatever we must to dull the awful sensations of racism—with drink, with cigarettes, with drugs, with sex, with video games, with sports, with music, with violence, with mistreatment to self and to others—a very vicious cycle, a treadmill we can never seem to escape—

NO ONE—*NO ONE*—SHOULD HAVE to live like this, think this, or be like this. No one should have to teach their children how to react if stopped by the police. No one should have to tell their loved ones "be safe" or "be careful" when they leave home, not knowing if they will ever return, not in the twenty-first century, not after all this nation has been through, not after all the many lives lost. No one, including me, should wake in the mornings wondering if this will be my last day on earth, if I will die at the hands of a police officer, or a White racist, or a deeply disturbed human being who is Black like me . . .

Yeah, it is utterly exhausting to have to navigate daily the macro and micro slings and arrows that are American racism. It is doubly exhausting to have to do so and also explain to good, well-meaning White people over and over again what racism is, what they can and should do and why, and then, in some cases, be expected to hold their hands emotionally. Black folks in America are sick and tired of being the emotional and spiritual help for White Americans who want to get it but do not. We are also sick and tired of being the historical mammy figure, or the postmodern nanny, forever catering to your needs while our needs get woefully neglected. You want to end racism in America and on this planet, my White sisters and brothers, now, and once and for all? You have got to do the work yourselves, in your communities, with people who are White like you. I can and will be your ally, your friend, will work in coalitions with you. But just like when I was first challenged, by women, to think about sexism and gender oppression as a man in a different way back in the early 1990s, I could not just expect women to do my work for me. I had to do it. Nor could I expect women to hold my hand. And I had to do this work with men and boys, not women and girls, primarily. Because I needed to go to the source of the power and privilege, not to the victims of that power and privilege. This is not easy work, challenging systems of oppression. But the choice of doing nothing or remaining inactive means a continued death of the American soul, of the American psyche, and an acceptance of the sickness that is within all of us. To be ignorant to what I am saying is a sickness. To think I am lying or exaggerating is a sickness.

To think you are somehow immune from all of this is a sickness. And to twist things around, to believe that you are somehow the victim, in sheer opposition to history and modern-day facts, is a sickness, a sort of mental and spiritual escapism devoid of truth and devoid of a desire for real healing and real reconciliation in America.

THE ABOVE SAID, THIS is so much bigger than #OscarsSoWhite or #BlackLivesMatter, although both are symptoms of the bigger problem. The Academy Awards are so White because America still believes it is so White, that White stories matter and that the stories of people of color do not, except on rare occasions, and with the same basic types of characters and plots. Rarely are we permitted to be complex, multilayered, thoughtful humans on film or television, except for the masterful producing work of, say, a Shonda Rhimes, that rare Black person shining in Hollywood. This is why I say Black lives do not really matter; because if they did, we would not need to say it over and over again. Who, precisely, are we trying to convince of this fact?

This is also so much bigger than how we perceive a Peyton Manning or a Tom Brady versus how we perceive a Cam Newton or a LeBron James; although we know White men can be angry, confident, sullen, rude, sore losers—no backlash for Peyton Manning after his Super Bowl XLIV loss and demeanor versus nonstop backlash for Cam Newton after his Super Bowl 50 loss and demeanor; we know White men can be fathers of children without being married to the mother and never accused of making babies out of wedlock, even if they did— Exhibit A is Tom Brady's first child versus Cam Newton's first child; same scenario but a different public reaction. And it is not mad cool when a famous or non-famous Black woman or man shows a range of emotions, including anger and confidence: she or he becomes a pariah, a thing to be marked, labeled, hated, condemned, and watched by false angels with dirty faces. Think of Serena Williams, think of Nina Simone, think of Sandra Bland when she was pulled over by that Texas cop. That said, we know a certain segment of the American taste-making machine likes its heroes to be heterosexual White men. So if you are, say, a heterosexual Black male hero, you must be the apolitical and socially detached Michael Jordan type. You cannot be Muhammad Ali, or someone like Ali in his prime like, say, Cam Newton. Nah. You cannot desire to be in control of your own career, your own life, and your own destiny, like LeBron. Nah. You must be obedient, you must be grateful, you must be an employee only, one who does not think or know your own value; you must be neutral, and you must castrate yourself and your dignity, by any means necessary—

And so, you see, that is why this is also so much bigger than a Donald Trump, although we know that Trump represents everything that is wrong with America, not just because he is an angry, foul-mouthed, disrespectful, opportunistic, racist, sexist, and classist heterosexual White male, but because he knows he has power and privilege, and uses it to injure others, without any remorse whatsoever. Trump's racism is the same racism of Barry Goldwater, of Nixon, of Reagan, of George W., of Paul Ryan, of Rudy Giuliani, of Chris Christie, of certain kinds of straight White men of means and access, who couldn't care less about middle-class and working-class White Americans, but who have conveniently created and spread a lie, in thinly veiled racial tones, that the enemy of these White folks in Middle America, in the American South,

is the Black folks and other people of color who threaten their freedoms, their jobs, their security, and their rights. Whether Trump really
means what he is saying or if he is simply being highly opportunistic is
inconsequential. Fact is he is saying those things, people feel and believe
him, and he continues a storyline that has brought great harm to America
for centuries now. Because the greatest trick of a racist is getting folks to
believe that racism doesn't exist in the first place, or that the people with
no power and no privilege are the real racists, the real oppressors.

BUT IN SPITE OF the questions in the title of this essay, and in spite
all I have written here, I really do have limitless hope for humanity, for America. It is in my spirit, it is in my bones, and it is in my
DNA. I have no other choice. I do not want to say the clichéd thing
about racism not ending in my lifetime, because I will continue to
do everything I can to help it end, before I die. And as I crisscross
America weekly, yes, I do hear the sad and sordid tales of racism on
college campuses, of Black student leaders and Black student athletes
protesting one insult after another. And yes, I do see, in innumerable
communities, people fighting the good fight against racism, against
hate. But I also see, as I speak at and facilitate public conversations in
places as different as Perrysburg, Ohio, and Minneapolis, Minnesota,
a genuine fatigue with the racism, with the hatred, with the fear and
ignorance and violence and division, with people not talking with
and listening to each other, especially when it is not comfortable to
do so. Yes, I have hope because of young people, the diverse groups
of youthful Americans I encounter everywhere I go, who at least

have a willingness to hear, to learn, to share. It is their fearlessness, their idealism, their openness that keeps me going, that makes me believe we can change history and change this world.

Finally, we have heard for years, at least going back to the presidency of Bill Clinton, this call for a national conversation on race. What I have come to realize is that that is a political football for certain kinds of political leaders to toss about when there is yet another racially motivated tragedy in our America. That if there truly is to be a conversation, a raw and real dialogue, that it must come from the bottom up, from we the people. I've said all I can say about America, about American history, about what racism has done to me, to my family. I am drained and near tears, to be downright honest, from writing this piece, because it forced me to revisit both new and old traumas, to revisit new and old wars with myself, with others, wars that I really do not want to fight. I want to heal; I want us all to heal. This healing work must happen with White sisters and brothers and it must happen with Black sisters and brothers, and sisters and brothers of every racial and cultural upbringing in America. Protests, rallies, marches should continue to happen as long as racism exists, as long as there is inequality, injustice, and the absence of opportunities for all people. They must. But we also must be conscious of how this racism cancer eats at us, how it destroys us from the inside out, how we must learn the difference between proactive anger and reactionary anger. Proactive anger builds bridges, possibilities, alliances, movements, and, ultimately, love. Reactive anger destroys bridges, breeds dysfunction, and spreads more madness and confusion. Yes, passion is necessary, and we should be

angry because of what I have described in this essay, for it is a natural human emotion. But that anger must not become the very hate
we say we are against.

For White Americans, this means you've got to reinvent yourselves if you are serious about ridding our society of racism. You've
got to ask yourself, Who and what was I before I became White?
What does it mean to me to be human, to be a human being, and what,
again, am I willing to do, willing to sacrifice, and willing to give up
to be a part of this necessary healing process? You must learn to listen to the voices of Black people and other people of color, you must
not feel the need, through arrogance or insecurity, to tell us who we
are, what we should be thinking or feeling or doing, and you must,
with love and respect, understand when we may be hypersensitive
to race, to racism, given the history and present-day realities of our
America. Shutting us down or ignoring us or un-friending us says
you do not truly want a conversation, as equals, especially if that
conversation makes you uncomfortable.

As for me, I just want to be at peace, I just want to see love in the
world; I just want to love and honor myself, who I am, without it being
considered an affront or danger to someone else, because of racism, because of hate and ignorance and fear. I do not want to be, forever, that
exasperation and anguish in Sandra Bland's voice on that video where
the Texas cop pulled her over, my life the heavy drag on the cigarette
she smoked, not knowing just a few days later she would be found
hanging in a Texas jail cell. I do not want to pick up a gun and commit suicide at the door of the Ohio statehouse because my demons got
the best of me like twenty-three-year-old #BlackLivesMatter activist

MarShawn M. McCarrel II. I do not want my life to end prematurely, at your hands or at mine, and I do not want my life to be in vain, because of what I am. I do not want my work for freedom, justice, and equality for all people to kill me, is what I am saying, to destroy me, to render me mute and useless, to myself, to others. That means I just want to be a whole human being, a free human being, and respected as such. And I just want to live in an America, and on a planet, where I can dream, forever, instead of being tired, irritated, uncomfortable, and scared, forever, that my life will somehow wind up as a nightmare—

The Day Our Prince Died

I finally shed massive tears for Prince a few days after he left us. Was not sure if I knew how to do so given the hole-in-the-heart sorrow I feel. I am sleepless, numb, and terribly sad that Prince is dead, gone from us forever. I have not been able to eat properly, or to think straight for extended periods; I just watch and listen to one Prince video clip or song after another. This is like the death of a family member, a close friend, someone you could not imagine life without—

I only met Prince once. It was back in 2006 and I was writing a cover story on comedian Dave Chappelle for *Esquire*. Chappelle presented at the Grammys and then got a personal call from Prince to come to his Los Angeles–area home for an after-party. At some point Chappelle and I separated, and as I stood alone marveling at the purplish-ness of Prince's mansion there he was to my left, sizing me up. "You're the writer, right?" I was stunned Prince knew me. I muttered "Yes," but could not look at him. When I finally gathered nerve to face him he had disappeared. I never saw him again that evening. A year or so later Prince's lawyer asked if I might be interested in helping the legend pen his autobiography. I was going through serious life struggles, so nothing ever came of it. I've always wondered what if.

You see, I am more than a fan; I am an admirer of Prince for the musical, social, fashion, and artistic revolutionary he has been for five decades. From disco and the birth of hip-hop and punk, to Kendrick Lamar and Katy Perry, there has been Prince, visible, in the shadows, somewhere. He has been a multigenerational global superstar when there have been few others in world music history, save the Beatles, Michael Jackson, Madonna, Bob Marley, Stevie Wonder, Nina Simone, Bob Dylan, Diana Ross; and maybe one day folks like Beyoncé, Ed Sheeran, Bruno Mars, and Adele.

I cannot say that I understood Prince at first. It confused me, as a ghetto youth, his very raw and public utterances in his lyrics about his racial and sexual orientation, the way he dressed, so very different than the average Black boy in the 'hood. But I paid attention because there was something behind the shiny permed hair, the thick mascara and make-up, the bikini underwear and androgynous clothes, the super high heels, and those big and round and hyper-animated brown eyes. Michael Jackson may have been more my superhero then, but Prince was the rebel, the troubled youth, the out-of-box brown-skinned Mozart only folks on the ragged edges of our own families and communities could truly appreciate. Prince represented for the nerdy kids, the weird kids, the bad kids, for the Black kids like me who were told we were "acting White" if we spoke a certain way or liked certain kinds of music. Nah, he was not acting White. He was being every part of himself, his whole self. Prince was post–Civil Rights America. He was that child integrating that public school, those kids sitting in at the lunch counters, the young freedom riders crossing state lines on a bus—Black students and White students, dreaming a world where a shining Black prince, named Prince Rogers Nelson, could be whatever the heck he wanted to be. Even if that meant being the sort of man, the sort of Black man, who refused to kowtow to someone else's definition of what a man was, or was supposed to be. Prince talked sex, he talked love, he questioned God, he questioned himself, he weighed in on social issues like AIDS and violence, and he had the balls, quite literally, to pose butt-naked, as a matter of fact, on the cover of one of his albums. So, Prince was, in a word, free, and it was electrifying and shocking to behold—

When *Purple Rain*, the movie and the soundtrack, fell like a piano from a skyscraper window in the Summer of 1984, it was also in that radioactive season that I began college. "When Doves Cry," the lead single, was everywhere. The sound was so distinctive, so hypnotic. Was not until many years later I learned Prince intentionally dropped the bass from the track at the last minute. And, yo, those lyrics, that song, pretty much every song he ever made, thirty-nine albums' worth in his lifetime—

What I am saying is Prince was a prophetic poet and a holy water preacher baptized by his ancestors' Louisiana gumbo and the good fortune to have a momma and a daddy who were both jazz artists. You think Prince, you think African griots chanting peace and love psalms in their village; you think Black slaves making melodies with the methodical movements of their perspiring bodies as they picked cotton from sunup 'til sundown; and you think Prince, you think Jelly Roll Morton on piano, Chuck Berry on guitar, and Ella Fitzgerald and Jackie Wilson borrowing the dopest sections of God's song-and-dance dream team to make the supernatural from scats of a migration jazz song: Louisiana swamps and second lines begat Minnesota frost and unfiltered funk.

Prince was, in a phrase, unapologetic Blackness like a molasses-tongued Mississippi Delta blues man; yet Prince was also Dr. King's mountaintop vision of the beloved community, too, a humanitarian for the human race, the flower-child hippie who might've also been down with the Black Panther Party, ya dig? That meant Prince was an Afro-ed soul brother who did not want to be locked and loaded as merely a Black musician but, still, he was very much straight outta Black mavericks like Little Richard, James Brown, the Isley Brothers, and Sly Stone.

Yes, Prince was a bridge builder, a mash-up of pop royalty pasts and pop royalty futures, a crosser and eraser of race, gender, class, and sexual identity boundaries, an imaginative and curious student of America, our America, from his Midwest stoop where the blatant racial hang-ups may not have been as hardcore in his hometown of Minneapolis as, say, the South or even New York City. That is why he told an exec from Warner Bros. Records, as a teenager, that not only was he going to produce his first album, but not to make him Black. Only a pint-size Black male secure in his swagger would dare say something like that to a multinational record label, to White men with power. As in, Do not tell me, Prince, that my music can only be one thing. Not when you are a prodigy, as Prince was; and not when he would be a one-man version of the Beatles, evolving from teen idol to serious adult arranger of his varied musical taste buds—taste buds that would come to fist-bump Joni Mitchell, Miles Davis, David Bowie, Jimi Hendrix, Laura Nyro, and even the rap music he avoided at the tip-off of his magical mystery tour—

This is why it is so hard to write this piece. I am writing about a very private dead man who may have been addicted to prescription drugs in the sunset of his life, a sunset none of us were prepared for mentally. It stabs and it cuts like a sharpened machete to say Prince is dead. Because I am writing about someone who, in spite of the world-wide adulation, and in spite of the revolving door of individuals who labored with him through the decades, may have been a very lonely man, emotionally, spiritually, still seeking answers, his Jehovah's Witness faith notwithstanding. *Nobody loves a genius child*, Langston Hughes once wrote in a poem. I also think we've called folks like Prince a genius so much that we make them loners and tormented and reclusive by default. We expect them to perform, to create, and make art, to entertain and mesmerize us, regardless if they are always able to or not. I wonder how Prince managed to get through his last live shows in Atlanta; I wonder about the alleged drug overdose on that private jet after the Atlanta shows; I wonder what years and years of leaps and splits and spins and dips, in high heels no less, had done to his puny body. Broken down, perhaps, the way an aging athlete plays and plays until the body just gives up and things fall apart.

No matter, what we should say now is that Prince was a man, very much his own man. That man twice married and twice also lost two children—one right after birth, one a miscarriage. That man withstood torrential public disses and humiliations because he chose to write SLAVE on his face and challenged his original record label, Warner Bros., for what he felt was an unfair contract for artists. That man who I saw perform live so many times I lost count, who hypnotized me speechless each and every concert, in large arenas, in small intimate spaces, because he looked and felt and smelled like music, like his very flesh was a polyester quilt of searing falsettos and space shuttle guitar riffs—

So I want to remember Prince as the greatest live performer I ever saw; for the good fights he fought to the very end; how he wrote that song for Baltimore after that city exploded in racial turmoil in 2015. How he continued to the very end to be a loud and present voice for the rights and power of artists to own and control their own destinies. How he mentored and supported so many younger artists, so many organizations and institutions, most of it very privately. How he acknowledged, loudly, the Black Lives Matter movement. And how he, Prince, remained true to himself in the nightfall of his days, as his heart and his breath stopped in that dusty elevator at his Paisley Park compound in the Minnesota he never abandoned, even as an entire planet bathed and washed him, time and again, with the very purple rain he had mind-sprayed on us.

That is because Prince, once an epileptic boy in a plastic bubble with a guitar and a dream, became in his fifty-seven years of a wonderful life, very much the kind of man, the kind of human being, who will never ever need to write the word SLAVE on his face where he is now—

A Letter to Tupac Shakur

Dear Tupac,

There is a lot I want to say to you, so much so that I do not know where to begin. There is rarely a day or week that I do not think about your life, and your death, since that fateful day on Friday, September 13, 1996. I have tried, at times, and with great failure, to block you out of my head, to ignore the people who've asked me mad questions about you, about the circumstances of your death. I've been utterly frustrated, even, when it felt, during these past twenty years, like my life, in some ways, and for whatever reasons, is at least partially linked to yours. Maybe I should simply start at the beginning.

When I first heard of you, it was when your debut album, *2Pacalypse Now*, had just been released. We were still in what we now call the Golden Era of hip-hop, when an incredible and diverse range of rap music was being produced, it felt, every single month, from one new artist or another. At the time, groups like N.W.A and Public Enemy dominated the art form, and in your lyrics I could hear the strains of both: you were very political and forthright, but also very much a street poet for the people in America's ghettoes. Only a couple of months after you released that album, a movie called *Juice* came out. I kept hearing about the performance of this young man named Tupac Shakur. At first, I did not untangle that you were the same young man whose rookie album had struck a chord with me, especially the songs "Brenda's Got a Baby" and "Trapped." I was living in Harlem at the time, the same uptown part of New York City where you were born, and where you lived until your early teenage years.

I went with a friend to a movie theater on Broadway, I think, and there were warnings of pending riots due to this film and its subject matter of young Black men and violence. There was a metal detector at the theater and police officers, including one with a ferocious German shepherd dog. I was perplexed by this because the movie theater where *Juice* was playing was not crowded. But as a twenty-something Black man, like you were, I understood we were perceived as dangerous, whether on a film screen or in person.

I sat in that dark theater and was mesmerized by your performance. I was struck by your acting chops, by your transformation from one of the boys in a local crew just kicking it, laughing all over the place, to this extremely troubled and villainous character, one who became reckless and evil and on a path toward complete self-destruction. When the lights were raised in that theater I sat there, my heart racing furiously, my eyes gaping at the soda-stained floor, musing on who you were.

A few days later I saw or read something about how you were upset that pressure from *The Hollywood Reporter* had led to Paramount, the film studio, removing the gun from your hand on the movie's poster. You thought this unfair and racist because there had been plenty of movies with White men posing with guns, but now it was suddenly a problem because a Black male had one. That is when it clicked for me that Tupac Shakur the actor was also 2Pac the rapper. This was 1992, the year in which two things happened to me that would change my life forever. First, I had been selected as a cast member on the first season of MTV's *The Real World*, a reality TV show. I had no idea what I was getting myself into, but because I had been a student leader and activist at Rutgers University in my home state of New Jersey, Tupac, I knew the history of America, the history of stereotypical images, and how Black folks had been depicted time and again. I vowed to myself that I would not go on national television and be some cartoonish buffoon of a Black man.

I did not know that some of the conversations and encounters with my majority White roommates would lead to wild and heated debates with them about racism, but I was clear that I was going to be my whole self, whatever that meant. The show became a ratings hit and took on a life of its own, I was both loved and hated for my so-called character, and I was told many times by young people, Black people and White people, that they had never seen a Black person like me on national television before. Meanwhile, as I was taping this MTV show, the legendary music genius Quincy Jones had formed a partnership with Time Warner to start a new hip-hop magazine. It would eventually be called *Vibe*. As rumors circulated about what Quincy was doing, I, a poet and journalist who had moved across the Hudson River to New York to pursue my dream of being a writer, was determined to get down with this thing called *Vibe*. All I wanted to do, Tupac, was get an assignment for a small record review, to be down with Quincy Jones. Perhaps because of my shaky self-esteem born of a life raised in the ghetto by a poor single mother, and perhaps because I did not yet know what I was capable of as a writer, I did not think big, did not think that something greater was waiting for me there at *Vibe*.

I did get a record review, but I was also asked to write a longer article about the hottest rap group in the nation at that time, Naughty by Nature, with a particular focus on its front man, Treach. I knew that Treach was your great friend, your homie, that he had also auditioned for the role of Bishop, your role, in *Juice*, and that your audition was so extraordinary that you wrested that lead role from Treach and everyone else. I also saw that you were in Naughty's music video for *Juice*, "Uptown Anthem." I never mentioned your name to Treach as I conducted that interview. I was as impressed with Treach as I was of you. In hip-hop, my culture, our culture, I knew that I had found the vehicle, through the rappers and deejays and graffiti writers and dancers, by which I could express everything I had ever felt in my life as a young Black male in America. Indeed, as a teenager I breakdanced and I also tagged with Magic Markers my graffiti name—"kepol"—on walls and school lockers, and here I was, through sheer determination, a journalist documenting the bravado and stress and excitement and recklessness and against-all-odds mentality. Treach represented that, and you represented that, Tupac, and I felt that artists like you, young as you were, young as I was, understood that.

Much to my surprise, 'Pac, that article on Treach and Naughty by Nature became the inaugural cover story for *Vibe* magazine, as it made history and sold out completely. It was now the Fall of 1992 and here I was suddenly well known because of MTV and *Vibe*. I did not know what to do with this newfound celebrity, was absolutely terrified of it, to be honest, tried to hide, at times, and knew, in my bones, that I had demons, many demons. Indeed, in that same September of 1992 that my *Vibe* cover story appeared, an essay I wrote for *Essence*, the Black women's magazine, was published called "The Sexist in Me." It was a raw and real account of what I was grappling with as a young man who, only a year before, had pushed a live-in girlfriend into a bathroom door in the midst of an argument. I did not know it then, Tupac, but I would never do that again to a woman, would become a man who not only challenged my own sexism, but would find myself working with men and boys of every background around how we defined manhood—on college campuses, at community centers, in prisons, with college and pro athletes. But in those days, I was merely trying to do my best not to die young, not to hurt myself, and not to hurt anyone else, even as I failed, miserably, many times.

Vibe's stunning success pushed it into becoming a full-fledged magazine. I cried when I was hired to be one of the three writers, because, since I was a boy, I dreamed of seeing my name in print somewhere anywhere, in that way. At our initial staff meeting, I was asked who I wanted to write about. Without hesitation I said you, Tupac Shakur, and put on the conference table a thick folder about you and your life that I had been keeping for over a year. I was ready. I had studied your mother, Afeni Shakur, I knew of her life in North Carolina, about her move as a young woman to New York City, how she joined the Black Panther Party and wound up in a scandalous case called the Panther 21, allegedly part of a plot to destroy several New York landmarks in response to the oppression of Blacks in America. It blew my mind that I, a young activist, had come across someone like you, Tupac, with your background in both activism and hip-hop. When I presented my idea to the *Vibe* team the reaction was indifferent. Truth be told,

Tupac, you were really only known by diehards in rap circles, and *Juice* was a cult film, and not considered on par with *Boyz n the Hood* in terms of critical acclaim and mainstream appeal, your remarkable performance notwithstanding. Regardless, I was disappointed, felt rejected, but dutifully accepted the task of reporting on Snoop Dogg, who was, in 1993, the most anticipated new music artist in America because of his association with Dr. Dre and the blockbuster album *The Chronic*. But I also quietly kept my Tupac folder close, and continually added things to it. And around that same period, in the Spring of 1993, we met for the first time.

I remember it vividly, 'Pac. It was in Atlanta, Georgia, at a crowded and electric music conference called "Jack the Rapper." It was named after iconic radio personality Jack Gibson, who, like other pioneering Black deejays and personalities in the 1940s and 1950s, would speak, live on air, in the same rhythmic patterns that hip-hop heads would deploy years later, on records. I was with my friend Karla Radford, who was the assistant to *Vibe* president Keith Clinkscales. We were in the conference's hotel lobby and there you were, surrounded by a gigantic throng of women and men, both equally in awe of who you were—rap star, movie star, the celebrity it-person of the moment. You were the polar opposite of most rappers because you were also a certified sex symbol, undeniably one of the most attractive and photogenic pop culture had seen. You were hip-hop's Rudolph Valentino, or Harry Belafonte, or Brad Pitt. There were the jet-black bushy eyebrows framing the top of your cocoa-colored face; there were the ridiculously long eyelashes fluttering whenever you smiled; there were the bulb-like almond-shaped ebony eyes and the meticulously groomed mustache and goatee; there was the sloped

Africa-meets-Native-America nose capped with a stud jewel on the left nostril; and there was the perfectly round bald head, either bare or crowned by one of your ever-present bandannas.

However, I was actually there at this music conference because of Snoop, but Karla knew how badly I wanted to write about you, and she prodded me to go over and meet you. I refused. I said I was not going to be one of the many people hero-worshipping you. Undaunted, and bold as she was, Karla marched across that lobby, shoved herself right in front of you, Tupac, and said you needed to know me, and that I needed to know you, because I was going to write a big story on you. To my surprise, 'Pac, you turned and looked in my direction, smiled that trademark toothy grin of yours, and said that you were a fan of mine from the MTV show, that you had my back whenever I was beefin' with the White folks, and that you would be happy to do an interview with me. And that is how it began, a three-year journey where our paths would cross in Atlanta, Los Angeles, New York City, and more changes for you and me than either of us could have ever imagined.

And it was because, ultimately, the leadership of *Vibe* came around to my profiling you, given that you could not keep yourself out of the news, or controversy. In that warped way we think in the industry, you were suddenly "hot." Our first sit-down interview, in Atlanta, Georgia, was at a house you either rented or owned, I do not remember. What I do recall was that there was barely any furniture, except for the sofa we sat on. And your mother, Afeni, was there, too. She was strikingly beautiful. Smooth chocolate-brown skin, wide, alert eyes, a smile and laughter as infectious as yours. Because Afeni was a single mother, the way my mother was a single mother, and from the South—North Carolina—the way my mother was from the South—South Carolina—I was divinely drawn to her. Your mother recounted for me what was in my notes: how she was arrested, while a Black Panther, and how she was in jail up until a month before you were born, on June 16, 1971, in New York City. How she was given scraps of disgusting food, was afraid she would lose you, her baby, her first child. When she spoke, when you spoke, you both smoked cigarettes. You both had a jumpy energy about you, like you both were always worried about time, about what you were supposed to be doing next. When I got to speak with you, Tupac, do you remember that one of the things you said to me was that you wanted me to be the Alex Haley to your Malcolm X? I thought to myself, with a wicked smile, "But what if I want to be Malcolm X, since I am an activist, too, and he is very much my hero?" However, 'Pac, I understood what you were saying, that you trusted me to tell your story, that I was the writer you wanted to give it to. I vowed that I would do my best and spent a lot of time with you and your mother, soaking up every detail of your lives, together and apart, not knowing, in that Atlanta house, that this would be the first in a series of conversations with you, Tupac. In that first article, I said you were the James Dean of the hip-hop era. Dean was rock and roll's rebel, and you were ours, with a backstory straight outta American history.

The traumas and difficulties of your mother and her family growing up in segregated North Carolina. The story of how your mother sat and watched, as she put it, the Civil Rights Movement, on television while there in the South. Why your mother up and decided, one day, to move to New York, not only to join other family members, but to also join the movement. How she was so drawn to the Black Panther Party, and admitted, with a girlish giggle, that part of it was because the men were so handsome and sexy in their all-black outfits. How

Afeni became radicalized and got involved in political and educational struggles in places like Brooklyn, New York; how she read and studied and got pregnant by your biological father, Billy Garland. How she got arrested and was charged, along with twenty other members of the Black Panther Party chapter in New York City, with several counts of conspiracy to bomb police stations, department stores, and other public places in New York. How your mother sat in that jail cell wondering, again, if you were going to live, wondering if she herself was going to survive. How you were born just a month after Marvin Gaye released his landmark album *What's Going On*, how that album could have been the soundtrack for you and your mother, Tupac. How your mother, in the tender caresses of her love, would sing a song by the Five Stairsteps, "O-o-h Child," to you, when you were a restless baby, and how you would sample that song for one of your biggest hits, "Keep Ya Head Up." How you and your mother and your little sister Sekyiwa moved around The Bronx, Manhattan, how you all struggled with poverty, and Sekyiwa's dad, your stepdad, the activist Mutulu Shakur, wound up in prison. How your mother told you that your biological dad, Billy, had died, and how you accepted that as truth.

How you and your mother and sister landed in Baltimore, how you found yourself, in due course, at the Baltimore School for the Arts, met your friend Jada Pinkett there, met yourself as an actor and rapper there, and then it was over and you and Afeni and Sekyiwa had gone again, this time to Marin City in the Bay Area. Leaving that high school shattered you and changed you. You were dejected, 'Pac, you told me, because you were leaving the one stable place you had ever experienced, that performing arts high school, and you were changed, too, because it was in Northern California that your

mother would succumb to a vicious crack cocaine addiction and you found yourself floating, a man-child, searching for a family in the gutters of your third urban ghetto.

This is the life that we lead, those of us who were born and raised and suffered and have died fast and slow deaths in the underbelly of American poverty. There, outwardly, is no hope, no possibilities, and no future for us, Tupac. We live day to day, we make it, with fear and trepidation, day to day. And we are given three lanes, as Black males, with which to try to escape: be an athlete, be an entertainer, or be some kind of a hustler, legal or illegal. There was no high school graduation for you, Tupac, there was no college education, there was no consistent support system except that which you found or stumbled into, like the local criminals, like Leila Steinberg and Atron Gregory, your first managers, like Digital Underground, the rap group that embraced you as a roadie, then a dancer, and finally gave you the break to be a rapper. That was your story, Tupac, but tragically, in post–Civil Rights America, in the America that has given us everything from the Reagan Revolution, to the Clintons' welfare reform and crime bill, to Trump's "Make America Great Again" mandate, it was and is abundantly clear, 'Pac, that Black boys like you and me were and continue to be on the receiving end of a sick and cancerous racism and inequality as old as this nation, and as hypocritical and hazardous to our existence as anything ever seen in so-called Western civilization. To remix one of your verses, we were given this world, we did not make it. These are our truths, 'Pac, and you spoke for generations alive and those not yet born in expressing our rage and our disgust and our anxieties with a system seemingly hellbent on detouring and arresting our development at every turn, simply because of the color of our skin.

Meanwhile, I watched you morph into a major superstar and also a young man with criminal cases spread from New York City to California. You never could stay out of fights or confrontations with citizens or the police, and never could quite control your raging emotions. I never shied away from you, because your anger was my anger, your pain was my pain, your demons were my demons, and you were caught up, and so was I. When any child, you, I, any of us, has experienced hurt, abandonment, abuse in multiple forms, 'Pac, it is going to come out of us in some way. For you and me that meant through our art, our writings, and through our actions and behaviors toward others. You fought, Tupac, and I fought, too. Your fight was far more public than mine, but my God did I know what it was to feel slighted or disrespected by people. My God did I know what it felt like to want to belong to something, to belong to someone, anyone, who would show love. And my God did I know what it felt like to feel as if you were attacked, always, for being who you were, because you were not understood, because there were forces out there who did not want to know or understand you as a whole human being.

And then you caught that rape case, that sexual assault case, Tupac. It devastated you, and it devastated your many women fans. Not Tupac, not you. You said you were innocent, that you of all people would never do that to a woman. You pointed to the lyrics in your song "Keep Ya Head Up," how it was an anthem for women, how it revealed that you were pro-choice, pro-feminist, anti-rape, and anti–street harassment. But something had happened in that hotel room, 'Pac—something. And while on trial for that case, a trial that did not include most of the other men arrested with you at the hotel that night, for whatever reasons, you were shot, five times, including in the head,

while entering a midtown Manhattan recording studio lobby with two
friends. They were not shot. I remember being awakened by the news,
dumbfounded that you were still alive. You gave a middle finger to
photographers who showed up instantly at that recording studio to
capture you as you were wheeled into an ambulance. You defied doc-
tors who told you not to go to court and showed up anyway, bandaged,
in a wheelchair, looking fragile and weak, but determined to beat this
case you maintained your innocence around to the very end. It did not
matter, as you were sent to jail anyway.

It was at that prison, the infamous Rikers Island, that I was sum-
moned to do a jailhouse interview with you, Tupac. Do you remember that scene, man, how you were wearing a white tee-shirt and the
prison pants, how you and I sat at a long table, and there also were
correction officers, your lawyer Michael Warren, your publicist Karen
Lee, and our *Vibe* photographer Dana Lixenberg? Do you remember,
'Pac, how you sucked on cigarette after cigarette, and how incredibly
stressed and anxious you were as you recounted every intimate detail of how you met the young lady at a nightclub in New York City,
how she performed oral sex on you on the dance floor, how you had
sex with her that first time at your hotel, how you thought that that
was it? Do you recall how you described the second hookup with her,
how you said your friends were more eager to see her than you were,
how you left her in the bedroom at one point, not knowing that your
friends, who you really did not know well, went in there, how you left
the room and passed out, and when you woke much later, how you
were told the police were waiting for you? Do you remember, Tupac,
how you shared, blow by blow, how you were shot that night at that
recording studio, how you were approached, targeted, hit with bullets?

Or how, bleeding, you got on the elevator after the shooting and went upstairs to the session that had been waiting for you, and the looks on the eyes of the folks there, famous music industry folks you would name, one by one, in this interview with me?

In the midst of all of this, Tupac, I did not know, fully, what I had gotten myself into with you. I believed in you, your life, and wanted to tell your story, fairly. That was it. I listened, in that jailhouse interview, when you admitted vulnerability, failure, and took responsibility for not protecting in any way that young woman in that hotel room. You were adamant that you did not rape or sexually assault her, but never before had I heard a man, of any age, let alone as young as you, say you should have stopped those other men. It did not matter, Tupac. You were convicted of something I cannot recall right now, and so was your close friend and road manager Charles "Man-Man" Fuller, and you were first there at Rikers, and then sent to an upstate New York prison. I cried when a new song by you, "Dear Mama," was released during this chaos, 'Pac. With your throaty baritone it was not only the most majestic and melancholy tribute I had ever heard a son give to his mother, but it was, like many of your best songs, an autobiography and a eulogy for your life—a life that I was praying, mightily, would not end soon.

I believed you, Tupac, when I left you that day in jail, when you said you were going to be a new person, that you wanted to be a leader, that you would learn from your mistakes. This was the beginning of 1995, but by the Fall of 1995, when you were bailed out of jail and now officially on Suge Knight's Death Row Records, something had happened to you. When I showed up on the set of the "California Love" video for you and Dr. Dre, the universe was off, and it felt like a torrential thunderstorm in that sunny Cali desert. There was talk everywhere now of a war between East Coast and West Coast rappers, and you were squarely in the middle of it, Tupac. When I reflect back on this "war," I think what I thought privately in the 1990s, that this was a classic case of divide and conquer of Black folks, of famous musical artists and executives. And I feel that there were forces unseen manipulating you, manipulating everything, for the sake of record sales, and also to undermine both your political legacy, 'Pac, and any unity and peace that could have been broached in the hip-hop nation. You became a willing pawn in that game, perhaps because you needed and wanted the money, and perhaps because you had become addicted to the celebrity, and to the drama and sensationalism that was your life. I knocked on your trailer on that video set, and when the door was swung open, a stink gust of marijuana smoke punched me in the mouth. The same Tupac who had told me in that prison interview he was going clean was smoking more weed than ever. You also were very distant in your limited chatter with me that day. Our connection was barely there, if not gone entirely. I was not given an opportunity for a sit-down interview during that trip to Los Angeles. I got to converse with everyone else for that "Live from Death Row" *Vibe* cover story, including Suge, Dr. Dre, and Snoop, but not you. I do not know why I was kept away from you, and little did I know that the set of the "California Love" video would be the last time I would ever see you alive.

Before I left California, I was told I could speak with you on the phone by the Death Row Records publicist George Pryce. Do you recall, Tupac? When you answered and realized it was me once more, there was distance, coldness. You told me to hold on while you got your cigarettes. You had been waiting months to get things off your chest. You told me that you were pissed that we had altered some of the names in the *Vibe* prison interview. I could not tell you everything, 'Pac, as I never wanted to cross that line between journalist and friend, but the fact is we had to change some of those names for legal reasons, because we, and you, could have been sued, and because, Tupac, I was trying to protect your life as best I knew how. You literally had named people as suspects or accomplices in that Manhattan shooting, with no proof whatsoever. We could speculate, you had your theories and I had mine. That did not matter to you. Your point was that you tried to give me the unfiltered and true story and I did not use it. We talked on, about your life after prison, about how you felt betrayed by so many, about your plans as an artist and businessman. When the topic flipped to the beefs between you and Suge's Death Row label and Diddy's and Biggie's Bad Boy Records, you were defiant and coy. Same with whether you had a relationship with Faith Evans, Biggie's wife. What I remember most, Tupac, is when I asked why you and Suge and the Bad Boy camp could not sit down and settle any differences, you said that yellow M&Ms and green M&Ms do not go together. You, a native son of the East Coast, of New York City, had eternally staked your claim in California, in the West Coast, and that was it.

Our phone call ended, and I stared blankly out my Los Angeles hotel window for a very long time, 'Pac. I would never speak with you again. That was December 1995. I followed you those final nine months of your life, but there was a great sadness that always hung over my thoughts of you like an ominous cloud. I saw you, Tupac, as someone who could have the multigenerational impact of a Bob Dylan, a Nina Simone, a John Lennon, a Joni Mitchell, a Bob Marley, your poetry was that powerful, that emotionally naked, your potential that limitless, that ridiculous. You were not the greatest rapper ever—no—but you had great moments fueled by a Black Panther's passion and a prophetic purpose. And in the annals of African American protest literature you were, with your one mic and your pen and pad, the working-class jazzy wordplay of Langston Hughes, the blunt, boisterous storytelling of Richard Wright, the preacher's slashing, quick-tongued prose of James Baldwin, and the ego-tripping literary gumbo of Nikki Giovanni. And you had the singular ability to be a bridge builder, or a bridge destroyer, depending on your Gemini mood. How many could say they were able to socialize with a Madonna or a Mickey Rourke, or walk the runway of a Versace menswear show in Milan, Italy, and be equally comfortable around dingy street corners, eyeless, ghost-filled alleys, and alcohol-infused house parties in America's inner cities? Yes, I saw you, 'Pac, but I did not see myself, falling. In May of 1996 I was fired from *Vibe* after getting into a series of arguments with staffers. I was devastated and cried long and loud in the office of the magazine's president. That Olympic Summer of 1996 I spent much of it in a drunken stupor.

Then, when I heard you had been shot a second time, in Las Vegas, right after a Mike Tyson heavyweight championship fight, something in me stirred. I first called *Vibe*, out of desperation, and asked if I could go to Vegas to cover your shooting. They flatly rejected me. I next reached *Rolling Stone*, where I had begun my career as a music journalist two years before MTV and *Vibe*, and I was promptly dispatched to Vegas. It was surreal, Tupac, that Las Vegas is where you laid, in a hospital, holding on to the shreds of your life. I was warned by several people to be careful, not to be seen, because of the ugly rap tensions between East and West. I ignored those warnings and went right to that intersection, Koval Lane and Flamingo Road, where you had been shot several times in the passenger seat of a car driven by Suge

Knight. I questioned how you were struck but he was not. I had a faint hope that you would make it, when I spoke with Kidada Jones, your girlfriend and the daughter of Quincy Jones, because she told me you would. I believed her, prayed to every god I knew of for you not to die, Tupac, not at age twenty-five, not with so much left for you to do. You had been gunned down on Saturday, September 7, and with each passing day that you held on there was a belief, throughout the country, that you were going to make it, again. Because you were our mythical hip-hop superhero who had withstood gunshots and lived. Because you were the boss behind "Thug Life," the 'hood movement you created, your version of Dr. King's Poor People's Campaign. Because you had turned your body into an artistic canvas crammed with tattoos as we had never seen before, those tattoos your shield, your bulletproof vest. But on Friday afternoon, September 13, 1996, I was sitting in my hotel room rewatching Denzel Washington play Malcolm X in the Spike Lee film when my friend and *Newsweek* journalist Allison Samuels called me. It was right during the part when Denzel, as Malcolm X, was heading to the Audubon Ballroom, where his assassination awaited him. Eerily, my favorite song ever, Sam Cooke's "A Change Is Gonna Come," played as this scene unfolded, and right then Allison's call: "Kevin, Tupac is dead. We have to go to the hospital."

I was numb. I did not cry in that moment. I was just numb, 'Pac. I was in a state of shock and had no idea what emotions should come out of me. At the hospital there were folks and commotion everywhere, including many cars, SUVs, and Hummers riding back and forth, blasting your music. When Suge Knight showed up, with no visible wounds, there was both terror and amazement. I remember, Tupac, that many of us, including me, shifted away from wherever

Suge was walking because, we thought, best to not be in the way of any bullets aimed for him. That night I went back to that intersection of Koval and Flamingo where you were gunned down, and prayed and bawled like a baby and drank liquor and poured some of that liquor out on the ground, as we do in the ghettoes, for our fallen soldiers. Tupac Amaru Shakur was gone.

I have not been back to Las Vegas since that day you died, 'Pac. I have not wanted to go, I could not bring myself to do so. That city is forever branded in my mind with death, your death. Twenty years have come and gone and I still do not know when I will return there. Six months after you were killed, Karla, the same Karla Radford from *Vibe* who had introduced you to me, called me in the wee hours of a March morning in 1997, and said, through tears, "Kevin, Biggie— They killed Biggie." Yes, The Notorious B.I.G., first your friend, then your rival, was killed, too, at a Los Angeles *Vibe* party Karla had event produced no less, under the same mysterious circumstances as your death, Tupac. We did not know where the bullets were coming from, and I was frightened that I would meet a similar fate because of my relationship to you. So I drank more, drank myself, for the next several years, through a debilitating depression, some of it because of the breathing and nasty scar tissues of my own life, Tupac, and some of it because of what had happened to people in my generation, like you, like Biggie. I did not want to live, tried, at times, to muster the energy to write a book about your life, but was always concerned about appearing to profit from you, from your death.

There were many problems with the estate set up after your passing, but I did my best to stay in touch with your mother and your sister, 'Pac, to be supportive. I was threatened with death, once, eyeball to eyeball, by one of those male friends who was with you the night you were arrested at that hotel, because he was enraged by my commentary in a video interview implying indirectly who I thought might have had you shot the first time, Tupac. I sincerely believed that he was going to make good on that promise. Somehow, mystically, and but for the grace of God, the threat disappeared.

Around that same time, I appeared on a BET program about your life and death, and Suge Knight was also a guest. Right on the show he tried to bully the other panelists, including me, and as we broke to a commercial the ghetto dude in me said, without blinking an eye, "Ain't nobody scared of you." After the taping Suge stepped to me and said we could settle whatever the problem was in a nearby bathroom. That did not happen, but I found myself, in the early years after you died, looking over my shoulder, mad paranoid that I felt too much, knew too much, and had invested too much of my life into your life, 'Pac. Nonetheless I accepted your mother Afeni's request to consult on the Oscar-nominated MTV documentary film that was made about you, using your own words. I tried as best I could to rid myself of you, Tupac, keeping it a hundred, because I did not want my life to be dependent on yours. I went back to my activism after finally coming out of that very bad depression, wrote as much as I could, and found myself doing speeches around the country, to help and heal others, to help and heal myself. Between your death and tragedies like 9/11 and Hurricane Katrina, the naïveté of my youth was gone forever.

Because of my lectures and activism, I traveled more than ever, and duly noted wherever I went, that your name came up everywhere, in some way. It was profound to hear folks in the West Indies, in Europe, in Japan, and in my first ever trip to Africa reference you, Tupac.

Like you were not dead at all. It was profound to witness the many documentaries and books come out, by some who knew you, by some who did not, purporting to tell the truth about your life, about your death. There was a hugely hyped but poorly conceived Broadway show based around your music. And I've mostly avoided prying journalists hoping to get something from me that would help prove their theories. I have sat on my interview tapes with you and your mother these many years, resisting folks' offers to purchase, or license. And only in the past few years, Tupac, have I decided, finally, to write a book about you.

But even with this book deal in place, I have wavered several times, about writing it, when to write it, or if I truly want to write it. Part of me does feel an obligation to tell your story the right way, Tupac, and part of me wants to walk away from it, and you, for good. I've even struggled with the thought of this new film about your life, a film that your mother was sued over to force her to participate in, because of the sloppy business dealings of her representatives, years back. Part of my soul does not want to see the film because I lived through this, already, 'Pac, I know the story, I know it as I know the blood in my own body.

So life goes on, and here I am speaking with you, again. The way I spoke to you maybe ten years ago when I just happened to be in the area of North Carolina where your mother had purchased an organic farm. When Ms. Shakur, as I always called your mother, heard I was there, she insisted I spend the night on her property. I was put in the guest-house right next to the tomb that contained some of your ashes, Tupac. I did not sleep well that night. I cried that night, too, and I listened as your spirit spoke to mine. It was not any special words, or message, just that old familiar connection. Earlier this year, when your mother died of a heart attack, unexpectedly, on a boathouse where she lived not far from that same Marin City neighborhood you all had moved to many years back, I cried for her life, too, 'Pac. The last time I saw your mother was, I think, in 2012 or 2013, I cannot remember which year, when she had invited me to this boathouse. We sat there and talked about you, about her, about life, about forgiveness, about love.

I always wanted Ms. Shakur to know I wanted the best for her, for Sekyiwa, for your memory, Tupac, that I was not one of those individuals who wanted to profit in any way from you or your life. She said she knew this, and understood. We hugged, I was very happy to see your mother, and every now and again I would get a message, in the time before she died, that she was thinking about me, that she knew what was in my heart. I wanted to pay my respects to your mother at one of the memorials for her, but circumstances and time did not allow that, 'Pac. I know she is at peace where she is now, because Ms. Shakur has been reunited with you, her son, the son she loved so dearly. In watching you and your mother through the years I have come to love and appreciate my own mother and what she went through and sacrificed so that I could live, Tupac. There is no greater love than a mother's love, even when our mothers are not always able to express or show that love.

Finally, you would be stunned by what has happened in America, Tupac. So much of what you rapped about, spoke about, were about, remains the same, or has come to pass. You once said to me that if the millions of diverse young people who bought your music ever voted, magic could happen. Well, that did happen, in 2008, with the election of Barack Obama as this country's first Black president. But we've also gone backwards, 'Pac. Racism is alive and well, and so are racial profiling and police brutality cases, like the one you experienced personally in Oakland, California. Violence against women and girls is worse than ever, and I have wondered how you would have evolved from the lyrics of "Keep Ya Head Up," from the sexual assault case, to a different kind of man, because there were multitudes who believed in you, who believed in your possibilities as a rapper, as an actor, as a leader, as a man.

You spoke to me regularly about the need for people to stand up and protest injustices. I think you would be very proud of efforts like Occupy Wall Street and Black Lives Matter, that that movement was mainly started by and is propelled by women, by Black women as powerful as your mother, Afeni. I think you would be in awe of the simple and quiet protest of football player Colin Kaepernick, that someone with his platform is as unafraid as you were to tell his truth, for the people. But there is so much hatred and fear and division and violence and ignorance out here, 'Pac, and I am sure you know, as I do, that that has always been the case. Yet, I feel, it is worse than ever, the dumbing down, of the music, of the culture, of our society. With the exception of, say, Kendrick Lamar, J. Cole, the Roots, Macklemore and Ryan Lewis, or Lupe Fiasco, hardly any major rap stars of this twenty-first century have your courage and your vision and your insatiable hunger to learn, and to think, out loud, and to grapple, out loud, Tupac, and to be a fearless voice for justice. That is why I've used you as an example in so many ways, when discussing race, or gender, or the pitfalls of fame, even mental health.

When it was revealed that Nate Parker, the director and star of the astonishing film *The Birth of a Nation*, had a college rape case in the late 1990s, though he was found to be not guilty, I reminisced obsessively about your case, about what toxic manhood means, what we men and boys must say and do, steadfastly, to end this abusive madness once and for all. I wondered what it would be like for you, Tupac Shakur, to be alive in the era of 24-7 social media and viral videos, given the intense and heavy scrutiny you faced in the 1990s. I have used your comments around taking responsibility for what you did not stop on behalf of that young woman in that hotel room in countless workshops and sessions with men and boys everywhere. I've pointed, time and again, to how you saw the splendor and dignity in your mother even at the lowest point of her drug addiction. Yours was a messy and complex life, sir, as it is with any of us. The difference is that you lived your life, at least the last five years of it, with a massive and unimaginable spotlight on you. You only wanted to hear your record on the radio, you told me in our first interview. Well, sir, you did that and more than you could have dreamed. In a world that often renders us poor Black boys as invisible, your name is permanently tagged on the erect, mud-smeared walls of history.

But you are us and we are you, Tupac, this I know, because you were very much a man, a human, and a person of the people, all people. There are many imperfect and damaged beings out here, my friend, as you were a very damaged and imperfect being. But what made you different, unique, is that you were never hesitant to speak your mind, never hesitant to show each side of who you were, 'Pac. You were an example of freedom and vulnerability in its purest forms. And just like you did not agree with everything I said or did, Tupac, I did not always agree with you or your actions, and I still cringe when I listen to some of your music or watch or hear some of your interviews with various journalists. I have had a chance to live, Tupac, past my twenties, and you did not. I got to work on myself, got to do years of therapy, and heal, emotionally and spiritually, in many ways you were not able to do in your lifetime. I am still doing that work, 'Pac, because the pain never ends. You were never able to do that work, to turn the corners you needed to turn, because yours was a short and fast life. I met your father, Billy Garland, a week or so after you died, the father you thought was dead until a couple of years before your own death. That meeting with him, clumsy, difficult, strange, sad, tragic, was the beginning of a long process of my coming to forgive my own father, 'Pac, because my dad was not there for me, either. You, I, we, Tupac, were boys, children in men's bodies, searching for ourselves, searching for fathers and father figures and, yes, love, here there everywhere, even when it took us to troubled and violent places, outside and inside ourselves. Thus, alas, I cannot deny that you have touched lives, millions of lives across the globe, including mine. And it is my humble opinion, Tupac Shakur, that in some small way, I also touched yours, and that wherever you are now, you know that I, your brother, have been carrying you around with me these many years since Las Vegas, because I have no choice. You are me, and I am you.

Sincerely,

Kevin

Why Is Baltimore Burning?

I am from the ghetto. The first thirteen years of my life I grew up in the worst slums of Jersey City, New Jersey, my hometown. If you came of age in one of America's poor inner cities like I did, then you know that we are good, decent people: in spite of no money, no resources, little to no services, run-down schools, landpersons who only came around to collect rent, and madness and mayhem everywhere, amongst each other—from abusive police officers, and from corrupt politicians and crooked preachers—we still made a way out of no way. We worked hard, we partied hard, we laughed hard, we barbecued hard, we drank hard, we smoked hard, and we praised God, hard.

And we were segregated, hard, by a local power structure that did not want the ghetto to be seen or heard from, and certainly not to bring its struggles out in plain sight for the world to see.

Indeed, my entire world was the block I lived on and maybe five or six blocks north south east west. A long-distance trip was going to Downtown Jersey City on the first of each month so our mothers—our Black and Latina mothers—could cash their welfare checks, buy groceries with their food stamps and, if we were lucky, we got to eat at Kentucky Fried Chicken or some other fast-food restaurant on that special day.

When I was about fifteen, I was badly beaten by a White police officer after me and a Puerto Rican kid had a typical boy fight on the bus. No guns, no knives—just our fists. The Puerto Rican kid, who had White skin to my Black skin, was escorted off the bus gingerly. I was thrown off the bus. Outraged, I said some things to the cop as I sat handcuffed in the backseat of a police car. He proceeded to smash me in the face with the full weight of his fist. Bloodied, terrified, broken in that moment, I would never again view most police officers as we had been taught as children:

"Officer Friendly"—

Being poor meant I only was able to go to college because of a full financial-aid package to Rutgers University. I did not get on a plane until I was twenty-four years old because of that poverty, and also because I did not know that that was something I could do. These many years later, I have visited every single state in America, every sort of city big and small, and every ghetto community you can name. They all look the same.

Abandoned, burnt-out buildings. Countless churches, funeral parlors, barbershops, beauty salons, check-cashing places, furniture-rental stores, fried-chicken spots, and Chinese restaurants. Schools that look and feel more like prison holding cells for our youth than centers of learning. Playgrounds littered with broken glass, used condoms, and drug paraphernalia. Liquor stores here, there, everywhere. Corner stores that sell nothing but candy, cupcakes, potato chips, soda, every kind of beer you can name, loose cigarettes, rolling paper for marijuana, lottery tickets, and gum—lots and lots of gum.

Then there are also the local organizations that claim to serve the people, Black and Latino people. Some mean well and are doing their best with meager resources. Others only come around when it is time to raise money, to generate some votes for one political candidate or another, or if the police have tragically killed someone.

Like Rekia Boyd in Chicago. Like Miriam Carey in Washington, DC. Like Tanisha Anderson in Cleveland. Like Yvette Smith in Texas. Like Aiyana Stanley-Jones in Detroit. Like Eric Garner in New York City. Like Oscar Grant in Oakland. Like Walter Scott in South Carolina. Like Freddie Gray in Baltimore . . .

Yes, we had the first Black president in the White House, but it feels like open season on Black folks in America once more. One hundred years ago this year, the Hollywood image machine was given a huge boost by a racist and evil film called *The Birth of a Nation*, a movie so calculating in the way it depicted Black people it set the tone, quite literally, for how we were portrayed and treated in every form of media for decades to come. One hundred years ago, it was common to see photos of African Americans, males especially, lynched, hanged from trees, as the local good White folks visibly enjoyed their entertainment of playing hangman.

One hundred years later, *The Birth of a Nation* has been replaced by a 24-hour news media cycle still obsessed with race, racism, racial strife, racial violence, but no solutions and no action steps whatsoever, just pure sensationalism and entertainment. One hundred years later, the lynching photos have been replaced by cell phones capturing video of Walter Scott running away from a police officer, like a slow-footed character in a video game, only to be shot in the back— *pop! pop! pop! pop! pop! pop! pop! pop!*

Except all of this is mad real. Black people in America—the self-proclaimed greatest democracy on earth—are being shot here, there, everywhere, by the police, in broad daylight, with witnesses, sometimes on video. And with very few exceptions, nothing is happening to the cops who pulled the triggers. No indictments. No convictions. No prison time.

And every single time one of these scenarios plays out, we are handed the same movie script: Person of color is shot and killed by local police. Local police immediately try to explain what happened, while placing most of the blame, without full investigation, on the person shot. Police officer or officers who fired shots is/are placed on paid "administrative leave." Media finds any and everything they can to denigrate the character of the dead person, to somehow justify why she or he is dead. Marches, protests, rallies, speeches. Local police show up in military-styled "riot gear." Tensions escalate. Folks are arrested, people are agitated or provoked; all hell breaks loose. The attention has shifted from the police killing an innocent person to the violence of "thugs," "gangstas," "looters." The community is told to be nonviolent and peaceful, but no one ever tells the police they should also be nonviolent and peaceful. Whites in power and "respectable Black voices" call for calm, but these are the same folks who never talk about the horrific conditions in America's ghettoes that make any 'hood a time bomb just waiting for a match to ignite the fury born of oppression, marginalization, containment, and invisibility. These are the same people who've spent little to no time with the poor.

If you aren't from the ghetto, if you have not spent significant time in the ghetto, then you would not understand the ghetto. . . .

No matter. Big-time civil rights organizations, big-time civil rights spokespersons, and big-time church leaders are brought in to redirect, control, and contain the energy from the people at the bottom. *Started from the bottom and now we here.* . . . But they really cannot, because the people have seen this movie a million times before. They know it is madness to be told to let justice take its course. They know it is madness to wait out a legal system that rarely if ever indicts and convicts these police officers who've shot and killed members of their community. They know it is madness to be told to stay cool, to be cool, when they have no healthy outlets for their trauma, their pain, their rage. They know it is madness to hear pundits and talking heads of every stripe on television and radio and via blogs analyze who they are, without actually knowing who they are. They know it is madness when middle-class or professional Black folks speak the language of the power structure and condemn the people in the streets instead of the system that created the conditions for why the people are in the streets. They know it is madness that so-called progressive, liberal, human-rights, or social-justice people of any race or culture have remained mightily silent as these police shootings have been going down coast to coast. And they know it is madness that most of these big-time leaders and big-time media only come around when there is a social explosion.

So: they do explode, inside of themselves, and inside their communities. They would love to reach areas outside their 'hoods, but the local power structure blocks that from happening. So: they destroy their own communities. I understand why. I am they and they are me. Any people with nothing to lose will destroy anything in their way. Like anything. Any people who feel as if their lives are not valued, like they are second-class citizens at best, will not be stopped until they've made their point. They, we, do not care if our communities have not rebounded from the last major American rebellions of the 1960s. We care that we have to live in squalor and misery and can be shot at any given moment by each other, or by the police, and no one seems to care. A rebellion, a riot, is a plea for help, for a plan, for a vision, for solutions, for action steps, for justice, for God, someone, anyone, to see our humanity, to do something.

Condemning them is condemning ourselves. Labeling the Baltimore situation a "riot" because it is mostly people of color is racist, given we do not call White folks behaving violently after major sporting events "rioters" or "thugs" or "gangstas," and Lord knows some White folks have destroyed much property in America, too.

It ain't a democracy if White people can wild out and it is all good; but let people of color wild out and it becomes a state of emergency with the National Guard dropping in, armed and ready.

Black lives matter, all lives matter, equally. I believe that, I believe deeply in peace and love and nonviolence. I believe in my heart that we've got to be human and compassionate and civil toward one another, as sisters and brothers, as one human race, as one human family. I believe that our communities and police forces everywhere have to sit down and talk and listen as equals, not as enemies, to figure out a way toward life and love, not toward death and hate; a way toward a shared community where we all feel safe and welcomed and human.

Yes, I love people, all people. But I also believe in justice, for all people. And I know that what has been happening in America these past few years is not remotely close to any form of justice, or equality.

Imagine, if you will, White folks being shot and murdered by the police like this, what the reactions would be?

Imagine if George Zimmerman had gone vigilante on a White youth with a hoodie in that gated Florida complex. Imagine White parents having to teach their children how to conduct themselves if ever confronted by the police. Imagine that Aiyana Stanley-Jones was a little seven-year-old White girl instead of a little seven-year-old Black girl, shot by the police as she slept on a sofa with her grandmother, in a botched raid? It would be a national outrage.

Baltimore is burning because America is burning with racism, with hate, with violence. Baltimore is burning because far too many of us are on the sidelines doing nothing to effect change, or have become numb as the abnormal has become normal. Baltimore is burning because very few of us are committed to real leadership, to a real agenda with consistent and real political, economic, and cultural strategies for those American communities most under siege, most vulnerable. Policing them to death is not the solution. Putting them in prison is not the solution. And, clearly, ignoring them is not the solution.

Cam Newton, and the Killing of a Mockingbird

The object of the artist is the creation of the beautiful.
What the beautiful is is another question.

—JAMES JOYCE, *A PORTRAIT OF THE ARTIST AS A YOUNG MAN*

I've wrestled with alligators. I've tussled with a whale. I done
handcuffed lightning. And throw thunder in jail.

—MUHAMMAD ALI

Bronn: What will you do?
Tyrion: I suppose I'll have to kill the Mountain myself.
Won't that make for a great song?
Bronn: I hope to hear them sing it one day.

—*GAME OF THRONES*, SEASON 4/EPISODE 7

Superman went to the Super Bowl, and he lost, and it was mad ugly. On that gorgeously sunny and mild date in February he could not skyrocket the way we knew he could, not over tall buildings, not over hulking defensive linemen or hungry linebackers with blood in their eyes and nullification greased on their lips. No, the man of steel would not be yanking open his shirt to reveal a giant "S" on his chest, not this day. Superman was overrun by raging Broncos kicking kryptonite into our wounded hero. He had had a marvelous season up to this point—an MVP season—and along the way football fans and everyday people from the Carolinas to Cali loved and revered him, or they feared and loathed him. The hate produced was particularly raw whenever his sculpted bronze face cracked into that toothy and dimpled Hollywood smile as he dabbed after his many scoring plays. Our heroes are not supposed to smile like that, or dance like that, some say. Some want our heroes to be predictable, one-dimensional, and, yeah, humble. Does not matter that our hero gives every single touchdown ball to a young kid in the stands. Does not matter that our hero routinely brings a meal to a homeless person without any attention or fanfare. Does not matter that our hero has transformed himself from a controversial bad boy number one draft pick into an all-everything behemoth of a man on a mission. Superman ain't 'spose to have fun being somebody's hero—

Hell, Superman is not even supposed to be complex and complicated in any way whatsoever. Please simply put on your tight-fitting costume and fly. This Superman named Newton, as in Cam, leads a team called the Panthers, just like fifty years ago another super man named Newton, as in Huey, was leading his own Panthers—the Black Panther Party for Self-Defense—in the very same Bay Area where Cam suffered defeat in this big game, Super Bowl 50. The revolution will not be televised, the poet Gil Scott-Heron once prophesized. But it was, and is: when Huey Newton and Bobby Seale cofounded the Panthers in Oakland as young men in their twenties, they knew, in their Southern-born bellies, that their political and legal genius had to coexist with image and fashion and style and swagger and soul and heroism, else the girls and boys in the 'hood would not be checking for them. They were right, and the Civil Rights Movement begat their party for the people: all eyes on them as White America, and Black America, and rainbow coalition America, supported or avoided them, saluted or attacked them, because they did not hesitate to tackle, hard body, uncomfortable things like racism and police brutality. They were young, they were gifted, they were Black, they were proud, they had free breakfast programs for kids, free health screenings for the community, a hugely popular newspaper that taught and represented culture and history through their eyes, and they were armed—with guns, because they knew their right to have them. Shoot, those Panthers were so ahead of the curve that the California law was changed, halting them from openly carrying weapons. But this is what happens when certain kinds of boys self-determine, without apology, what kind of men they are going to be. When Cam Newton, still merely twenty-seven years old, decided he indeed was going to be a professional quarterback in the National Football League, mixing and matching the brain gymnastics and physical fearlessness of a QB, and the video game darting and daring of a running back, and the WWE theatrics of a barreling, brawny tight end, with image and fashion and style and swagger and hip-hop and heroism mic dropping inside his heart, he, in a single bound, became a one-man revolution shot round the globe before millions of fans weekly, including nearly 112 million on that Super Bowl Sunday last February. Cam Newton is young, he is gifted, he is Black, he is proud, he has a foundation for youth, he hosts a self-esteem-boosting hit television show for children on Nickelodeon, and he is armed—with a charisma, a rock star aura, a Yoruba god's focus, and a supermodel's spectacular poses that could not be manufactured anywhere or by anyone, except in the home of his momma and daddy. And, yep, Huey and Cam are brothers of the same mind: equally comfortable hanging with the masses from the gutters of America's ghettoes as well as the rich and privileged with the Hermès wallets and Lana Marks purses. Yep, Huey and Cam equally calculating and stupidly handsome in that way that makes both women and men swoon and stare. Yep, one could say that Cam Newton is "pretty," the way Huey Newton was pretty. And one could say that Cam is a trapped pretty boy, the way Huey Newton wound up being a trapped pretty boy, imprisoned by the facts of his life and the myth-making of his hero worshippers.

But none of this mattered to the thirsty throng of media awaiting Cameron Jerrell Newton for his post–Super Bowl press conference. Every make of cameras, lights, microphones, digital recorders, iPhones, iPads, and Androids was aimed in Cam's direction as he took his seat, alone, at the dais, in front of what must've seemed to be a titanic and endless ocean of journalists. Cam wore a blue Carolina Panthers hooded sweatshirt, the hood part was atop his head, and his mood and energy were that of a man who was bare-fisting the brick walls of an agonizing depression. He bowed his head several times; his left hand reached inside the hood to rub or scratch his scalp; sometimes he made eye contact with the media, most times he did not; he spoke in a hushed monotone; he could not hide the disgusted smirk that was graffitied on his face. Cam did not want to be there, did not want to participate in his own crucifixion. Superman had been humiliated, and they had questions for him. He had answers for them, too, and they were short, cryptic, to the point, defensive, noncommittal.

"We'll be back."

"No."

"Got outplayed."

"Got outplayed, bro."

"They just played better than us."

"I don't know what you want me to say."

Reporter: "Can you put into words the disappointment you feel?"

Cam: "We lost."

He felt attacked. He felt dissed. He looked like a severely bruised caged bird yearning to fly himself away from the humans with the weird gadgets pointed straight at him. Did not help, either, that the poorly constructed partition between his press conference and that of the winning team, the Denver Broncos, meant he could overhear one opponent after another boast about how they harassed and shut down his game. He who had thrown for 3,837 yards and 35 touchdowns, and rushed for 10 additional TDs, in his MVP season. He who in his first five years in the National Football League had total stats that rivaled the first half decade of surefire Hall of Fame quarterbacks Tom Brady and Peyton Manning, while only missing two games—one because of injury and the other due to a car accident. He who had almost magically placed an entire team on his Paul Bunyan shoulders and made that squad, and football, relevant and electrifying in the college basketball–obsessed state of North Carolina. Yes, Cam had had a bad game. Yes, that bad game happened to be his worst of the entire season, at the worst possible time. And yes Cam, admittedly, is a sore loser. But who actually enjoys losing? So there was Cam, no smile, no teeth, no dimples, no expression, suddenly a man-child in this promised land, facing a restless and relentless jury that had been waiting for Superman to fall from the sky. And Superman had crashed and burned, terribly.

"I'm done."

PRESS PAUSE: ON THIS day, it was not clear how prophetic Cam Newton's words and actions would be. Almost like he would become undone by the hype of his MVP campaign and that unsightly Super Bowl loss, leading to this current dismal season, one stilted and awkward press conference after another, a concussion and much punishment to Cam's body, to the point of him pleading directly to National Football League commissioner Roger Goodell for help, and protection—

PUSH PLAY: AND WITH that, Cam Newton got up and ended the press conference after less than three minutes. As his muscular, chiseled frame rose one could see he was still wearing his white football pants soiled with the grass and dirt from the fifteen times he was hit and the six times the Broncos had manhandled and sacked him. Superman ain't 'spose to have a bad attitude, and the reactions were swift. Super Bowl–winning commentators such as Joe Theismann and Deion Sanders and every couch potato with a remote control and access to the comments section of a website condemned Cam. "Immature." "Unprofessional." "Arrogant." "Unacceptable." "Polarizing." "Egomaniac. . . . "

CAM NEWTON HAD PERPETRATED the cardinal sin. Not only did he lose, but he lost without grace and class, so they said. Manning, the winning quarterback on this day, once walked, angrily, off a Super Bowl field after his then Indianapolis Colts were beaten by Drew Brees's New Orleans Saints, not shaking hands or congratulating anyone, and that gesture has been deleted from memory. New England Patriots Coach Bill Belichick has mumbled his way, often disrespectfully and sarcastically, through many press conferences over the years, with a permanently sour demeanor, but that does not register scathing rebukes of his character. But as Cam had said himself a few days before the Super Bowl, "I'm an African American quarterback, that may scare a lot of people because they haven't seen nothing they can compare me to." In other words, he had been dealing with heavy criticism throughout his MVP season and his career—don't dance, don't smile so much, don't be so happy, don't be so hip-hop, stop acting like you are Superman, because you are not. . . .

Finally, the self-anointed Superman had been humbled and silenced, before a worldwide audience, by Von Miller and the Broncos' vaunted defense, in the last game, no less, for the legendary Manning, with the third-biggest television audience in United States history. Newton had completed a lowly 18 of 41 passes for 265 yards, with one interception and two fumbles. On one of those fumbles Newton hesitated, looked at the ball as it sputtered on the ground, actually took a step back, then made a half-hearted effort to go for the football, with the game on the line. It was too late, and the Broncos had the ball, and the victory. No matter how unfairly that one fumble would be replayed over and over, across multiple platforms, it cemented for some the notion that Cam Newton, the most remarkable and supremely talented athlete in America other than, maybe, Serena Williams or LeBron James or Mike Trout, was not only a sore loser, but a quitter, too.

LOS ANGELES IS WHERE people go to be stars. It is in this rambling Southern California municipality of 3.8 million that the cocktail chasers of film, television, music, media, and sports march and herd, searching for money, fame, or, sheepishly, the unfussy prospect of being seen, or seen as anything but their true selves. LA, the Hollywood edition of it, is the Mickey Mouse glass house of movers and shakers and hustlers and fakers. It is a place of perfect Mediterranean weather, United Nations–heavy ethnic diversity, majestically picturesque mountains, swaying, lazy palm trees, and fertile, beige beaches along each congested freeway drive, and as many billboard ads for new movies and TV shows as there are for plastic surgery and breast implants. The sexy, magnetic pull of Los Angeles is a thrill seeker's wet dream: the shiny, overpriced automobiles; the über-trendy, upscale restaurants; the velvet VIP opportunities to grind elbows with the wealthy and the wannabes.

Cam Newton retreated to LA after that Super Bowl disaster to engineer his second career while still in the prime of his first: his new Nickelodeon program, *All In with Cam Newton*. Much of the first season's twenty episodes are set amidst the sun-kissed days of Los Angeles. The youth are an assortment of ages and cultures. This seems to be intentional, perhaps to counter beliefs that Cam has mostly Black appeal, that he is only able to relate to African Americans. The show is good,

MY MOTHER. BARACK OBAMA. DONALD TRUMP.
AND THE LAST STAND OF THE ANGRY WHITE MAN.

81

vastly appealing, kinda like *Mister Rogers' Neighborhood* meets Peter Pan, where Cam morphs into a witty and mild-mannered sidekick helping youth to achieve their dreams in life, or to get them closer to their dreams. Here you see a side of Cam rarely depicted in the media: he still has his washtub chock-full of charm and gusto, but he is also funny, very funny. And he is at ease with these children, who include an aspiring weatherman, a budding politician, a singer with the voice of a Broadway diva, and a girl basketball player. We learn that Cam is deathly afraid of snakes in two episodes, that he is actually shocked and nervous that he has gotten an audience with First Lady Michelle Obama for the politician named Rosie; and that he, ever the big kid, loves to spit booger jokes. But more telling, to me, is the fact that Cam is liberated in this space with the kids. It is here that he smiles brightly as one boy dabs, here that he makes thinly veiled references to his disastrous post–Super Bowl press conference, here that his compassion cup runneth over as these children talk about the pressures of life, and here that he does not blink when it is obvious one of the kids has two mothers, two queer parents. In a word, Cam is free. I can imagine little Cameron visualizing being a professional football player and wishing his ten-year-old self would have had a TV big brother like him. And I imagine taping this show has been healing for Cam, because in kids, yes, you do get unfiltered and raw conversations; but missing is the brutal judgment and condemnation Cam has been shouldering from media and haters his entire adult life, since he was a highly touted teenage college recruit. Therefore, Los Angeles serves a dual purpose for Cam Newton: it is a place where he can test the waters of his superstardom in a different way, with the children's show, to gauge what else may be possible as a host, a personality, maybe even a multimedia juggernaut like past pigskin luminaries Howie Long and Michael Strahan. And Los Angeles is likewise a protective bubble so loaded with other household-name celebs that it allows Cam to be looser, and himself.

I THOUGHT OF THESE things as I walked around the annual Gatorade Player of the Year Awards inside the L.A. Hotel Downtown, right near the Staples Center where Kobe Bryant retired from basketball a couple of months before. This yearly celebration for the top female and male high school athlete in America, kick-started back in 1985, is granted based on athletic ability, academic achievement, and high character. There is chatter if Cam Newton, scheduled to co-bestow the male Gatorade Athlete of the Year, will actually show up. His agent had previously told me Cam was definitely not going to the ESPYs the next night, in spite of being nominated for Best Male Athlete and Best NFL Player. Thus, I wondered, too. Still no Cam as soccer's Landon Donovan, football's Todd Gurley, and basketball's Karl-Anthony Towns mounted the stage to announce the boy winner. Just as the trio was reading the teleprompter, Cam Newton strolled out, looking self-conscious, very late, blaming his tardiness on the immovable parking lot they call Los Angeles traffic. An audible gasp went through the Gatorade banquet at Cam's sudden appearance, he grinned shyly, and stood with his hands folded obediently in front of him. He is wearing a black suit jacket, a white rose in his lapel, a white shirt, a multicolored bowtie, and gray slacks, with black shoes and his trademark wrist accessories of a watch and colorful Lokai beaded bracelets. As always Cam is clean shaven, save his meticulously clipped goatee. He dives in and announces St. Louis native Jayson Tatum, bound for college bas-

MY MOTHER. BARACK OBAMA. DONALD TRUMP.
AND THE LAST STAND OF THE ANGRY WHITE MAN.

83

ketball at Duke University, as the boy's national winner. During the photo opps with the girl and boy awardees, Cam, the court jester, pretends to give five-foot-eight Landon Donovan a boost so he can be as tall as the other athletes on stage. We are then ushered, with great difficulty, from the banquet to another room where a rapid-fire round robin of media interviews will happen for the ten Gatorade finalists, and the pro athletes, too. If Cam moves, the crowd moves. But if Cam stops, then the crowd stops. Clearly, most of the media and others in attendance want to speak with and listen to Cam. No matter, several times I hear Cam mouth to his agent and the Gatorade reps "Are we done yet?" as he does not want to do this. Cam constantly checks the two cell phones in his goliath, leather-brown palms. "Come on, man! We only half-done?" The one moment Cam seems himself, and at ease, is when he sits in the middle of the room with the Gatorade high school athletes and jaws with them about sports, about their massive responsibilities. He is animated, he is excited, and the young athletes are in awe that they are convening in a tight circle with *the* Cam Newton. Then he is back up, back into the shift of interviews, back to his handlers and Gatorade reps announcing in five-minute intervals or so "ROTATE! ROTATE!" to us journalists, to say your time is up with Cam or the other athletes. It is something of an assembly-line effect that I have not experienced in many years. I've asked for as much time as I can get, but Cam's agent has made it clear to me, before I speak with his client, that that ain't happening, and that he is not happy about something that recently appeared about Cam on ESPN.com. I have no idea what the agent is referring to, precisely. I am told I get ten minutes—

When I finally sit down with Cam for the first time, in this heated haze of activity, I have the feeling he is looking through me, not at me, that he sees me as another cardboard media cutout. To help him align his eyes and his attention, I speed-dial my intro to Cam: that I have written about American idols like Tupac Shakur and Dave Chappelle through the years, that I am a diehard hip-hop head like him, that I want to tell his story differently, tell it as the whole human being he is. Something in Cam wakes up, his body language softens; he really sees me, and is listening, and talking. . . .

"Me growing up, if somebody asked me a question of how would eighteen- or seventeen-year-old Cam, you know, going back and look-ing ten years or however many years later, would I imagine being in this point, I would have said Yes! But with it, that was just me dreamin'. . . .

"Nobody else could tell me that I was not gonna make it to the NFL. And, you know, oftentimes I hear so many people say have a Plan B a Plan C. Well, I didn't. I turned my ear to that because I just wanted to have a Plan A and finding ways to master Plan A. . . . "

I wanted to go far deeper, but it was ridiculously loud in this make-shift media room, and I duly noted that every single time I asked Cam a question, or he answered one, his handlers, already on edge, leaned in, just as they had done with every other media pit stop before me. I had never seen an athlete or entertainer so closely monitored. What were they afraid of? Was it because they knew they could not entirely control Cam, who he was, what he might say? Or was it because Cam is many things, and it is difficult to gauge which Cam you are going to get on any given day? Like the city of Los Angeles where we were, Cam Newton is a tale of two frequencies: he is, no doubt, South Los Angeles and East Los Angeles, where Black and Brown working-class people, like the family from which he comes, wrestle with finances, mediocre public schools, gang and street violence, gentrification, and a dreadful police-community saga that includes the Watts rebellion of 1965 and motorist Rodney King being savagely struck with cop batons, on videotape, over eighty times in 1991. It was the acquittal, in April 1992, of those police officers who beat King that led to the infamous LA riots. But then there is the Los Angeles where Cam Newton is incubating his big boy power moves, where you never know who or what someone is, whether they are real or make-believe, where one moment they can be friendly and accessible and the very next glum and remote, a non-person with an attitude. Maybe Cam Newton, like this city of angels, permanent tans, and cigar-colored smog, is both, because that is the nature of things in this swath of territory bracketed by that mountainous HOLLY-WOOD sign and its addictive myth-making machine.

CAM NEWTON HAS FINISHED his worst football season ever. It flared up noisily like cheap firecrackers in training camp when a *GQ* magazine cover story appeared and Cam proclaimed, naïvely, that racism did not matter any longer, that America was "beyond that." Not sure if this was Newton's reaction to the avalanche of negative attention he has received as "an African American quarterback," or because the Carolina Panthers hired, a couple of years ago, a Republican strategist and public relations advisor named Frank Luntz to work with him and the team. Yes, the same Frank Luntz who has molded the messages of right-wing crusaders like Rudy Giuliani and Newt Gingrich, and who once said of Newton, "With the right language he can help cement his place in the NFL as one of the great franchise quarterbacks, like Brady, Rodgers, Favre." However, Cam Newton's racial moonwalking in *GQ* backfired and social media, principally "Black" twitter, went in on the Panthers' leading man, with many labeling him "sell-out," "coon," and "Uncle Tom." People were surely not buying Cam's logic that "one-eighth of an inch" should not be the reason why there is racism in America, given that "under that, we're all the same color." Not when Black folks experienced two extremely traumatic police murders this past Summer, in Louisiana and Minnesota, both on vid-eotape, both heartless and excessive, and both Black men in trapped, vulnerable positions. And not when Cam's quarterback buddy Colin Kaepernick elected, during training camp, to make the courageous and controversial move not to stand for the national anthem as these police murders of Blacks continue to occur in one random American locale after another. But Cam seemed to be confused, or unable and unwill-ing to find a clear and consistent way to talk about race and racism, even resorting to wearing a Dr. King tee-shirt before one early season game in the aftermath of yet another police shooting, this one right in Charlotte where the Panthers play, and on the heels of that *GQ* blun-der. People were not buying that either, the MLK tee-shirt, or Cam's use of the word "oppression," or his Republican-like analysis around Black America and personal responsibility, either.

On the field Cam Newton plainly has not been the same player. His offensive line has been decimated by injuries, the receiving corps and the running game have swung between missing-in-action and there just barely enough, and the defense is a shell of its former self, beginning with upper management's foolish resolution to let All-Pro cornerback Josh Norman sign with the Washington team. With Cam Newton and his very unique journey to NFL superstardom we have a football player who once won the Heisman Trophy, a national champi-onship at Auburn University, and was the league's number one overall draft pick in a span of six months; and whose journey, in only the past ten months, has gone from Most Valuable Player, Super Bowl QB, and the new face of the National Football League, to embarrassingly mediocre stats and embarrassingly mediocre play. The fall from the mountaintop has been swift and it has been harsh. Is Cam Newton a target in various ways? Oh yes, just look at film of games in the 2016 season where he has been hit high, hit low, and opposing players have squarely aimed for his head. Why, again, did Cam appeal to Commissioner Goodell for protection? Case in point is the recent Monday night affair where Newton got matched against former teammate and sparring partner Norman. On a scramble Cam was torpedoed, helmet-to-helmet, by Washington linebacker Trent Murphy, while sliding to avoid being popped. Disgusted, the quarterback bounced to his feet and chucked the ball in Murphy's direction. Cam Newton was flagged for unsportsmanlike conduct, while Murphy received no penalty. This has been the pattern throughout the season, and if one examines past years, this has perpetually been the pattern. Maybe Panthers' head coach Ron Rivera is correct in saying the assumption is that because Cam is such a big man, specifically for a quarterback, he can absorb the body blows, the way players used to beat up on the freakishly gargantuan Shaquille O'Neal during his basketball career. Or maybe it is because Cam Newton is forever hotly debated and widely disliked, because he is seen as arrogant, aloof, "an uppity nigger" to some in White America and detached from the reality of what it is to be a Black man, or "a real nigga," in Black America.

Think W. E. B. DuBois's classic breakdown of this country's racial double consciousness and you get Cam Newton, essentially: Black folks want Cam Newton to be Blacker, stronger, and White folks do not want Cam Newton to be too Black, too strong. And then there is

the sentiment that Cam Newton is overly pampered by the Panther hierarchy, that he is permitted to do whatever he feels, whenever he feels,
because of his cozy father-son relationship with owner Jerry Richardson. Or is he? In arguably the weirdest coda of this doomed season
Cam was benched at the coin flip of a Sunday night game against the
Seattle Seahawks, for violating a team rule. His violation? Not wearing a necktie during a team flight. His replacement, Derek Anderson,
promptly threw an interception and it was run back for a touchdown on
the very first play; and although Newton came in for the Panthers' next
series, Carolina was thoroughly defeated in this nationally televised
contest. So bad has Newton been this season, so inconsistent, that his
stats are worse than what they were in his first or second years in the
NFL, when young quarterbacks traditionally go through the tortuous
growing pains of learning the difference between the college game and
the pro game. And so bad has Cam Newton been at times that broad-
casters and writers are questioning everything about him, including
his footwork and throwing mechanics, his purported sore right shoulder, and whether or not he relies too much on his "natural talents."

All of this is problematic, no doubt, because playing football is Cam
Newton's golden parachute to fame and fortune, and the hope is he will
have a long and successful career. He is a man who also stands on the
shoulders of Black athletes who came before him, like Curt Flood, baseball maverick and father of sports free agency; like Oscar Robertson,
basketball god and basketball role model; like Doug Williams, the first
Black Super Bowl–winning quarterback back in 1988, none of whom
could have conjured what Cam Newton has: a $103.8-million-dollar
contract with $60 million in guaranteed money; endorsement deals with
major brands like Gatorade, Under Armour, Microsoft Corporation,

General Motors, and Dannon Yogurt. This plus Cam's Nickelodeon gig means this product of Georgia makes additional millions outside the lines, that someone recognizes and respects his marketable combination of Muhammad Ali and Huey Newton prettiness, evident leadership qualities, family-friendly values, and an ability to be a zealous cheerleader for others, be it those kids on his Nick show, or his teammates on the field, or anyone that excites and motivates him. All of this making Cam Newton a pitchman who might very well transcend the millions Peyton Manning still corrals in his now done sports career. If he can maintain, and survive, on and off the field—

BLACK ATHLETES HAVE NEVER had it easy in America, even with otherworldly star power or sudden and exorbitant wealth. They have a history of being seen as different, problematic, someone or something to be contained, told what to do, and how to do it. This is why Jack Johnson, the first Black heavyweight champion of the world in the early 1900s, was considered notorious, evil, cancerous. He dared to give America the middle finger and an unforgivable Blackness, in the Jim Crow era where Blacks were being roped up and hung from trees, no less. Johnson was a kind of Black man, a kind of Black athlete, who had never been seen before, who was not only wildly triumphant as a boxer, but who also openly and brazenly dated and sexed White women. It made White America afraid, uncomfortable, angry, and eventually Johnson was taken down, for his sexual escapades, by the Mann Act in 1912. In between the over twenty-year span of Jack Johnson and Joe Louis, there was not another Black heavyweight champion, and Blacks were fundamentally banned from the major sports of baseball and football and basketball as well. Once he became boxing's new world champ in 1937 Louis—aka the Brown Bomber—represented the kind of Black male athlete White America could love: he was quiet, shy, buttoned-up, servile, obedient, controllable, and the only place he truly did his speaking was in a boxing ring. And Joe Louis went out of his way to show his patriotism by doing whatever he could for World War II efforts. In spite of his well-behaved persona Louis aged dramatically, had substantial debt, and he was reduced to being, for a spell, a senior citizen casino greeter in Las Vegas. Just like how Jesse Owens won those four gold medals for America in the infamous 1936 Olympics in Hitler's Germany, and the best his country could offer him to earn a living after, as a human being, as a man, was, among other indignities, foot-racing against horses.

That is why, when I look at a Cam Newton, who could quite possibly go down in the annals of athletics with the same level of fame and impact as Jack Johnson, as Joe Louis, as Jesse Owens, I also feel he has a bit of a kinship to Muhammad Ali. Like Ali, Cam has always been outgoing, since he was a boy. Like Ali, Cam was a class clown, a man blessed with an Olympian physique and the competitor toolbox of a Jim Thorpe, a Jackie Joyner-Kersee, a Magic Johnson. So great is Cam's sway that his Number 1 jersey is one of the biggest sellers in the National Football League, and he had a legion of fans doing the dab, even kids at the National Spelling Bee last year. This is what American football has become, our new national pastime, long ago surpassing baseball. It is because football parallels so many things that are unique to the American social fabric: speed, power, the warrior mentality, hyper-masculinity, and, yes, violence. Football, our football, is the postmodern gladiator sport for those who enjoy the crunching of

MY MOTHER. BARACK OBAMA. DONALD TRUMP.
AND THE LAST STAND OF THE ANGRY WHITE MAN.

91

bones, the pounding of flesh, and the busting of heads. It is a ferocious and abusive sport; it hurts to play football, and it hurts, in a way some could never fathom, to religiously watch and digest football, too. The sport has grown from a barnstorming league into a global billion-dollar conglomerate many of us have come of age with. When I was a child in the 1970s my idols had names like Roger Staubach and Tony Dorsett of the Dallas Cowboys, and Fran Tarkenton and Chuck Foreman of the Minnesota Vikings. We youth played our version of football in my hometown of Jersey City, New Jersey, sometimes in the park, sometimes in a nearby cemetery with plenty of grass, and sometimes on the streets with the piss-smeared concrete and dented parked cars. We did not care if we broke noses, dislocated shoulders, or demolished our knees. It was our pathway into our manhood, this game called football, because if you could withstand this, on an actual team or the pick-up games around the way, then you were truly on the road to being a man. I did not know, when I was a youth, about concussions, about chronic traumatic encephalopathy (CTE), or the other everlasting injuries that would assault and arrest the post-career lives of these he-men. I saw this as I flew on a flight to California maybe a month before I met Cam Newton. To my surprise the plane was filled with former Cowboys who had played for the team in the 1970s, the 1980s, and the 1990s. They ranged in age from forty-something to their early seventies. They were men of all sizes, and some were White and some were Black. But what they had in common was how uncomfortable they seemed, their battered selves, these tormented years later, sitting in the legroom-challenged coach class. I spoke with two of the players, one from the 1980s, one from the 1990s, and both complained of several persistent body aches. And how they were making their living, predominantly, doing autograph signings and picking up speaking engagements wherever they could. Cam Newton would say to me at that Gatorade event, "I got to maximize it on the field as much as I can as well as off the field." Because the truth is we do not know if Cam will make it as a football player to forty, as Peyton did, as Brett Favre did, as Tom Brady is doing. This is because the average player is lucky to survive in the National Football League, injury-free, maybe three to five years, and a small percentage make it past age thirty. I think there is no question that Cam wants to go down as one of the greatest players ever. But I also think it is clear that his off-the-field activities mean he is likewise aware he needs to have a life beyond football, especially when it was Magic Johnson who once told me that something in the range of 80 percent of professional football and basketball players wind up dead broke after their careers are over.

And of all the Black quarterbacks who've come through the revolving door of the National Football League, there has not been one like Cam Newton: he is a stud athlete plus a fashion icon plus a dream for Madison Ave marketing specialists. Perhaps that is why his handlers leaned in on every single interview at the Gatorade Awards, especially after the debacle and humiliation of the Super Bowl press conference. It was said in the immediate aftermath that Cam's reputation and stock could be affected by his lack of sportsmanship, that he would lose deals, that brands would shy away from his far too risky and unpredictable persona, and clearly someone somewhere had gotten to him to say he should not screw up this golden parachute sitting right before him. But what price does one have to pay to play one's sport and to be a man, a holistic man, too? Ali sacrificed everything, by refusing induction into the army to go to the Vietnam

War. He was stripped of his heavyweight title, lost his best years as a prize fighter, and struggled to earn an income of any amount, doing speaking gigs wherever he could, and even winding up on Broadway as an unexceptional actor. And Ali boxed well past when he should have, was badly managed financially, and spent his silent years as he suffered from Parkinson's making public appearances—in some cases ones he did not want to make—and signing autographs with his shaky hand so that his family, as he put it, could eat.

As for the highly successful Black quarterback, there are few real precedents for Cam Newton on the field, unless you retreat back close to a century, to the very first Black quarterback ever, Fritz Pollard, and the position was not even called that in the early 1920s when pro football truly caught on. Frederick Douglass "Fritz" Pollard, named after the distinguished abolitionist and orator who was born a slave, played in the NFL when it was still called the American Professional Football Association (APFA). Pollard was a running back who would ultimately get under center to get the ball, the prototype for the modern quarterback position. As a star athlete at Brown University, Pollard had become, in 1916, the first African American ever to play in the Rose Bowl. He later competed for the Akron Pros, the team he would lead to the APFA championship in 1920. In 1921, Pollard became the co–head coach of the Akron Pros, while still maintaining his roster position as running back. The following year, he once more proved a dominant player while doubling as the first African American coach in the league. The APFA was renamed the National Football League in 1922, and Pollard served as one of its primary gate attractions over the next few years, much the way Cam Newton is today, because Fritz could both throw and run the ball. However, Pollard, along with the nine other Black players in the NFL in that era, was removed from the league at the end of the 1926 season, never to return again. By 1933, Blacks were all but unofficially banned from the National Football League entirely, not to show up again until 1946. And before, since, the shadowy whispers of Black quarterbacks come and gone would hut-hut-hike their plea to be. . . .

Fritz Pollard . . . George Taliaferro . . . Willie Thrower . . . Charlie "Choo Choo" Brackins . . . Eldridge Dickey . . . Marlin Briscoe . . . Onree Jackson . . . James Harris . . . Joe Gilliam . . . Vince Evans . . . Doug Williams . . . Warren Moon . . . Andre Ware . . . Randall Cunningham . . . Jeff Blake . . . Kordell Stewart . . . Donovan McNabb . . . Steve McNair . . . Michael Vick . . . Daunte Culpepper . . . Vince Young . . . Russell Wilson . . . Colin Kaepernick . . . Robert Griffin III . . . Tyrod Taylor . . . Cam Newton . . . Jameis Winston . . . Dak Prescott . . .

Many Black quarterbacks, instead of being given an opportunity to field the position, were turned into or became, out of necessity or desperation, running backs, cornerbacks, or wide receivers, as former Oakland Raider QB Terrelle Pryor did for the Cleveland Browns in 2016. Quite a few had to escape to the Canadian Football League, a de facto Negro Leagues for Black quarterbacks, to prove they had the maturity and intelligence and skill sets to pilot a team. There are countless stories of mentalities and conducts being interrogated; of anger repressed or exploded; of a Black quarterback like Joe Gilliam of the Pittsburgh Steelers, in one of the golden eras of the 1970s, becoming so disillusioned with losing the job he'd won from Terry Bradshaw, that he was out of the NFL by age twenty-five, followed by a troubled and damaged life wrecked by drugs and alcohol and homelessness. There are also stories of Black quarterbacks drafted or signed, but when you look at their career stats, they never played a single game at quarterback, or barely got in. Quarterback is the glamour position of professional football, the kingpin, the general, the sheriff; and given the history of racism in America it is little wonder that certain kinds of owners and sports media did not think Black men were intelligent enough, or qualified enough, to be quarterbacks, never giving most of them a fair shake. And the only colleges providing Black quarterbacks a legitimate shot were schools running the option offense (because of the historic judgment that each and every Black man is a naturally gifted athlete, and, thus, naturally fast) or historically Black colleges and universities, like Tennessee State, where Gilliam was the star and his dad was the defensive coordinator. Indeed, Steve McNair remains one of only three HBCU quarterbacks taken in the first round—alongside Eldridge Dickey and Doug Williams.

Outside of attending a Black college, which Cam did not, the only other thing that could have prepared him for any of this was his own family history and traditions and methods of survival. His mother, Jackie Newton, had her roots in St. Mark's Parish, South Carolina, before her family migrated to Statesboro, Georgia, by the early 1900s. His father, Cecil Newton Sr., has kin steeped in the rust-brown dirt of Georgia going back to 1816. As with so many Black people made in America during and after slavery, it is a history of victories and losses, of sorrow and joy, of great highs and traumatic lows, of making something from nothing, of often having nothing but each other. There was Talbot Carter, great-great-great-grandfather of Cam Newton, a Black man who signed an oath book with an X (he could not read or write) in 1867, swearing that he had not rebelled against the state of Georgia during

the Civil War, so that he could vote. About a dozen years later, Talbot
Carter, in 1880, was tilling sixty-nine acres of land, which he rented on
a fixed income. There were a range of occupations for Cam's clan that
included domestic workers, a porter in a shoe store, and farmers, some
of whom owned the land and some of whom did not. There were some
relatives who referred to themselves as "mulatto," or, rather, mixed
race, instead of colored or Negro or Black, because anything except full
Blackness gave them some social wiggle room in terms of employment
or the ability to navigate through a racist and hostile environment.
There was one family member who wound up, during the Great Depression of the 1930s, in a mental institution, something Black people
did not discuss then, and rarely discuss in these times either. There was
Talmadge Wilder, Jackie's father and Cam's grandfather, who had been
a bricklayer, a soldier during World War II, and who was arrested for
"simple larceny" in the late 1940s, spending two years in jail. In those
days that could have meant a petty crime, maybe, or it could have meant
that Cam's granddaddy had pissed off the wrong White police officer or
White judge and been given that sentence; kinda how so many Black
males, myself included, have been charged with "resisting arrest" when
we had done no such thing. Even more fascinating is that Talmadge
Wilder was once listed as "mulatto"; but in the aftermath of World
War II he chose to identify as Black. It was the time period of the great
migration and the first warning shots of the Civil Rights Movement.
Bishop Talmadge Wilder would go on to found Holy Zion Holiness
Church in Savannah, Georgia. It was there in the swamp-like humidity
of that river city that Cecil and Jackie met as college students at the his-
torically Black Savannah State University. A football player at school,
Cecil had pro tryouts with the Buffalo Bills and Dallas Cowboys in the

early 1980s, but nothing stuck and his career ended. A regal and proud
Black man, he and his wife had three boys, Cecil Jr., Cam, and Caylin. Cecil Jr. was mostly on practice squads in his short NFL career as
a three-hundred-pound offensive lineman, and Caylin is in his senior
year as a high school quarterback. Cam, the middle child, was born on
May 11, 1989, under the sign of Taurus, one that claims leadership, daring, but also mule-like stubbornness and turbulent emotions. Taurus
folk like Cam crave stability, family, but also get bored very easily. Cam
was that kind of child, from peewee football through high school. He
was blessed, he would tell me, to have his father in the home, especially
when so many around him did not: "My dad is one of those dads that at
least—I can't even put a number on 'em: They call him Pops. I call him
Pops, my best friends called him Pops."

With that foundation, and an Atlanta full of possibilities for Black
people—mayors and other elected officials, thriving entrepreneurs in
every field imaginable, the explosion of entertainment empires rang-
ing from L.A. Reid and Babyface to Jermaine Dupri, the Dungeon
Family, and Tyler Perry, to every kind of Black person in every kind
of occupation, little wonder that someone like Cam Newton growing
up in that environment would think highly of himself, would think
anything was possible. Add to that the revolution of hip-hop as the
dominant music and youth culture of the past four decades, where a
young Cam, as he made his way between school and practice, between
home and church, and in the confines of his room, more than likely
had a steady diet of Atlanta-area rap figures such as Goodie Mob, Outkast, Kriss Kross, Organized Noize, Ludacris, Lil Jon, Bone Krusher,
T.I., DJ Drama, Killer Mike, Gucci Mane, Migos (as in "Look at My
Dab"), Skippa Da Flippa, Peewee Longway, and Rich the Kid. This

art form has impacted what is now multiple hip-hop generations, of all races and colors and backgrounds. Cam was and is no different. It is a music, it is a culture, it is our blues, our jazz, our rock and roll, our language, our value system, our way of seeing the world. It is from that culture, that was created by poor African Americans, poor Latinos, and poor West Indians, the same poor folks whom Dr. King, that other Atlanta dreamer, warned us not to abandon at the end of his life, that we get the hairstyles, the tattoos, the creative ways Black athletes don their uniforms and accessories; where we get the bald heads and the dreadlocks, and, yes, where we got Cam Newton doing the dab, got him wearing colorful, eye-grabbing clothes, and shutting down press conferences when he no longer wants to be bothered. It is a culture of resistance, was created as such, it is a culture of doing for self, of winning on our own terms, and its roots can be found in the field hollers and spirituals of slaves and farmers like Cam's ancestors in South Carolina and Georgia, in the bebop of Charlie Parker and Dizzy Gillespie, in the daring base stealing of Jackie Robinson, in the take-no-prisoners running style of legendary Cleveland Browns fullback Jim Brown, in the poetry of Muhammad Ali and his hype man Drew Bundini Brown, in the call and response of the Black churches many of us grew up in, including Cam's parents; it is in the rhetoric and speech patterns of Huey Newton, Bobby Seale, Fred Hampton, and the Black Panther Party; it is found in the way Michigan's Fab Five amplified the trend of extra baggy basketball shorts, in the way Deion Sanders danced and two-stepped whenever he made a great play, in the way the late great Stuart Scott, he of ESPN lore, did his reports as if he were a dope emcee with just one chance to rap the funkiest rhymes in the history of the genre. This is hip-hop, our church, our gospel. And

MY MOTHER. BARACK OBAMA. DONALD TRUMP.
AND THE LAST STAND OF THE ANGRY WHITE MAN.

99

the Black church, yes, is itself the other space of liberation for Black folks who are not able to express themselves freely. It is there we can cut loose. Spiritual therapy, I call it, where, if your church has no restrictions whatsoever, is not embarrassed to be Blacker than Black, you will see choirs swaying, parishioners dancing and crying and running laps around the aisles as the Holy Ghost gets all up in them. When you hear Cam Newton say he is going to be who he is, he is talking about where he came from, where in that Black church excellence was expected of you, and greatness, too, in everything you do. You smile, you dance, you celebrate, you be your unabashedly African self. In the Black church, as in hip-hop, you do not care who is watching you, who is listening. Whatever you are you are, and we keep it a hundred, as we say. And in a world where the National Football League has been densely populated by Black male bodies who either grew up in urban America or rural America, who have some relationship, more than likely, to both hip-hop and the Black church, to Black spiritual practices of some sort, it is inevitable, really, that our culture and our values would clash with those of White America. But many of us do not care because we know we've got one opportunity, often, to be who we are. As Cam had said to me, there is no Plan B or C—

So, like those Gatorade national finalists, Cam would break several records at Westlake High School, and would be heavily recruited by schools like Oklahoma and Virginia Tech and the University of Florida. He wound up at the University of Florida, as an understudy to Tim Tebow. In the midst of that he did something very dumb, something I have done, that many young people have done. He took something, a laptop computer. Between that incident and allegations of academic dishonesty Cam was forced to leave Florida and landed at tiny Blinn Col-

lege in Texas. He put up huge numbers, he won a national junior college championship, and he decided on Auburn University in Alabama
as his primetime move. This is where it once again got dicey. Rumors
circulated that his dad was auctioning his son's college services to the
highest bidder. What is fact or fiction is still muddled, but this carried
on throughout Cam's lone season at Auburn, as he crushed quarterback passing and rushing records, became a lightning rod and a cult
hero, won the Heisman Trophy as college football's best player, and
topped it off by leading Auburn to the national championship with a
win over Oregon in Glendale, Arizona. All along, Cam's eligibility
was held in the balance, and eventually Cecil Sr. was banned from the
Heisman ceremony and the national championship game, too. Cecil
would later say he had to fall on the sword to protect his son, and
in other interviews Dad would comment about how unfair amateur
athletics was, how much money was made from these unpaid college
kids. Revealing, kind of, when you think about it. And perhaps some
truth to the rumors that Cam's father was peddling his son's services,
known or unknown by Cam. After all, Dad himself had played football, knew the demands and rigors of the sport firsthand, knew that
the window of celebrity is small and can close at any time. And as a
proud Black man, Cam's father was keenly aware of how big-time
college sports, specifically basketball and football, make millions of
dollars off these athletes, many of whom never get their college de-
grees, and all but a few of whom actually make it to the pros.

Cam did, even as the pundits said he was not pro football quarterback material, and definitely not the number one overall draft pick, and
not even someone worthy of the first round, either. We've heard this
song before. But Jerry Richardson, owner of the Carolina Panthers,

saw and felt something about Cam Newton. Like Cam, Richardson is also a product of the South—Spring Hope, North Carolina. He played his collegiate football at Wofford College in South Carolina, and was a member of the Baltimore Colts' illustrious championship team of 1959, led by the crewcut–wearing storybook of a dude christened Johnny Unitas. Richardson would go into business, making a fortune in the food franchising and food service industry, and in 1995 he purchased the Carolina Panthers, now worth $1.5 billion, for $206 million. Mr. Richardson, as Cam calls him, asked his star quarterback not to be so outwardly hip-hop—no earrings, no visible tattoos, no wild hairstyles, no hair on his face, save that trademark goatee. Cam said he could do it, and the naysayers notwithstanding, in his first season Newton broke all-time NFL rookie records for passing and rushing yards. He became the first NFL quarterback to throw for 400 yards in his opening game, shattering Peyton Manning's first-game record by 120 yards. He also broke Otto Graham's sixty-one-year-old record for passing yards by any quarterback in an NFL debut. Newton would go on to become the first rookie quarterback to throw for 4,000 yards in a season, as well as the first rookie quarterback to rush for 700 yards. He also ran for 14 touchdowns, more in a single season than any quarterback in NFL history, breaking Steve Grogan's thirty-five-year-old record.

At six feet five inches and weighing 245 pounds, Cam is built like his favorite target, tight end Greg Olsen. But that size does not inhibit him. He has the running ability of Gale Sayers, the arm strength of Dan Marino, the on-field mental toughness and know-how of Joe Montana, the strategic vision of John Elway, and the swashbuckler sense of joy and adventure of Brett Favre. That he is Black doing this, in a country and in a football league that has never quite seen the likes of a Cam Newton, means that the pile-on is mad real, folks searching hard for some hole or quirk in his game or personality, some way to knock that chip off Cam's shoulder. Not coincidentally, Cam's rise to national fame began in that 2007 first year at the University of Florida, just as another trailblazer, Barack Obama, had announced his first bid for president of the United States. Like Obama, Newton has been on a national stage ever since. Loved, hated, scrutinized, misunderstood, dissed, disrespected, his leadership and intelligence and aura questioned all over the place. Ellis Cose once titled a book *The Envy of the World*, referencing how Black men are looked upon and treated, in our America. A kind of gaze that makes one wonder if people see us, or simply see what they want to pin on us. But where previous Black quarterbacks faltered or failed or simply were not up to the job, or had brief moments of brilliance, Cam, season after season—and despite his substandard sixth season—is, as he put it, something we've never seen before. This is not to take anything from the Seattle Seahawks' Russell Wilson, but Cam is simply different, and that is OK. This is not to say Colin Kaepernick, who has a White mother and a Black father and was raised by two White surrogate parents, is somehow Blacker than Cam Newton because Colin openly protests America's racism and Cam does not. There is no uniform Blackness, no one way of being a Black man or a Black athlete. The old game of good Negro versus bad Negro, of Floyd Patterson versus Muhammad Ali, of Michael Jordan versus Charles Barkley during their playing days, is as old as the slave master pitting Black slaves in the big house against Black slaves working in those cotton fields. There always has to be a counterpoint, someone to go against the Black person who makes Whites so very uncomfortable, to prove it is that Black person, not them, or their racism, that is the problem. This is why it is such a difficult thing for Cam Newton to be seen as the face of the National Football League, even if Peyton Manning, long that face, said as much last year. Much of the fan base who can afford those tickets are White. Many of them are White males. Many bring with them the worst possible stereotypes about Black people, about Black men, and are only comfortable with Black men shooting and dunking basketballs, or throwing and catching and running footballs, or tackling each other, hard, à la the battle royal scene in Ralph Ellison's *Invisible Man*. A Black man who is able to look you square in the eyes, say what he feels without apology, and smile in a very different kind of way than how Magic Johnson smiled, will make you uncomfortable. I love and admire Magic, as the revolutionary basketball player he was, as the revolutionary businessman that he is; but his smile was more of the Rodney King can-we-all-get-along smile, whereas behind and inside Cam's smile is a smile his grandfather Bishop Talmadge Wilder more than likely also wore, throughout his life, one that says I am not afraid or intimidated of you, you do not own me, and you never will—

IT HAS BEEN SAID that as the American South goes, so goes American politics, American history, and, I would add, American sports. As a child I was terrified of the American South. I was terrified by the stories of water hoses and barking dogs and Dr. King getting gunned down on the balcony of that Memphis motel. I was terrified of the stories of people, Black people, dying under mysterious circumstances, the stories of the ghosts of ancestors and this relative or that relative walking, yes, walking, hundreds upon hundreds of miles, to get away from danger, although it was never quite explained why. I was terrified of the long, lonesome dirt roads, and I was terrified of those silent trees that seemed to keep secrets only God and the birds could comprehend. But I also know there is a beauty and magic and poetry to the South, too. It is the home of the Bible Belt, of biscuits and gravy and macaroni and cheese and fried chicken, of fireworks and barbecues, and it is the home of football, American football, the kind of prideful smash-mouth football that unites people, towns, counties, states, regions, this team or that team, this school or that school, because football, as Cam Newton learned when he starred at Westlake High and Auburn, is where you can make a name for yourself. The American South, quite literally, and culturally, is a farm system, a breeding ground, for American sports, be it baseball, or basketball, or football, in a way no other locality of the nation is.

As I ease my rental car from the Charlotte airport, and drive on 85 South to Spartanburg, South Carolina, where the Panthers have their training camp, I reflect on this. Like Cam, my entire family tree is also rooted in the American South—proud Geechees from the Low Country of South Carolina—a quick drive across the Savannah River from where Newton's granddaddy founded that church in Georgia. The American South is weighted by history, love, hate, rigid belief systems, and in-your-face contradictions. There is Southern hospitality and then there is an impenetrable embrace of the Confederate Flag, of words like *plantation*. There you find the hideous residue of slavery and segregation, and there you find the source and birthplace of the Civil Rights Movement. There is a worship of Jesus, that prophet of peace and togetherness, and then there is brick-wall resistance to full racial integration, still, to marriage equality, to immigrants, to "foreigners." And there is an almost mythical and steady stream of astonishing Black athletes, athletes who transformed their sports, athletes breast-fed Down South, but who did not make their names as professional sports icons, by and large, in the American South, like Willie Mays, like Hank Aaron, like Muhammad Ali, like Michael Jordan, like Steph Curry. No, they each may have been shaped by the American South in some way, but outside of Cam Newton, no Black pro athlete of his stature has ever been an ultra-dominant force in this part of the nation, as he was during his MVP season, and as he has been for much of his career. There is the one example of Michael Vick, he of Virginia and for a brief time the heralded quarterback of the Atlanta Falcons, but we know how badly and how tragically that ended, for both Vick and his dogs. The only other example we can point to is Hank Aaron, back in 1973 and 1974, near the end of his Hall of Fame career, as he approached Babe Ruth's homerun record. Aaron, from Alabama, was playing for the Atlanta Braves after the bulk of his résumé had been spent with the Milwaukee Braves, before the team moved to ATL. Hank Aaron learned quickly and firsthand how sacred Ruth's mark was to White America, to the American South, as he fielded every kind of death threat and hate mail imaginable. And this in the face of Aaron being the polar opposite of Cam Newton, if you will: quiet, soft-spoken, a throwback to the era before Black athletes were inspired by the likes of Ali and Jim Brown and Curt Flood to speak up for themselves, fearlessly, unashamedly. So in this sense, too, Cam Newton is a pioneer, a native son of the South treading water in this new territory.

This is where Cam Newton practices and plays and eats and sleeps and dreams football. South Carolina is as big a fan base for the Carolina Panthers as North Carolina, where the team hosts its regular season games. As I walk slowly toward the practice field there is a sea of

White faces and bodies and I wonder who amongst these many fans screaming Cam's name are hardcore racists themselves, who believe the South was right during the Civil War, who own a Confederate Flag or two or three, and who only applaud for Black men if they are playing one sport or another. I bring my mind back to Spartanburg, where the team holds its preseason training camp on the grounds of Wofford College. It is a spongy green campus, lined with redwood and sequoia trees; it has a statue of Mr. Richardson on the patio of the Harley Room in the Richardson Physical Activities Building; and it is a school that has just under two thousand full-time students. It is a cloudy and overcast morning, smells like rain, as Southern folks are prone to say, but that is not going to stop the session from happening. As I walk from the parking lot to the practice field, I do a quick Google check and see that in the city of Spartanburg, 21 percent of the residents are Black and 74 percent are White. This is evident, perhaps, by the majority of White fans, of all ages, who've shown up here as early as 7:00 a.m., 8:00 a.m., to get a look at their heroes, mostly Black men. It is not an unfamiliar sight to me, as I have been to many football and basketball games through the years. But sports, it is assumed, is the great equalizer, and, I was told from my youth forward, a place where people of different backgrounds are in fact on even-level playing fields, but I simply no longer believe that, and have not for years—and it doesn't matter how much I love sports and see it as an outlet for my blues. As is the case wherever I have traveled in the South, the people are polite, respectful, say "sir" and "ma'am" to initiate or punctuate most sentences—everyone from security guards to interns to local police officers are friendly and helpful to me. Many of the fans are wearing Carolina Panther player jerseys, with Cam's Number 1 being the most visible. As the players stream in, either by foot, or in golf carts, the fans scream for their favorites, like Greg Olsen or Luke Kuechly or Kelvin Benjamin. Then Cam Newton shows up sprinting onto the field, head down, white bandanna tied around his forehead, red practice jersey and white practice pants, as the too many to count children pushing along the practice field let out an infectious CAM! CAM! CAM! Tons of children out here, and nearly half the crowd are women, further illustrating that women and girls are the fastest-growing demographic of football fans in America. Like his TV show, these children are Newton's real fans. They love Cam, really do see him as larger than life, as a Superman. I watch Cam horse around with teammates, stretch, go through sprints, and then a series of plays with backup quarterbacks Derek Anderson and Joe Webb. Every chance Cam gets, he slyly eases his way to the section where screaming kids are, posing for a quick picture here or there, then moving back onto the field. There is a media throng, too, local and national media both, including CBS's *60 Minutes*, which has been tracking Cam much of the year. Cam, the boy who grew up in the church, has a foul mouth, and has rebelled very slightly against the rules about his clean-cut image: he has dyed his goatee blond and lets the f-bomb fly several times in practice. Like the fans, I wait for Cam to exit the field once practice is over. He decides to do extra foot and speed work with the backup quarterbacks, then slowly makes his way toward the fans clamoring for photos, or for him to sign their shirts, hats, footballs, or even somewhere on their bodies.

CAM! CAM! The children's voices shriek again.

Cam Newton does his best to see, touch, high-five, or sign something for every single person standing behind the fan area. When he leans in, they lean in, when he moves on, a dejected sigh is voiced from that particular section. When Cam gets to a group of military personnel in uniform, each holding a football, he takes his time to thank them for their service, and carefully signs each of their footballs, then offers them a word of encouragement. You can see the joy in the eyes of the fans, of the military folks, of everyone who either clears a path for Cam, or who eagerly follow behind him as he makes his way back to the dorm building where the entire team is staying. Like his television show, this is Cam's comfort zone, his sweet spot, where he is free, completely free, and he soaks in the adulation. The glow for Cam is so colossal that it is almost as if the other players do not exist. Cam is truly in his own universe, Elvis to their Jordanaires, Michael Jackson to his brothers, Prince to his Revolution. You know they are there, you know the music would not happen without them, but everyone is always looking for the hero, hoping something about that hero will miraculously rub off on them—

ON THIS SWELTERING AUGUST night in Baltimore, there is the mood and feel of a regular season game, probably because it is Cam Newton and the Panthers the home-team Ravens are playing. In a booming M&T Bank Stadium, there is purple everywhere. And there is Cam Newton on the near sideline, jumping up and down, pumping up his teammates as he always does. Cam is only going to play one series tonight, and he is already in midseason form, or so it seems. He completes crisp passes, and the only errant throw was a missed touchdown toss to Ted Ginn Jr. Rest of the half I follow Cam as much as I can on the sidelines, but he is a spirited soul. The man simply cannot sit still for more than a couple of minutes at a time. When a teammate intercepts a Ravens pass and run it back for a touchdown, there is Cam running down the sideline, bursting with glee. Except he does not realize he is on the turf. The refs huddle, and a penalty indicates that Cam was flagged for being an illegal substitution on the field of play. That touchdown is erased. Indeed, as I watch and hear the Panthers and Ravens crunch and clobber each other, in pads, as they sweat and yell, I wonder how many of these players, in the years yet to be seen, will suffer from CTE, will have arthritis, will barely be able to get out of bed each and every single day. And I wonder if these players know, or even realize, or even care, that the NFL fan base is 83 percent White and 64 percent male. These are people who pay staggering amounts of money to watch Black men have their bodies pummeled on the field. So as long as these Black male athletes run and hit and tackle, keep their helmets on and their mouths shut, then they are acceptable to the White mainstream public. However, when Black athletes choose to point their defiance not toward each other but to systematic inequalities, that's when the backlash begins. Or if they dare to, like Cam Newton, have a chip on their shoulders, then they are crucified, even before they get into the league. . . .

"Very disingenuous—has a fake smile, comes off as very scripted and has a selfish, me-first makeup. Always knows where the cameras are and plays to them. Has an enormous ego with a sense of entitlement that continually invites trouble and makes him believe he is above the law—does not command respect from teammates and always will struggle to win a locker room. Only a one-year producer. Lacks accountability, focus and trustworthiness—is not punctual,

seeks shortcuts and sets a bad example. Immature and has had issues with authority. Not dependable."

> —*Pro Football Weekly*'s Nolan Nawrocki, a White gentleman who played linebacker at Illinois (Spring 2011, the year Cam was drafted)

These are some of the kinder things that have been said about Cam Newton through the years. I recall the first Black professional football player, Charles Follis, who was nicknamed "The Black Cyclone," a six-foot, two-hundred-pound halfback. I think of how he must have felt, from 1902 to 1906, when he played for the Shelby Blues of the Ohio League. To have fans threaten your life before, during, and after the games. To have players, White players, do everything they could to purposely hurt or injure you. To know that you were carrying not just the burden of your own destiny, but that of an entire race of people. One of his White teammates on that Shelby team in 1902 and 1903 was a young man named Branch Rickey. Rickey was a student at nearby Ohio Wesleyan University. Years later, in the 1940s, and as general manager of the Brooklyn Dodgers, it was Branch Rickey who signed Jackie Robinson to be the first Black baseball player in the modern era. You have to wonder what he saw of Follis that affected Rickey's life. Follis only lived to age thirty-one, dying of pneumonia in 1910, but it is in the ancient footprints of men like him, Black men like him, that Cam Newton walks, whether he knows it or not.

For the second half of the game I decide to sit in the media press box upstairs. I look around several times and notice that the vast majority of sports media are White men, a few diverse women, and less than five are Black males, counting me. I think about that stat of the National

Football League being over 70 percent Black males, yet most of the folks working for sports newspapers, radio shows, television programs, websites, and podcasts have little to nothing in common with these Black men, and many, based on the media I have absorbed since I was a child, do not really even know or understand the America they, we, come from, and that is clear by the coverage. You wanna ask, Have you ever spent significant time in any Black community, be it working class or middle class? Ever set foot at a majority Black high school or historically Black college or university? Do you have a working knowledge of both American history, inclusive of all people, and also Black history, particularly given you have such strong opinions about these Black athletes? Ever thought about slavery, segregation, the crack epidemic, the prison-industrial complex, or how integration may have both helped and hurt Black America? Any knowledge, beyond the surface, about Black music, Black art, Black culture, Black spiritual practices, like the Black church or Black folks who might be Muslim? Any consideration to how Black English, to us, and hip-hop, to us, is our culture, our way of being, whether you like or understand it or not? You ever been pulled over by the police, harassed by the police, beaten by the police, racially profiled by the police? And do you have any idea what it is like to grow up in a world, an inner-city world, where the bulk of these Black male athletes come from, where you are essentially given three life options, as Black males: be an athlete, be an entertainer, or be a street hustler? This is the crux of the problem, historically, from Jack Johnson, to Kareem Abdul-Jabbar, to Cam Newton; these White male sports gatekeepers do their duty, so they feel, both consciously and subconsciously, of placing on the heads of Black male athletes what is moral or immoral, what is mature or immature, what is a good attitude and what is a bad attitude, what is acceptable behavior and what is not acceptable behavior, and what constitutes model citizenship and what does not. In other words, it is their value system, their culture, these Black men are expected to adhere to, from generation to generation, if they want to have any real and sustained success in American professional sports. The great irony, of course, is that these Black male athletes, many of them, anyhow, are simply emulating definitions of manhood obtained from White males with power and privilege, like the owners of their football teams, like America's political and business leaders: the money, the material goods, the entourages, the women as sex objects or caretakers or punching bags—or all three, the accumulation of as much authority and influence as possible. But they are not the owners, they are the players, so the owners get to tell the players what they cannot do, directly, or via the league office. Call it whatever you want, but it is clear to me, from NFL Draft Day to how a Colin Kaepernick has been ridiculed, maligned, isolated for speaking out against police brutality, that it feels a lot like slavery, at times. But they are high-paid athletes, you say? But, if we are mad honest, we know that what these athletes are paid is peanuts compared to what the league and the owners and Commissioner Goodell make, and that no amount of compensation will make up for the permanent injuries, including those to the brain, none too few of these modern-day gladiators accumulate like war wounds during their playing years. I think of this as I watch Cam Newton on the sidelines of this preseason game with the Ravens, and it makes great sense why his handlers are signing every deal imaginable, why they are going out of their way to clean up the perception of Cam that was intensified because of his rotten Super Bowl 50 press conference. You just do not know how long the window of opportunity will be open for Cam

Newton, for any Black athlete. In the words of the immortal rapper Ice Cube, they'll find a new nigga next year—

Perhaps that also explains, after the Ravens game, why Cam Newton stepped into the media room for the press conference, gripped the podium adorned with the NFL logo—tight—closed his eyes, then breathed for just a few seconds, before taking questions from the media. It is the kind of breath his ancestors might have taken when they were on those slave ships bound for states like South Carolina and Georgia. Or the kind of breath they drew when they were working those fields or in the big houses of those plantations. Or the kinds of breath inhaled when they bought, built, created land and schools and churches to call their own, under the daily threat of White domestic terrorism in the form of lynch mobs, or legal doctrines, or the denial of their right to vote, even as they paid taxes like everyone else. It, too, was like the breath of every single Black man who has been told, in his lifetime, that he has a chip on his shoulder, that he is uppity. It is that breath we drew when we could not say what we really felt for fear of being spat upon, or punched, or stabbed, or shot, or hanged from a tree, simply for having the nerve to talk to a White man like he was our equal. Cam, in his blood and his bones, knows this all too well, not simply because he is a native son of the American South, but because he was born in America.

We've come a long way from Fritz Pollard and other Black men being run out of the National Football League for good. We've come a long way from Jackie Robinson having to suppress his anger, his rage, his true feelings, and being told not to fight back, to the point that it probably hurt him more than anyone else. But we've still got a long way to go before a Cam Newton is treated with the respect of a Peyton Manning or a Tom Brady. Manning can be accused of sexual misconduct during his undergraduate years at the University of Tennessee, have those sexual allegations trail him for years, but they do not stick to him. Tom Brady can have a first child of his without being married, just like Cam, but no one questions Brady's morality, no one declares that he is having babies out of wedlock. There remains, in our America, a confounding double standard when it comes to White men and Black men, and in few places is that played out so clearly than in our beloved sports world. Again, we love to say all is equal on a playing field or a court, but we know, if we are truly honest with ourselves, that it is not. Long since Fritz Pollard in the 1920s and the Rooney Rule of the 2000s, the National Football League still barely has any Black men as coaches or executives, and not one African American owns a majority stake in any of the teams. Over 70 percent of the players, yes, but in the prized position of quarterback Black males by and large are not trusted to run much of anything. Dak Prescott, the Dallas Cowboys' highly regarded Black rookie QB, had a couple of bad games in spite of propelling the 'Boys to one of their best runs in team history, and there has been ever louder chatter to have him replaced with the former starter, Tony Romo, in spite of Prescott being a superior player, obviously. Yes, Black men are leaders, too, can lead, and Cam Newton destroys that mold because he is an unabashed general, and he knows he can be whatever he wants to be because his God and his momma and his daddy and his church and his Black community in the ATL told him so. Why would he be any different once he got to the University of Florida, or Blinn College, or Auburn University, or the Carolina Panthers? You cannot suddenly erase who've you been your entire life, a Black boy who was taught early on that his Black life mattered, too, and was the equal of yours. This is where it

MY MOTHER. BARACK OBAMA. DONALD TRUMP.
AND THE LAST STAND OF THE ANGRY WHITE MAN.

115

hurts, this is where it eats at you, this is why, I believe, an immensely gifted quarterback like Joe Gilliam sunk into that depression and self-medicated for so many years on things that would trash his body.

Because this is what racism does to Black people, to Black athletes: you work twice as hard, three times as hard, ten times as hard, and still you are told you are not good enough, that you have been rejected. Has there been progress in sports? Without question. Thanks to that Black baseball rebel long ago, Curt Flood, there is free agency and some ability to determine the course of your athletic career. Cam Newton is making a salary that a Curt Flood could have only dreamed of. These players, without question, are pampered and privileged, and have become heroes, to people of all races and cultures, as people's first heroes, their only heroes, in a way that could not have been conceived when Fritz Pollard and other Black players were run out of the NFL. But I also believe the doors opening, the opportunities, the successes, have come at a price for many Black athletes. Think of what Jackie Robinson endured, per Ken Burns's recent and brilliant two-part documentary film. Jackie could never fully be who he was. Yes, he succumbed to diabetes, but I also feel that Jackie Robinson died, at just age fifty-three, and looking twenty years older, because he had swallowed so much racism in his life. Cam Newton is doing his best to avoid that fate. Perhaps that is why he shows so much joy and enthusiasm on the field, because he is trying not to die a slow and miserable death due to the game he loves. Perhaps that is why he lets his guard down around children, because Cam remembers what he was like as a child, what it was like for all of us as children before we began to realize that race matters, and that some lives do not matter. So there he stands, at that podium, and I think of the Cam we saw at that Super Bowl dais, just sitting there, limp and defeated. This Cam, on this boiling August night, was anew with his fashionista alter ego, but it really hit me that between January and this August night something had shifted in Cam Newton. He was wary, tentative, as a matter of fact, because he just did not know what would happen to him next, because he was, is, at the mercy of people who could make or break his image. It wears you down, the constant barrage of scrutiny, the smugness of some of these reporters, and, yes, in some cases the outward disdain and racism. If you say what you really feel, then you are the problem, not them. I am sure Cam would love to tell folks, straight up, to kiss his butt. I am sure Cam is angry every single time someone White refers to him as "immature" in their sports commentary, as a second-tier quarterback with that MVP trophy sitting in his home. I am sure he is angry when someone, anyone, online, refers to his partner Kia Proctor, the mother of his son and their new baby, negatively, and habitually posts pictures of her from her days as an exotic dancer, with no discretion what-soever, and the lewdest and most sexist observations. Maybe that is why, in this press conference after the Ravens game whenever Cam hears a question he does not like, or does not want to answer, he says, simply, stoically, "Next question." He is not going to take the bait, not any longer, he seems to be saying. But when does this become the extreme, when does this become a kind of prison, a kind of death, in and of itself? Not every athlete, regardless of race, has the gift of gab and the courage of a Muhammad Ali. Not every athlete is or will ever be as fearless as Ali was, able to push back and challenge the media, and dictate to the media, with a wicked left-right verbal combination, who he is, and who he wants to be. Cam actually does possess an incredible speaking voice, an understanding of the media and how it operates, but you feel that he is torn between being completely real and blunt and playing it safe so as not to screw up his potential standing as the new face of the National Football League, and so that he will have money, wealth, for the rest of his life, unlike many former and current players. And the reality is there has not been a Black football player with the same star power qualities in at least the past twenty-five years. Not Jerry Rice. Not Randy Moss. Not Steve Mc-Nair. Not Adrian Peterson. Not Russell Wilson. Cam's son may be named Chosen but it is actually Newton himself who is the chosen one for these baby steps of the twenty-first century. Because Cam carries with him an uncontainable Blackness that up until him was the reason why many Black athletes, and especially Black quarterbacks, were never given an opportunity to shine. It is enough to make you wanna holler, and to make your momma, who done seen some things in her own lifetime, as mine has, as Cam's has, want to jump in front of that moving truck she can see coming right at her son—

ONCE AGAIN, I AM told I only have about ten minutes to walk and talk with Cam Newton from this Baltimore press conference to the team bus. Essentially, I have been working on this Cam Newton piece since the Super Bowl last February and have spent the better part of six months reading, watching, listening, observing, and traveling to different parts of the country to get from Cam and his handlers the eleven minutes and forty seconds in Baltimore and the twelve minutes and ten seconds I got in Los Angeles. And, I need to add, this piece was originally with another publication, went through mad changes, and now it is here. My changes, this article's changes, Cam's changes . . .

As he and I stroll in the underbelly of the Ravens stadium one of the Panther communications folks trails us closely, and, yup, I feel like the entire conversation is being monitored. What, for God's sake, are they afraid of? I ask Cam a corny softball question on purpose—

Me: "Where did you get your sense of style with your clothes?"

Cam: "I'm a preacher's son. And having an old grandma it was always a point of emphasis to put your best fine linen on going to church. And it just stuck with me."

Next, I try to get Cam to open up about that report calling him a second-tier quarterback. "No sir. It's just personal opinion for so many people. I know who I am. That's it."

We are interrupted a few times by stadium maintenance workers wishing Cam good luck, and by his stop at a table holding bags of Popeye's fried chicken for the Panther players to grab as they head for the team bus. I am actually a bit stunned that world-class athletes are being fed greasy fast food. After Cam gets his bag of chicken, I am told I cannot go any further with him, after initially being offered the walk to the bus. I am flustered, I sigh inwardly, I suck it up. I go straight to the question in my head about Black athletes like LeBron James, Carmelo Anthony, Chris Paul, and Dwyane Wade taking a public stand at this year's ESPYS, the ones Cam skipped, with them challenging their fellow athletes to get more involved in their communities. Cam smiles mischievously, adjusts his bag of Popeye's in his left hand, and ponders what to say for a second or two.

"Uh, that's a publicity stunt. I'm not saying that those athletes are not doing something. For me to just try to go over and beyond to make it known that I'm doing something in my community, that's not who I am. I am authentic. I have a foundation that has done much for the community. These facts need not be publicized in all instances, but if you search, you will find."

I think about how Cam Newton quietly went to Charleston, South Carolina, after that racist church massacre, to show his support to the victims' families. I think of what Cam does for people at Thanksgiving, of his surprising both children and adults during the Christmas season with visits, with presents, with meals. He is, in fact, a philanthropist, a giver. However, this is part of the Cam Newton people often do not see, and often do not acknowledge. And this is why, I believe, many have publicly and strongly urged him to speak louder, to use his big platform, including, at the tip of this season, Seattle Seahawk defensive end Michael Bennett.

I thank Cam for what he did for those folks in Charleston, tell him that the pastor of that church, the Reverend Clementa Pinckney, was from my family's hometown in Ridgeland, South Carolina, and then Cam repeats, once more, what is now his standard mantra about community and giving back. We shake hands, I wish him a great season, and just like that Cam Newton and his humungous burgundy Pharrell Williams hat are being rushed away, even as more Raven employees oooh and ah in his direction, and he smiles back in theirs. And then he is gone to get on the bus.

I sigh again and wonder what is to become of Cam Newton. Fast-forward a few months later, we know the disaster of a season he and his team have had. We know the physical beating he has taken from opponents. We know that he seems confused and uncomfortable at times when he has to deal with the media or otherwise express himself in public. Perhaps there will be more MVP awards, more endorsements for Cam. Perhaps there will be a Super Bowl victory one day. Perhaps there will be more love, and more hate, too. I wonder about that concussion that forced him to sit out a game this past season, I wonder about concussions we do not know about, and I wonder what will become of Cam Newton's brain and body as he ages, particularly since he has wavered between not seeing any real dangers to playing football and urging his teammate Luke Kuechly to go easy with his own return from a concussion. I wonder if Cam Newton will forever say "next question" when something comes up that he does not want to talk about, or if he will evolve, as Ali did, as Colin Kaepernick has, by actually becoming fully knowledgeable about the world in which he lives. I wonder if Cam Newton, playing there in the state of North Carolina, will ever publicly take a stand around voting rights, voter ID laws, marriage equality, equal access to bathrooms for transgender people, and if he will ever openly embrace Black Lives Matter in some form as other Black athletes have done. Right now, I know that I am not qualified to throw a football in the NFL just as Cam Newton is not qualified to speak about race and racism in America on any profound and layered level, or any social issue, for that matter. He has a right to his views, but unlike, say, Kareem Abdul-Jabbar, it is very obvious that Cam does not read, does not study, has never been exposed, in a real and consistent way, to conversations that would challenge him to think, and to think critically. What Cam is is another mega-celebrity with a platform, ill-prepared, sadly, for the magnitude of that platform. Exhibit A is the Super Bowl postgame press conference, and Exhibit B is the disastrous quotes in that *GQ* cover story. Exhibit C is pretty much most of the things he has said and done, very awkwardly, this past season. In a way Cam Newton is,

MY MOTHER. BARACK OBAMA. DONALD TRUMP.
AND THE LAST STAND OF THE ANGRY WHITE MAN.

121

and has become, a prisoner of his own meteoric success, his own gigantic fame. And how free, truly, is Cam Newton, and how free can he ever really be, no matter the amount of notoriety and money and access to the super-wealthy, if he can never consistently speak his mind for fear of alienating White America, especially that part of White America with power and privilege and the ability to make or break him whenever it chooses, or so he and his handlers believe?

But because of the dynamic personality and talent and swagger Cameron Jerrell Newton possesses, the thought is that he can be more, so much more, than a celebrated athlete. Paul Robeson more. Jackie Robinson more. Jim Brown more. Muhammad Ali more. Yet, alas, Cam is not a revolutionary, nor is he an Uncle Tom, either. It is hard to say who or what he is because I do not think he knows, really, himself, not as of now, regardless of the fame and money and global branding maneuvers. What he is is Black, man, and a Black man. And, plus, either description—revolutionary or Uncle Tom—is dangerous, is just too easy, and speaks to an emotional, intellectual, and spiritual laziness so embedded in our American social fabric. For we Americans are always searching high and low for heroes and villains, and sometimes the hero and the villain are the same person. What I saw, as Cam Newton was ushered away from me beneath that Baltimore stadium—and what I witnessed in Los Angeles and South Carolina, too—was a young Black man in America trying to find his way amidst the sound and the fury, and also trying to figure out how to fly, like Superman—

The Liner Notes for the
A Tribe Called Quest Greatest Hits
Album That Never Happened

I don't really mind if it's over your head / Cuz the job of
resurrectors is to wake up the dead / So pay attention, it's not hard to
decipher / And after the horns, you can check out the Phifer
—Q-Tip, "Jazz (We've Got)"

Back in the day, when George H. W. Bush was president and the crack epidemic was deferring and devastating dreams in urban America, four young lads birthed from the loins of New York City—Q-Tip, Phife Dawg, and Jarobi from Queens and Ali Shaheed Muhammad from Brooklyn—struck b-boy poses in Afrocentric garb, determined to make a way out of no way.

They were baptized A Tribe Called Quest, and the crew, a mash-up between Sun Ra's spacey imagination and Miles Davis's sonic experimentations, were beamed smack-dab into the middle of hip-hop's Golden Era. Roughly covering the years 1985 through the late 1990s—from Run-DMC to Tupac, Biggie, and JAY-Z—that period was animated, dynamic, and as necessary as the glory days of rock and roll in the 1950s, and the Motown Sound and British Invasion of the 1960s.

And just as New Orleans incubated jazz and its innovators like Jelly Roll Morton and Louis Armstrong generations before, New York boroughs like The Bronx and Queens hatched a cultural revolution heard round the world, with little more than microphones and crafty wordplay, turntables, spray paint and Magic Markers, cardboard or linoleum to dance on, and the vinyl record collections of their parents.

Yes, hip-hop America was created from practically nothing, in the aftermath of Dr. King's assassination and the Civil Rights Movement, in the midst of the neglect and decay of New York, yet magically propelled by the fearless agitprop genius of its children like the members of A Tribe Called Quest.

At the time, the Golden Era had bumrushed the show, the culture was routinely producing major rap acts and musical game-changers like Public Enemy, N.W.A, Salt-N-Pepa, Queen Latifah, the Geto Boys, and MC Lyte. Such was the diversity inside hip-hop's Golden Era that Tribe belonged to the artsy, funkadelic wing known as the Native Tongues, whose membership featured De La Soul, the Jungle Brothers, and UK import Monie Love.

Self-emancipated from any restrictions as they recalibrated bohemia with working-class Black pride and Beat Generation poetic explorations, A Tribe Called Quest, in one surrealist brushstroke after another, spit humorous lectures, life meditations, and social commentary into ripe ear holes, on how cool it was to be intelligent, whimsical, silly, a sports fan, a lover of love and sex; but they were also brain-digging pop culture archeologists able to reference cartoons, history, politics, and TV sitcoms in a single bound; and the members of Tribe were unapologetic music geeks who knew and sampled obscure jazz masters like Weldon Irvine ("Award Tour") and Grant Green ("Vibes and Stuff") while also verbally bouncing off the beat-making wall of their Japanese peer Towa Tei ("Find a Way").

Tribe's two front men, Q-Tip and Phife Dawg, were not just the vocal leaders but had known each other since they were tiny toddlers in Queens. Phife and Jarobi met as teens in that same Q-borough and shared a love of basketball and hip-hop, while Tip and deejay-producer Ali Shaheed Muhammad crossed paths at the Murry Bergtraum High School for Business Careers in Manhattan.

Although Jarobi would depart for a culinary career after Tribe's first album, *People's Instinctive Travels and the Paths of Rhythm*, Tip often referred to him as "the soul of our group." In subsequent years, Jarobi would rejoin the squad for reunion shows, the spiritual glue that has kept this band of brothers rolling into the twenty-first century.

But A Tribe Called Quest was new millennium before it existed. Be it Q-Tip's prophetic, nasal chants that snapped in our minds a selfie nicknamed The Abstract ("Mr. Incognito"), or the hyped-up rude boy rumblings and braggadocio of Phife aka The Funky Diabetic ("Oh My God"), Tribe represented for both the boyz n the hood and the college boys on the yard with a breezy effortlessness, while also keeping it seductive and mad real for the ladies ("Electric Relaxation").

Possessed with that bottomless, ancestral vision and inventive nimbleness that negated the fact they were mere twenty-somethings, A Tribe Called Quest generated five albums in eight years (plus numerous remixes, demos, and movie soundtrack cuts), impacting along the way major musical trailblazers like Pharrell Williams, the Beastie Boys, Beck, Outkast, the Roots, Common, Eminem, Lauryn Hill, Erykah Badu, and Kanye West.

Tribe is not simply one of the great collectives in hip-hop history, the group is American artistic royalty, its street-level dissertations as mandatory as the Pulitzer Prize–winning plays of August Wilson. The crew's influence is far-reaching, global, multicultural, multi-generational, a rhythm nation as revolutionary and triumphant as the Beach Boys' majestic milestone *Pet Sounds* and the Beatles' landmark *Sgt. Pepper's Lonely Hearts Club Band*. No doubt Tip and Phife are hip-hop's Lennon and McCartney, standing eyeball to eyeball, swapping vocabularies, intentionally and matter-of-factly stepping on each other's utterances, a rites-of-passage kinship born in the tradition of African griots, Caribbean toasters, Southern bluesmen, street corner preachers, and homies on the block talkin' ish and blowin' melodic musings into the wind.

That they chose to make jazz the root and tree stump for their art meant Tribe could do what Miles did in his journey: brazenly maneuver from straight-ahead jazz to rock, funk, and soul fusions. Be it those bumpy jazz riffs over a breakbeat ("Same Ol' Thing"), stripped-down acid jams ("1nce Again"), or R&B in its raw essence ("Stressed Out"), A Tribe Called Quest, divested of the African garb of their early career and now wearing the uniform of the everyday homeboy, deftly defied prepackaged stereotypes of the Black man-child. Tribe be Langston Hughes and Amiri Baraka, yes, but Tribe also be Dylan Thomas, Allen Ginsberg, and bebop, too: free, loose, wildly unpredictable.

That they could be all of this, and still also give us the greatest rap posse cut ever ("Scenario"), teach a master class on storytelling ("I Left My Wallet in El Segundo"), manipulate metaphors to express their love for women and a certain body part ("Bonita Applebum"), and slyly reconstruct the call-and-response tradition of the Black church ("Can I Kick It?") says, loudly, that A Tribe Called Quest were far, far ahead of the game, and far, far ahead of their time.

JAY-Z and the Remaking of His Manhood. Or, The Crumpled and Forgotten Freedom Papers of Mr. Shawn Carter.

Woke up this morning with my mind
Stayed on freedom
Woke up this morning with my mind
Stayed on freedom
Woke up this morning with my mind
Stayed on freedom
Hallelu, Hallelu, Hallelujah . . .
—CIVIL RIGHTS MOVEMENT SONG

VOLUME 1.

When I was a little boy my mother, ever-protective of me and the world outside of our ghetto windows—the criminals, the hustlers, the drug addicts, the winos, the adults who "messed with children" in inappropriate ways, the violence, those police who might kill us simply for being Black and, consequently, dangerous—would quote the Bible, in her own way, warning me, more times than I can count, that the truth will set you free, or a liar is a thief, or a lie will leave you dead, or something to that effect. My ma's point, which I have hauled with me my entire existence, is that we must always fight for ourselves, for truth, always fight to tell our own stories, otherwise someone else will do it for us, often to our devastation and demise. Because the ghetto is not merely a sunken place savagely pistol-whipped with poverty, fear, hopelessness, despair. It is also an emotional space, a cataclysmic nightmare pretending to be normal; and if you live there long enough, a nightmare that becomes mighty difficult to shake, for no matter where you go, there you are, trauma, pain, scars. Like I was there the first thirteen years of my life, in my hometown of Jersey City, New Jersey, which I have learned, because of much movement and travel in my adult years, is no different than the poorest parts of Brooklyn, or Detroit, or Washington, DC, or New Orleans, or Atlanta, or Miami, or Chicago, or Houston, or Seattle, or Los Angeles, or Oakland, or any other urban enclave one can name. The ghetto is the ghetto, and it is not merely about life when you are born and seemingly trapped there, unless you get fantastically lucky. It is simultaneously about survival however possible, legal, illegal, spiritual, diabolical, whatever it takes to withstand the uninterrupted barrage of insanity that gets at you. Not like we are given a blueprint, a boxful of tools, physical or mental, or otherwise, to navigate and negotiate the madness. For sure, we spend our lives looking over our shoulders. I know I do, in spite of everything. Because I am a Black man, because I am a writer, because I am an activist—someone inevitably hates you for one or more of these reasons. Thus, you spend your woke hours doing a "stick and move stick and move" as The Notorious B.I.G. once muttered. But you are eternally like those big bloated black rats my mother and I had in every single one of our tenement buildings, sprinting and squeezing from space to space, from hole to hole, and bumping into one wall or one object or another, hoping that you do not get killed, in some way, or kill yourself, so that you can make it to the next day. You are conditioned to believe that you are going to die young, before your time as the elders say, as one of my friends recently did, in his forties, from a terrible and insatiable liquor habit, because it was the one thing, for him, that could dull the damage he had been conceived under as a fetus, quite literally, and what had circled and harassed him his entire short life, like a punch-drunk prizefighter slap-boxing with the devil. Slow suicide, I call it, when we are not able to be honest with ourselves, when we do things that destroy us, that destroy others, because we do not know any better, or because we just do not care, or because we have given up.

Add to that being a Black man drop-kicked into a globe dominated by a mountaintop of things White male-ish and rinsed in power and privilege, and your definitions of manhood, from certain kinds of White males, on television, in film, in popular culture, in your school textbooks, via the various levels of government—like everywhere—means you've got to figure out your own definition of manhood, which, in the main, is a bootleg definition of that powerful and privileged White manhood. Their power is your power, their privilege is your privilege, and their material possessions become your wet dreams, your aphrodisiac. You want what they have, not every White man but, yes, the ones with the power and the privilege, the ones who truly are the bosses, the innovators, the superheroes, the saviors, the anointed and hailed rock stars. And if a poor Black male, you hardly stand a chance if, like me, if, like JAY-Z, you inherited nothing except the color of your skin and a target on both your forehead and your back. And the ghetto you were given and in which you feel that you are stuck, permanently. For this is what American racism and American classism have wrought,

what has been created, maintained, spread, like crack cocaine and the
AIDS virus back in the day, coast to coast. Call it whatever you want to
call it—ghettoes, inner cities, underprivileged populations—it doesn't
matter. What matters are the people who are trapped in these spaces,
as I felt I was in the Greenville section of Jersey City, as JAY-Z felt he
was in Marcy Houses in the Bedford-Stuyvesant section of Brooklyn,
New York. And what we children of the ghetto feel, without fail, no
matter where we land, is a need to tell our truths, to clutch the spiked
bloody hand of survival, to step to those who would try to injure us or
otherwise box us in, and to do battle with them, and with ourselves. I
would be straight lying to you if I said that despite twelve books and
hundreds and hundreds of published writings and probably at least a
thousand speeches across America and internationally over the past
two decades that I still do not tussle ferociously with the dark shadows and long nightmares of my past. I do. The physical violence and
uncontrollable bursts of raw rage are not there any longer, have been
long gone, thanks to years upon years of therapy and my spiritual practices, but the internal wars go on around self-esteem, staggering bouts
with sadness, with depression, and triggers sparked by mean words
my mother hollers, even now, or thoughts about the tremendous emp-
tiness I endlessly have because of my father's disappearing act when I
was eight. This leaves you, if you are a man, if you are a Black man,
also struggling with issues of intimacy and self-expression, of trying
to figure out, often with little help from others, how to be a man who is
not a human lethal weapon, to self, to others.

And then there are the secrets. Those of us who were verbally
abused, or beaten viciously at times, or physically and emotionally
abandoned, or all of the above, like me. Those of us who might have

been raped, or sexually assaulted, or molested. Those of us who cried loudly for that father love, but our pops could not teach us to be men because they had no idea either. Those of us who did not tell the family secrets, or our own secrets, who wore the masks to cover up that trauma, to cover up that pain, to pretend to be what we were not, just to survive. And yeah how the wounded prey on and maim each other. Passed from generations before, passed amongst each other like a bottle of liquor or a marijuana joint, I have since learned these many years later that this applies not exclusively to poor people in America, or working-class Black males in America, but also to middle-class and super-rich Americans of all backgrounds, too. Because we live in a nation, in a world, that does not encourage truth-telling, or honesty, or healing, or self-empowerment in a manner that is holistic, that is healthy. What is encouraged, supported, spread like the latest trending topic on Twitter, is rugged individualism and individual success stories that leave out the garbage-stink back alleys of life; what feels nurtured, supported, encouraged, is darkness, is dysfunction, is self-sabotage, is a culture of dishonesty and dissing of self and dissing and outing of others; and is a dependency on being so unwell that the unwell is celebrated or sensationalized or both, while those who are trying to sort through the bull____ and heal are considered, well, crazy. And when you are labeled crazy, the price of the amusement park ticket is people trying to fix or distract you in some way. With the Lawd. With Jesus. With corrupt and crooked preachers and corrupt and crooked politicians. With prayer cloths and prayer oils. With that drug. With that liquor. With money. With unwise and irresponsible sexual adventures. With video games and television shows and movies and music that freeze your brain cells. With food that will one day give you diabetes or a heart attack or a stroke or cancer. With anything and everything that would, allegedly, take the pain away, and make you feel better. But those things are merely temporary Band-Aids; for the larger problem is that there is just no way to survive, and win, no matter who you are, in a way that is human, that is whole, physically, spiritually, emotionally, if you have not been taught how. I know I did not know, which is why I found myself, in my twenties, in my thirties, into my forties, yes, regrettably like those ghetto rats crash-landing into objects and walls and each other. Because you are forevermore in search of yourself, forevermore in search of a hero or shero, beyond yourself, forevermore in search of a meaning to your life, to your soul. And even the fortunate ones amongst us are not immune from the charade that is this thing we call life, Black or otherwise, as made in America.

We know why, if we ain't afraid of the truth: Racism in America has worked so well, for so long, that it can proudly sit back in its leather recliner, kick its cobwebbed feet up, and watch us crush ourselves and each other, daily weekly yearly for entire lifetimes. The oppressed will always believe the worst about themselves because they have been taught well by the oppressor. It is the obvious that JAY-Z points out, light versus dark, rich versus poor, those with access to mainstream America versus those without, but it is also the meanness we see, today, on social media. The folks—White Black everybody everybody—who make it their business to dis those they do not like, who they do not agree with, in the worst ways imaginable. I've been on the receiving end of quite a bit of this, and it stings, badly, especially coming from people Black like you. As I am sure it hurt JAY-Z as a child, as a young man, in these times, to be called "ugly" over and over because he has full African lips and an expansive African nose and does not fit someone's hateful vision of what it is to be handsome or cute. Imagine what that does to the psyche of anyone: you are ugly because we said so. . . .

So, when I came to JAY-Z's thirteenth and newest album, *4:44*, I came with no expectations, but thoroughly intrigued by his marketing genius that had us wondering, for weeks on end, why *4:44* was plastered everywhere, who put these numbers there, and what did it mean, precisely? But then we found out it was JAY-Z: it was the time JAY-Z woke up to pen perhaps the most mind-blowing apology from a man to a woman ever heard in pop music history, as the title song. As an album *4:44* is as abrupt a departure from JAY-Z's lyrical norm as *What's Going On* was for Marvin Gaye. What they have in common are real-world events that forced them to stand nose-to-nose in the mirror in ways they never had before. For Gaye that included the Civil Rights Movement, the Vietnam War, and the riots and protests happening everywhere. There was the turbulent marriage to his first wife, the sister of Motown Records founder Berry Gordy, where there was misery, where Marvin, as perhaps a somewhat misguided exit strategy, made explicitly sexual music that touted his affairs with other women, including a teenager. And then there was the tragic death of his beloved singing partner Tammi Terrell. Marvin had no choice but to reimagine and reinvent himself, else he might have perished far sooner than he did. "What's Going On" was his plea to us, to himself, his rebel yell for help. We know Marvin never really got that help, and by the time he was close to JAY-Z's age, his own father shot him down during one of their many heated arguments. The love-hate of father and son, the father blasting a son who had spoken very candidly about his depression and drug use, but could never quite get off that corner, dead at the hands of his father. . . .

For JAY-Z it has been the symbolic and historic presidency of Barack Obama and the many doubts about that president's allegiance to those Black like him; rampant, out-of-control police murders of Black folks (countless ones captured on video) and the siren scream of Black Lives Matter; the explosive and angry rise of Donald Trump's America; the Black-on-Black violence in the Brooklyns of America; JAY's father longing, the father longing of far too many Black males in post–Civil Rights America; the prison-industrial complex that has gleefully gobbled up the lives of men from communities like JAY's Brooklyn; and JAY'S now-admitted extramarital affair in spite of his stunningly beautiful and business-savvy wife being the most famous music icon on the planet Earth. This is a rapper, an artist, who has declared in his past lyrics that he did not know how to cry, that he had to let the song cry. But here we are with *4:44*, an album by a man, about manhood, one that feels like part of a trilogy that includes his sister-in-law Solange's *A Seat at the Table* and Beyoncé's *Lemonade*: Black folks, in an ecosphere riddled with racism, sexism, and toxic manhood, trying to figure ourselves out, and out loud. But *4:44* is its own unique thing, too, because JAY-Z, born Shawn Carter, had no choice but to eyeball his demons, alone. *4:44*, save some readily recognizable samples of Nina Simone, Stevie Wonder, and Donny Hathaway, is a minimalist magnum opus with only one producer, No I.D., one of Chicago's pioneering hip-hop beatmakers. There are no major party anthems here, no ridiculously magnetic boom-baps for the sake of having that boom-bap. Think MTV's stripped-down series *Unplugged* and that is *4:44*. You have to listen to the words because there really is no other option. It is clearly planned, it is a record, yeah, but it is also the autobiography of a forty-seven-year-old man who has had everything except peace and truthfulness in his roller coaster of a life.

For sure *4:44* is a breathtaking achievement, one that I have digested a few dozen times. It has elements of Public Enemy's agitprop
political manifestos, and Tupac Shakur's smoke-y 'hood sermons are
there, too. You also can feel the force of N.W.A's and Ice Cube's anti-
authoritarian middle fingers as well. Like always, I marvel at JAY's
verbal imagination, as his boundless genius means he has never written
lyrics down, like never; but it is also clear that Big Daddy Kane, my
favorite rapper ever, and one of Brooklyn's finest, has been a contin-
uous influence on JAY-Z's diverse vocal stylings. JAY was there with
him, unknown, when Kane was the mega-star, and in the pantheon
of BK hip-hop legends it is Big Daddy Kane, The Notorious B.I.G.,
and JAY-Z, in that order. Little wonder that JAY has, time and time
again, referenced or vocally sampled Kane or Biggie wordplay in his
own lyrics. He is forever a student of his art form, and what JAY-Z
has given us with *4:44* is a blueprint on how to make a hip-hop album
in the second decade of the twenty-first century that is a message to
the masses, a confession of an ex-abuser of people, an apology to his
wife, his sister-in-law, his mother, all women, while never quite losing that ego-centered palm grip he has had like forever on his private
parts. He is vulnerable, yes, but he is also, in a word, free, fighting for
his freedom, on his terms. Money don't buy you freedom. And money
can't buy you love. What money does for JAY is give him access to the
therapists most will never be able to afford or see, the SoulCycle spin
classes he pops up in when in Los Angeles, and a circle of influential
and deep-pocketed friends, including men, to bounce all this ish off of.
He wants to get saner, better, because, I believe, JAY in his heart not
only wants us to get saner, better, but also because he suffers from the
same survivor's guilt that any of us who have escaped the ghetto carry

around, including me. Like why me, God, and not my man over here, or him over there? When you hear JAY spit, on the 2011 Kanye West collaboration "Niggas in Paris," "we ain't even 'spose to be here," if you are from where we are from, you overstand, as we say, immediately. Like from the gutter to Paris, like why, like how? And you find yourself engaging in the trappings of that success because no one ever bothers to tell or warn you that the entertainment industry, like the concrete jungle many of us have fled, is as hazardous as any ghetto could ever be.

I was shocked, like for real, the first time I listened to *4:44*, because I have long had an ambivalent relationship with JAY's music. I am a fan, yeah, because half of my life has been lived in Brooklyn, and there is mural-like Brooklyn pride and swag. I am a fan, yeah, because I always want to see another brother succeed who comes from where I come from, who has survived what I survived. And I am a fan, yeah, but my emotions have been all over the place because of this record. Every listen I hear different things, feel different things, see different things, in JAY-Z, in myself. But I remain conflicted, too. I mean it has always been evident that he is super-talented, that no rapper has ever had the career run as he has had, solely as a rapper. The running joke has been that a hip-hop artist is lucky if he is able to squeeze two or three albums out of a career, and if he does not diversify from there into other business ventures, then his career is over. Like Queen Latifah. Like MC Lyte. Like Will Smith. Like LL Cool J. Like Snoop Dogg. Like Ice Cube. Like the Roots. All began making songs, all do many other things now where rhyming on records is no longer their primary thing. Hip-hop has been said to be a young person's game, a game where we are so fickle, so easily persuaded, like sheep, that it is pretty impossible for any rapper to survive beyond a few years of glory because the next big thing is waiting to exhale. Given that JAY-Z's first CD hit us in 1996, and it is now 2017, twenty-one years and thirteen platinum solo albums later, he has shattered that notion, and then some. Jigga really is the Michael Jackson or Michael Jordan of hip-hop, that rare pop culture action figure with crazy crossover appeal and a multi-generational and multicultural fan base. He really is hip-hop's Grateful Dead all by himself, able to tour whenever he feels like it, knowing that legions of diehard admirers will flock to his shows. He really is hip-hop's Frank Sinatra, that rare artist not only able to make hit record after hit record, but a shrewd business, man, trafficking in several entrepreneurial lanes, dabbling in entertainment, sports, artist representation, technology, real estate, wherever JAY, like Sinatra before him, can expand and amplify his throne.

What I have felt listening to *4:44* is a range of emotions, as I have lived through and written about many of the same things. The poverty. The violence. The absent father. The single mother struggling to be whoever and whatever she is. The inability to commit to relationships, fully. I have never been a cheater in the way JAY-Z indicates he has, but before my very recent marriage, to an absolutely amazing woman, my relationships with women, through the years, have been a great adventure, to say the least. As JAY-Z says, not like we were given the skill sets to handle any of this. And success in whatever form does not equal maturity for us men. If anything, it entrenches us in the dysfunctional behavior, toward ourselves, toward each other, toward women. We in essence become successful damaged goods, cheating on women, lying to women, beating on women, wounding women. It makes sense to me now, when I think back to that infamous eleva-

tor video of JAY-Z and Beyoncé and Solange, two things: Why Solange was so angry. And why Beyoncé stood there, motionless and
indifferent, as her sister kicked and punched at JAY-Z on that elevator.
Like he had it coming. Women, Black women, love hard, and when
you burn a woman, a Black woman, you are going to feel her wrath,
hard. Thus, Solange's album. Thus, Beyoncé's *Lemonade*. Thus, all the
women who challenged me when I screwed up, as a young man, as
my wife does. I believe in my heart of hearts that most Black women,
without fail, love Black men, want to see us heal, evolve, grow, often
to their own detriment and mental health. But I also hear, loudly, as I
crisscross America, as a speaker, as an activist, as a writer, that there
is a great fatigue with waiting for us men to get it, to grow up. This
juvenile behavior, in our twenties, in our thirties, in our forties, even
into our fifties and sixties, has got to end. The stunted growth has got
to end. The excuse-making has got to end. That limbo area between
being men and being boys must end. As I have heard in my travels,
boys play all the time, men know when to play. This is perhaps why
many are referring to *4:44* as "grown-up hip-hop" or "adult hip-hop."
I respectfully disagree. I feel *4:44* is a portrait of an artist who has made
a conscious decision to reject the material trappings of success, first,
for his own sanity and spiritual health, and, second, and equally as important, for the sake of the love for his wife and children. Must it have
been humiliating and humbling to have your wife openly sing about
what happened on her last album, while you have to sit silently, as a
man, and deal with it? One can only imagine that.

But I also do not have to imagine how my mother reacts, to this
day, when my father's name is mentioned, because of the hurt she
feels, the unreconciled anger, the way she felt, as Beyoncé did, simi-

larly wounded and discarded, as if her life, and her feelings, did not matter. There was no *Lemonade* for my mother; like most women, my ma had to suck it up and keep going. Which is why I overstand the massive reaction to that album, and the excellent short films that accompanied it. People can say whatever they want about Beyoncé, but she, too, was growing, stretching, as a human being, as a woman, as a Black woman, as an artist, and serving notice to everyone, including her husband, what is and what is not acceptable. Whether Beyoncé is a feminist or not is none of my business. Neither is it my business what she and JAY-Z have decided to do together, as a couple. This is not the first famous marriage or partnership where there has been infidelity, nor will it be the last. Yoko Ono once told John Lennon to leave, to go do what he had to do, and after a year or so of doing so, he came back and was a different sort of man. The tragedy, of course, is the sacrifices both famous women and not famous women, like Yoko, like Beyoncé, make for the sake of the love of a man. But that is their choice, not ours. JAY's responsibility, Lennon's responsibility, is to not ever take for granted again these women who love them from the depths of their souls. To understand that manhood is not, in fact, power, privilege, sex, rock and roll, hip-hop, violence, ego gone wild, material things, money, any of that. That manhood should be about love, peace, nonviolence, respecting women as our equals, because they are, that manhood is about being honest, about being open, available, exposed. As JAY-Z struggles to be on *4:44*, as John Lennon struggled to be many times in the last years of his life, where he owned up to having been a "hitter" who violently beat women, including his first wife Cynthia, because he was, as JAY-Z admits about himself, downright ignorant about what it was to be a man.

VOLUME 2.

The first time it dawned on me that JAY-Z was a major star was in the late 1990s, after the killings of Tupac and Biggie, and while I was in the midst of my own downward spiral with liquor and violence and a grudge match with low self-esteem in the aftershocks of those unsolved murders. I stumbled upon a party in New York City, it may have been a New Year's Eve joint, and the vast majority of the attendees were White. And their soundtrack was one JAY-Z song after another, and they knew every single word to every single song. I thought I was dreaming, because the hip-hop I had grown up with, that I had known, even during my years as a writer for *Vibe*, had largely been populated by the African American, West Indian, and Latino communities who created the culture in the first place. But something had shifted, mightily, and this thing, this energy, now belonged to everyone. Pop goes the culture . . . I was both proud and mortified. Proud because Jayhovah, one of the many nicknames he calls himself, had come up from the ghetto, had escaped a life destined for an early death or prison, to become, as he put it, the best rapper alive. And as we know, the life options for the products of our environment are perpetually reduced to these three things: be a rapper, be an athlete, or be a criminal in some form.

But I was also wary of JAY-Z because of the things he was saying, how apolitical much of his music was, how visibly comfortable he was with the word *nigga*, how comfortable these White folks at that party were, and many parties I would roll to in the years to come, with all the foul things JAY was saying about his own people. It was as if he consciously, purposely, dumbed down his lyrical content to meet the masses where they had been pushed to, with no regard for anything except his own power and money and pleasure principles. We saw a tease of awareness, like when he would wear a Che Guevara tee-shirt or a red, black, and green wristband (the colors of Black liberation) during performances, or when he boldly detailed police racial profiling on his high-voltage song "99 Problems," but otherwise JAY-Z chose to be silent, invisible, to not rock the boat of the America that was embracing him. This was maddening to many, particularly as he built, brick by brick, what was Blaxploitation on record, mind-spraying the most graphic tales about drugs, violence, and super-size ego boosts, while pushing forth an assembly-line montage of racist, sexist, and materialistic lyrics, with no remorse whatsoever. Save his Roc-A-Fella and Roc Nation inner circle, there seemingly was no community for JAY-Z, at least not in his music, it was just him against the world.

But obviously something has been lying dormant since the 1990s. JAY-Z and I are not that far apart in age, and we grew up in the same eras, the soulful 1970s, the crack madness of the Reagan '80s, the Golden Era of hip-hop that saw the explosion of socially conscious rap by acts like Public Enemy and Boogie Down Productions, as well as that muscular political statement by N.W.A with "F___ tha Police," to this day the most concise and unapologetic anti–police brutality record ever made. So, JAY-Z was not mad uninformed, I do not believe. I believe he made a deliberate decision to sell the music that would be permitted by the powers that be. Because, to my thinking and observations, by the late 1990s, hip-hop culture had not only become the dominant art form in the world, but also a threat, as it not only woke up the poor people of color who midwifed it, but it was reaching far beyond its ghetto origins to the suburbs, to White America, to an entire multicultural universe. I believe, in my gut and in my heart, that hip-hop was intentionally redirected, and made to be, well, mostly stupid and directionless, the balance once present was water-hosed and coon-danced away, and it was split into two—hip-hop culture versus the hip-hop industry. Hip-hop culture, led by those poor people Dr. King warned us at the end of his life not to forget, was about life, about hope, about communities making something from nothing, about winning on their own terms; but the hip-hop industry, as it ambushed and surpassed and transplanted the culture, peddled mayhem, beefs, turf and coast wars, drugs, guns, violence, and hatred and a despicable disrespect for women and for queer people, and a kind of reckless and irresponsible disregard for life, in particular the lives of Black and Latino folks most affected by this shift. JAY-Z was the right artist at the right time to emerge in the midst of this chaos and confusion. He did not have to pretend to be from the streets, he really was. He did not need a ghostwriter because, lyrically, JAY-Z is as gifted as they come with unwritten wordplay that is a cross between Brooklyn barbershop and ball court banter, the hellfire comedic bursts of Dick Gregory or Chris Rock, and an uncanny ability, like the writers Richard Wright and Chester Himes before him, to convey the everyday realities of the forgotten America. Keeping it a hundred, that is what has kept me listening to JAY from the jump: he is the people's poet, as Tupac Shakur was, as Kendrick Lamar is, and even without the fearless social justice vocal bombs of 'Pac or KL, I could always count on JAY to say something that made me respond with *Damn*.

But be that as it may, my activist life and my woke-ness around American and Black American history would not permit me to ignore the many ways the hip-hop industry, led by the creative cleverness of JAY-Z, was no different than the minstrel shows concocted in the 1800s, which became the most powerful and most visible entertainment in America for a century. Think excessively Blackened faces because Black was 'spose to be ugly, perpetual mockery of thick lips and large noses, mumbled words trapped and loosened from the mouths of racist White entertainers and self-hating Black entertainers who saw Black folks as the running joke of these United States. It made White people a fortune, this industry of minstrelsy, and some Black people got paid, too, but that damage persists to this day. . . .

Good hair versus bad hair
Bloods versus Crips
East Coast versus West Coast
Black Americans versus West Indians
Dominicans versus Haitians
Your block versus my block
Your projects versus my projects
City folks versus country folks
Your fraternity or sorority versus my fraternity or sorority
This Civil Rights leader versus that Civil Rights leader

And no different, either, from those many Blaxploitation films of the 1970s: over and over, with exaggerated facial expressions, exaggerated words, our bodies, our spirits, our lives, depicted as oversexualized, violent, dangerous, with no morals whatsoever. Shuffling, jiving, Aunt Jemima, Uncle Tom, Black mammy this or Black buck that, bugged-out eyes, scared Negroes even scared of they own shadow; macks, pimps, whores, so super fly that we could possibly be nothing more than that presented to us, like the greasy fast-food spots that overwhelm every inner city in America. The hip-hop industry, determined to put the balance and diversity of the Golden Era firmly in the rear-view mirror, was simply doing it all to one hot musical track after another. JAY, like the drug dealers he and others were before they went legit, was crafty enough to peep the supply and demand game perpetuated by the hip-hop industry, and he flipped it. I got memories of what heroin and crack did to my people, excruciatingly dreadful memories. And I am clear what the hip-hop industry has done to my people since the 1990s, mad clear. Be it a drug or entertainment, if it is meant to hurt and destroy, it will. And those who participate in it, on whatever level, wind up having blood on their hands, too. That means all of us—

JAY-Z got out of the drug game and it now seems he is trying to escape from the hip-hop industry, too. He knows it is a sham, as demonstrated by his harsh criticisms of it throughout *4:44*. He knows it is a sham when he says they will probably kill him for saying all of this. Well, yeah, strange ish happens to truth-tellers in these parts. And JAY's truth is about power, who has it and who does not, and why. Cannot be mad at the boldness of JAY-Z's positions. As we say, he has earned the right to say whatever he wants. For myriad reasons, few rap artists ever make the kind of money JAY-Z has made, and never will. But if you come from nothing, financially, spiritually, and your one shot to make a name for yourself is to denigrate you and people who look like you, to sell your soul to the devil, you are going to do it. Poor people do not want to be poor. This is the crux of what I felt JAY-Z was doing before *4:44*, a very sordid dance with the devil, benefiting himself, his small circle around him, and hardly anyone else. Yes, I knew that he was quietly supporting Black Lives Matter with monetary donations. Yes, I knew about his foundation, his support of Barack Obama, and other charitable things. But because I am from the same ghetto as JAY-Z, I also know that history of local drug dealers who sell death and devastation to the people daily weekly monthly yearly while also providing them with turkeys at Thanksgiving or children's toys for Christmas. The criminal-minded amongst us know that we as a people have sunk so low and are so desperate for help that they can say or do anything to us, and we will be happy with the crumbs, even as they are killing us and our communities, then showing up at our funerals to offer their respects to our families—

But I also believe that people can change, I truly do. *4:44* is in the nakedly confessional tradition of *The Autobiography of Malcolm X*, Claude Brown's *Manchild in the Promised Land*, Piri Thomas's *Down These Mean Streets*. It is a man facing the many devils inside himself with the very first song "Kill Jay Z," a trembling open letter spoken in the third person where he concedes his sins and offers up a laundry list of how he has ducked and dodged himself. I mean, the man once more admits shooting his own blood brother and how cray cray it was to stab Un Rivera. There are echoes of the landmark rap album *De La Soul Is Dead* within the tune "Kill Jay Z," or, even, the Black church. That we have to be born, again, to have a different path, and sometimes we have to discard our old lives and our old identities without fear, without hesitation. *4:44* is part lecture, part spoken-word performance art, as if it were battered and fried right on the asphalt outside the Nuyorican Poets Café. Think Malcolm X coming back from Mecca saying he will work with anyone who is about justice and no longer calling White folks devils; think Martin Luther King Jr. breaking ranks with scared Negro leadership and condemning the Vietnam War. This is what this Brooklyn boy named Shawn is doing with *4:44*, shocking the world, and himself, and attempting to be a new he, even if he is not quite clear how, or why, as yet. *4:44* makes me think once more of that other other-worldly pop icon I mentioned earlier, the Beatles' John Lennon: shaving the hair from his soul, trying to make peace with his fame and success, and how that fame and success blocked him from being a whole man, a different sort of man. John never got to speak with or about his mother in his music except in sheer terror and anxiety and wounded-ness. But there is JAY telling us, forthrightly, that his mother is a lesbian, been a lesbian, who, like him, had been living in the shadows, hiding her true self for much of her life. It is remarkable to hear a man who has spouted anti-LGBTQ lyrics say he loves his mother no matter what, regardless if that love is with a him or a her; to hear him speak plainly about his mother who, like him, is living a life that is not completely her own, that was once fake, manufactured. Equally remarkable to hear that mother speak, at the end of "Smile," calmly, confidently, as she reads her personal emancipation proclamation on a song by her son, arguably the most famous hip-hop artist in the world.

VOLUME 3.

As I have listened to *4:44* over and over again, and hear it blaring out of cars and SUVs, on the subways, at restaurants and cafés, it is quite clear this work of art has struck a deep nerve. Even the hatred for JAY-Z and this album are real. Some are referring to him as going soft or corny, as this work being gimmicky, as him being "controlled by Solange and Beyoncé." I have been there, and I am still there. When I pushed an ex-girlfriend into a bathroom door in July 1991, my life changed forever. I apologized to any and all, over and over, and apologized to her many years later, and feel as if I have been living a nonstop apology with what I say and do with regard to women, including my mother, ever since. I simply did not know any better, and that is what I am hearing with *4:44*. JAY merely did what he knew, did what he saw. Even if it meant suppressing any political and social thoughts he may have had along the way. And the fact that he spends so much time on the album talking about financial wealth, financial literacy, about ownership, says that he still, in the main, thinks money is the great equalizer, that hyper-capitalism is the only true path to freedom. While I certainly never again want to experience the kind of horrific poverty I have endured in my lifetime, I also think what JAY is missing is that all the money and material possessions and property in the world mean nothing if you are also not actively engaging your community, your people, the people who have purchased all these millions of records of yours. And there is a way to talk about economic empowerment without constantly rubbing one's things in the faces of those of us who do not have what you have. That is the other corner JAY-Z, to me, needs to turn. There is nothing wrong with having wealth and privilege, if that wealth and privilege are tied to a sense of humanity, if that wealth and privilege are used to uplift those other than yourself and your immediate family. No, I am not into that celebrities need to do this and that with their money talk. What they do with their money is their personal business. Nor have I been duped into believing that just because someone has a huge platform, that means he is automatically a leader. No, you cannot be a leader if you do not read and study and travel in a way that makes you accessible to the very people you claim to represent. What made a Tupac Shakur threatening, for example, or makes a Chuck of Public Enemy threatening still, is that they were very much of the people they were rapping about, on the streets and in the communities with them on the regular. That cannot really be said about JAY-Z, at least not yet. As Bono said, giving money to causes is charity, no matter how well intentioned. Anyone can do that. But if you are serious about social justice, then you join the people, in the trenches. Like Paul Robeson did. Like Harry Belafonte and Joan Baez and Bob Dylan and Nina Simone and Bob Marley and Fela did. Like Dick Gregory did. Like Jane Fonda did. As Susan Sarandon, George Clooney, Bruce Springsteen, and Rosie O'Donnell do. That is when you truly become a different type of artist, one who understands your greater calling beyond one album or one movie or one television show or one video.

And we need Black artists, specifically, who think like Langston Hughes and Zora Neale Hurston, who are as forthright as Miriam Makeba and Jesse Williams, who take stands, whether we agree with all of them or not, like Lauryn Hill and John Legend. *4:44* is clearly influenced by these types of artists, as I hear elements of them, and of the Watts Prophets, Arrested Development, Camille Yarbrough, and Sonia Sanchez, across the ten tracks. But we also cannot pretend that "Black capitalism" is new (it is not), or talk about money, about capitalism, without also having a very serious critique of capitalism. Ghettoes exist because of capitalism, on purpose. The "old Brooklyn" JAY rhymes about is gone because of greed and gentrification, fueled by the nastiest aspects of capitalism. In our ghettoes everywhere, we see fast-food restaurants, liquor stores, churches, rent-a-centers, check cashing places, bad food options, food deserts, little to no

places at all for our youth to exist and thrive, diabolically, because
of capitalism capitalizing on the misery of the people. There is something wrong with any society where a handful of us get to "make it"
and the rest of us remain stuck in that misery, living check to check,
EBT card to EBT card. It is not merely a case of one person working
harder than the rest. Most people I know work hard, but still have
nothing to show for it. There has to be an even more honest convo
about how some who are wealthy got their wealth, and hold on to that
wealth, on the backs of the rest of us. So, it is one thing for JAY-Z
to scold us about being smart with our money, about not wasting it
on dumb ish. I endorse that public service announcement. But it is a
whole other thing to talk about power, who has it, and why, and who
does not, and why. JAY alludes to this when he references the fight
over Prince's estate and name-checks Black attorney Londell McMil-
lan, and also when he name-checks White music mogul Jimmy Io-
vine. He is right: Why should White people get to automatically own
what we Black folks build and create like it is no big deal? He is right:
Why do some Black folks participate in the selling out of their own
people, their own creativity, with seemingly no remorse? As JAY-Z
rapped these words I immediately thought of "Black Wall Street" in
Tulsa, Oklahoma, and the history of Black folks doing for self in the
face of obnoxious racism and segregation. I thought of Black folks
from both the South and the Caribbean who, in our history, have
supported each other financially, put together formal and informal
economic cooperatives and lifelines for each other, owned things big
and small, who have made a way out of no way. That is why there was
no need for JAY-Z to fall into a very unwise stereotype with regard

to Jewish sisters and brothers around wealth and credit. If JAY was reading more books, or people around him were having far deeper dialogue with him, he would know to name-check Black Wall Street, and Madam C. J. Walker, the first self-made woman millionaire in America, and Reginald Lewis, America's first Black billionaire. Part of being free, to me, is also having knowledge that is rooted in self, not the history and value systems of people who are not you. So even as JAY waxes poetic about legacy and Black excellence throughout the album, his lack of knowledge of his own history remains striking. White people, no matter who they are, have never been and never should be the litmus test for Black possibilities. We need to look to ourselves and know ourselves. This is what ultimately separates *4:44* from, say, the work of Public Enemy or KRS-One or Tupac Shakur or Nas. You can find them referencing Black sheroes and heroes all over the place. As they should have, and as we should. It is not an either/or to me. I love Black people and I love humanity, I love all people. But financial empowerment alone does not mean freedom if your mind and spirit are not truly free as well.

Legacy legacy legacy legacy JAY says on the final track of *4:44*, as he converses, lovingly, about what he wants to give to his daughter, his new twins, his family. Yes, Legacy legacy legacy legacy, but if Malcolm X, while sitting in prison for seven long years, could read book after book and make it a point to become a student of history, of life, in a manner that would permit him to become an intellectual giant and a magnificent spokesperson for the forgotten, then JAY, with all the luxuries and amenities he has at his disposal, including those therapy sessions he references and those SoulCycle spin classes he loves, has a responsibility to do the same. No, I neither expect nor want rappers, or singers, or athletes to be the leaders of our communities. Most are simply not qualified to be leaders or spokespersons in that way, unless you happen to be a genuinely well-rounded and well-read renaissance person like, say, Paul Robeson, or Sam Cooke, or Kareem Abdul-Jabbar. However, if you are going to step out there and say something, then you do need to be as prepared as possible. Otherwise you leave yourself open to folks wondering why you are talking about Jewish folks or calling little people "midgets" on *4:44* like it ain't no big deal. Either you are going to go all the way with the transformation of self, or you are not. Either you, we, are for love and equality and justice for all people, or we are not. Ain't no in between, especially not in this age of Trump—

VOLUME 4.

So, we need to also say that *4:44* is a community public therapy session because JAY was publicly embarrassed by that elevator episode with Solange and by Beyoncé's *Lemonade*. The album is both an action and a reaction. An action because he is doing inventory on his entire life. A reaction because you wonder if JAY would have made an album like this had Solange not stepped to him on that elevator video that went viral, if Beyoncé had not so audaciously made a record like *Lemonade*. Moreover, he lands where many of us men land when we are not happy in our marriages: We are doing it for the kids. We say things like what JAY says, that I never thought about how women feel or how I treated women until I had a daughter myself. What he, we, need to understand, is the crux of the problem itself. That sexism, and our definitions of manhood, never consider the lives of women and girls, except as appendages to who we are. What women said to me when I was younger, what my wife says to me today, is that we men need to consider the humanity and equality of women on the regular, not merely when it is convenient for us. There has to be a vigilance to ending the sexism Beyoncé speaks of on *Lemonade*, and that burden cannot fall squarely at the feet of women. JAY-Z, you, me, we, need to be able to say sexism. JAY does not even say the word once on *4:44*. As teachers of mine like bell hooks and Eve Ensler and Gloria Steinem and my mother have said, in their own ways, what we men and boys do to women and girls daily weekly monthly yearly—many of us our entire lives—will not end until we make a sustained and unafraid effort to make sexism end. Otherwise, just like Beyoncé's father cheated on her mother and JAY-Z cheated on Bey, some man at some point could do something that violates Blue Ivy. This is the thing we've got to come to understand if we are serious. That we've got to remake manhood all the way, not just part of the way. What I was given, what JAY-Z was given, was patriarchy, sexism, misogyny, violence, a hatred and reckless disregard for women and girls that gives us a false sense of power and privilege that not only hurts and destroys women and girls, but us, too. All the money and fame and success in the world does not erase toxic manhood. Rather, as heard on *4:44* and from the person in the White House right now, it actually exacerbates the twisted behavior.

Like America itself and everything before it, hip-hop has always been a male-centered and male-dominated culture. America's so-called founding fathers matter-of-factly left out any mention of women. Women in America have only had the right to vote for less than one hundred years. Women are told what they can and cannot do with their bodies, by men, when it is their bodies, not ours. Violence against women and girls is at epidemic proportions, in America, globally. You cannot constantly refer to women in disparaging ways in your words and deeds and that not be a reflection of how you really feel. You cannot be a famous Black public intellectual many of us have heard of—not JAY-Z—who routinely espouses how much he loves Black women, but is so pathetically addicted to sex, to cheating on his wife, that from coast to coast it is common knowledge this man's hypocrisy and infidelities, as he is more or less the R. Kelly of Black scholars luring younger women with the spoils of his fame and access. I have witnessed women and men both enable and make excuses for this man, the way we make excuses for the legions of those who live dirty and blatantly contradictory lives while our eyes are wide shut. So, they go on, refusing to do the self-therapy JAY-Z is trying to do on *4:44*. And the list of famous men who've engaged in toxic manhood is a virtual Who's Who. Say their names. . . . Pablo Picasso, Marlon Brando, Frank Sinatra, some of the Kennedy men, Roman Polanski, Woody Allen, Reverend Jesse Jackson, Bill Clinton, Bill Cosby, Johnny Depp, Rob Kardashian . . . Clearly, JAY got busted, as we all do, eventually. Clearly, many of us men never get the memo that things like sex, violence, drugs, alcohol, money, and ego are the main things that destroy men of all backgrounds over and over. JAY, it seems via *4:44*, nearly destroyed his marriage, his family. As someone who just got married myself, I think daily, my flaws and all, about how I treat my wife, how I speak with her and to her, and I think about something her grandfather said to me a couple of years back when I asked how he made a marriage of over fifty years endure: "I made a commitment."

Jarring, weighty, real, those words spoken by that grandfather have rung like a freedom bell in my ears ever since. *I made a commitment. . . .*

But it is hard, I admit, to make a commitment, if, as a man, you feel few have made commitments to you in your life, in this dog-eat-dog world. That is why what JAY lays out on *4:44* is all the more valuable. Because we men are not encouraged to be honest, to be vulnerable. We are encouraged to lie and cheat, as evidenced by all the men—and women—of the Trump administration, and quite a few of those masquerading as financial geniuses on Wall Street. It is hard to say if JAY is now a feminist, or if his wife is, either, for that matter. Only they know who they are, not those of us who gaze at celebrities as if we know them when we do not. What I see and feel are two Black folks who had no idea, a decade and some change ago, that, together and apart, they would be this wildly successful, this wildly famous, and this wildly rich. If I may, feminism means women and men are equals, yes, but to my understanding it also means that women have the right to do whatever the heck they feel, on their terms. So if for Beyoncé that means working it out, via *Lemonade*, via her pushing JAY on *4:44*, with their public art, and in private, too, the contours of their relationship, then that is her right, their right, and, frankly, none of our business, whether they are public figures or not. Do I condone cheating in a relationship? No, especially because, in my lifetime, I have been cheated on, and I have cheated. I do not like how it feels either way, the spiritual filthiness of it all, and it is not something I would do to my wife, now, ever. I think if someone cannot commit, if someone cannot be honest, then one should not be in a relationship. But this is my journey, my path, not JAY-Z's. He is figuring it out, aloud, for himself, on *4:44*, the way Malcolm X was

figuring out ish in his autobiography. The way Marvin Gaye was figuring out ish on *What's Going On* and *Let's Get It On* and *Here, My
Dear.* The way John Lennon was figuring out ish, post-Beatles, until
his untimely murder at age forty.

The above said, a step is better than no step at all. As it is an
important first step, that public apology from JAY to Bey; it says
that we are indeed human, at least some of us, that at least some
of us have the ability to empathize and feel for what women go
through. Because I do believe that *4:44* is the album JAY has had
in him for a very long time. And fact is, rappers in their teens and
twenties have said many of these same things going back to folks
like Melle Mel, Slick Rick, the Geto Boys, Outkast, others. What
JAY has done, what any great artist can do, is to capture the energy
of our times, and to transcend those times. That is what makes *4:44*
a game-changing achievement, in spite of the flaws. He has become,
as we say in activist circles, a young elder, a master teacher, no question, and I am sure there is no way that JAY could make a song and
ridiculously uncomfortable animated video like "The Story of O.J."
if he were not at least somewhat familiar with the history of minstrel shows, Malcolm X's classic 1963 speech "Message to the Grass
Roots," and the Last Poets' "Niggers Are Scared of Revolution."
But also telling that JAY centers himself in the video as Jaybo, as
in Sambo, virtually declaring that he, too, has allowed himself to
be used, the way Stepin Fetchit and Bill "Bojangles" Robinson and
a roving army of Black entertainers have been used, then and now,
just to make a dollar, and to get closer to and inside the big house. If
we say we despise these Black men and Black women who have den-
igrated and disrespected themselves for White America, for fame

and money, why is it then all good that JAY-Z has been calling us niggas, over a symphony of hypnotic rhythms, for the past twenty years? Is casting himself as Jaybo in "The Story of O.J." animated video an admission that he has played an undeniable role for White America for two decades, and now wants to be free? Well, that freedom might begin with letting go of the word *nigga* once and for all. Cannot be free of someone else's big house if you still publicly use the master's words to describe yourself and your people. Because there is a mad thin line between self-love and self-hate, and it begins with our very fragile self-esteem, whether we are light or dark or rich or poor or real or fake. Because wherever you go, there you are. And, to me, it is bugged irony "The Story of O.J." song sampling Nina Simone's "Four Women," a feminist psalm by a person who spent her life resisting being a nigga, or a nigger, or a nigguh, to the point where it drove her off the edge. You wish someone would give JAY and all rappers a copy of Jabari Asim's book *The N Word: Who Can Say It, Who Shouldn't, and Why*, so whether JAY or Drake or Kanye or a mumble or trap rapper, you at least know where the word came from. Save the children, Marvin Gaye said to us, not teach the children to call themselves niggas through your music. . . . Nothing wrong with ignorance, but definitely something wrong with enthusiastic ignorance. JAY is not ignorant, we know this. Loaded with melancholy throughout, you feel on *4:44* that there is almost a resignation that in spite of all he has accomplished, JAY-Z understands, plainly, how he will forever be viewed by some because of the color of his skin, and because of where he is from. Because that is the truth. JAY-Z does not want to be O.J. Simpson, or Michael Jordan for that matter, either, Black men who have done whatever they can not to appear to be Black, or too Black, terrified of losing the favor of White America. We know what happened to O.J., and the jury still shadows the calculated movements of M.J. because it is clear he ain't totally cozy wearing his dark skin color on the daily, no matter how much money he has earned. It is when I sink into songs like the O.J. one, like "Marcy Me" and "Family Feud," that I get, finally, he is a man, a brother, Shawn Carter, trying to figure out how to pivot, next. Like his athlete brothers LeBron James and Carmelo Anthony and Chris Paul and Dwyane Wade, it is about controlling his own destiny. I feel the exact same way. Black people did not survive capture and kidnap in Africa, the middle passage, slavery, segregation, second-class citizenship, to be slaves or suckers or butt-kissers to someone else our entire lives. We want to self-determine for us by us, which is really no different than what Stokely Carmichael was shouting fifty years ago with those two little words, "Black Power."

But no matter the color or context of power, it has to be rooted in love, in responsibility, and yeah, in commitment. Took me three long weeks since the release of *4:44* to work through all my feelings about JAY-Z, and I am sure this is just the beginning. I do not know if JAY is the best rapper alive, but he certainly has been the most fascinating one for a very long time, and he is not going anywhere. I feel *4:44* is JAY-Z's true masterpiece, a work of art we will be discussing and debating for years to come. Without saying any names, we've watched a lot of myth-making and half-truths and outright lies happen lately with hip-hop, on television, in movies, in media interviews. Now that hip-hop is the dominant music and culture around, that will only continue, as it has with jazz and rock before it. I wonder, I am not going to lie, how much truth JAY-Z is telling, and if, also, he is attempting, in 2017, and in the aftermath of the episodes with Solange and Beyoncé, to bring a different image of himself, as an artist, as a man. Only JAY knows what is truly in his heart, only he knows the depths of his own soul, as I know mine. There are no tools for any of this, no blueprint, we make it up as we go along. That is why it was not lost on me when he rejected, on *4:44*, some of the older men before him, for cartoonishly taking selfies on social media, like Al Sharpton, for hanging themselves with their own rope, like Bill Cosby. Not lost on me, either, that JAY talked about those who did not help him, because that father hurt remains, even though he is a father himself. This album seems to be his coming-out party, his attempt to help those behind him, his way. It makes you want more, seriously. Like imagine if a JAY-Z and other male musical artists and male athletes could spend some quality time with men like Byron Hurt, Antonio Tijerino, Jackson Katz, The Good Men Project (from whom I borrowed part of the title for this piece), Joe Samalin, Charlie Braxton, Ed Garnes, Charles Knight, Juan Ramos, Quentin Walcott, Tom Keith, Michael Kimmel, and others I can name who have been doing this work around self-examination, around remaking manhood long before *4:44*. Imagine if these artists and athletes were far more connected to those on the front lines of social justice, the way it was in other times, and the way it ought to be. Imagine if *4:44* were not merely an exciting and brilliant musical moment, but also the start of a movement to truly march manhood toward peace, love, nonviolence, and respect for women as equals.

Finally, I say be you, Shawn Carter, be the man, the Black man, you 'spose to be. It is your choice now where you go from here. Do you continually evolve, as an artist, as a man, as John Lennon did, as Stevie Wonder did? Or do you get derailed or remain stuck, as it happened to Marvin Gaye, unable to leave and turn even more corners? Freedom is a road seldom traveled by the multitude, said Frederick Douglass, said the Bar-Kays, said somebody. And we been known freedom ain't free. At the end of it all only you, JAY-Z, know what will truly set you free—

Me and Muhammad Ali

I lost a piece of my youth when Muhammad Ali died. I don't remember when I first heard his name, but I do know that there are certain things connected to Ali that I shall never forget from my early years:

Those d-CON roach spray commercials in which the fast-talking Ali burst through our rundown black-and-white television set and made me feel as if he would singlehandedly rid our Jersey City neighborhood of those pesky creatures . . . The many times we sang, in grade school, the song "The Greatest Love of All"—the theme, we were told, for the biopic of Muhammad Ali, a film I did not see until years later . . . The frigid winter night in February 1978 when my mother and I gathered ourselves in front of that TV and stressfully watched, through a constantly moving thick black line, an aging and out-of-shape Ali succumb to a much younger Leon Spinks . . . And the seven months later when my ma and I, anxious about every jab, hold, and counterpunch, were overjoyed to see Ali regain his heavyweight championship a record third time, from Spinks. His victory was our victory; his comeback was our comeback.

It was the late 1970s, an eternity since Martin Luther King Jr. and the Civil Rights Movement had died, and unbeknownst to me at the time, Ali was one of the last shining symbols of a historic era of immense Black pride and achievement. I worshiped the way the man spoke—confident, bold, highly intelligent, funny, and Southern-fried chicken poetic, just like my momma and them.

I was a Black boy with my self-esteem already ruthlessly damaged by poverty, violence, and a complicated relationship with my mother. And my community was besieged by heroin, neglect, hustling preachers, and crooked politicians. Except for the few examples of positive Blackness I gleaned from television programs such as *Soul Train* and the blockbuster miniseries *Roots*, Ali was teaching me, with his words, mannerisms, swagger, to believe in myself. Perhaps this is one reason that "The Greatest Love of All" became the one tune I whisper-sang nonstop during my dark and troubled adolescence. Somehow, I felt those lyrics from that movie in which he played himself might one day also free me.

The other reality was I had no father and no male role model the first eighteen years of my life. My mother and father never married, and she was forced to raise me alone on welfare, food stamps, and government cheese. I saw my father a few times until I was eight years old, then he was gone forever. I cried mightily inside for a male presence as a boy, and the only place I could get some semblance of that was from sports or entertainment figures.

That is why Ali was a giant to me—my own Crayola-brown Superman—and why he became one of the only Black male heroes I had. His name and face were everywhere, and I would stare in awe at his photos. Yeah, this dude really was as "pretty" as he said he was. Over time I would watch and study each of his boxing matches, sixty-one in total. When I was thirteen, I took up boxing at a local Police Athletic League gym. I pursued it aggressively for maybe a

year or so, thinking-hoping-praying that boxing would bring me the
fame, fortune, and love it had brought Ali. When you are born in one
of America's ghettoes, and you have very few life options readily in
front of you, there are basically three choices: become an entertainer,
become an athlete, or become a criminal. In Ali's journey, I saw a
glimmer of possibility for my own. If he could do it, why couldn't I?
I studied boxing and its history with the same shameless enthusiasm
that led Ali to say he was the greatest.

I eventually abandoned the idea when it became clear what boxing
had done to Ali by the time of his next-to-last fight, against his former
sparring partner Larry Holmes. Again, my mother and I watched in
utter horror as Holmes brutalized Ali. I wished he would quit and move
on with his life. He had proven what he could, I thought, and he had
been an encyclopedia of lessons to me about never giving up, of always
trying your best, of never making excuses. I could not view, at the time,
Ali's last fight ever against Trevor Berbick, as I was terrified it would be
similar to watching a blood relative taking a vicious beating.

When I got to Rutgers University in the mid-1980s, I learned Black
history in a way I had never been taught it before. This, despite attending
the so-called best public schools in Jersey City. I read what remains the
most important book of my life, *The Autobiography of Malcolm X*. I was
stunned to hear that Ali, who was born Cassius Clay, had been mentored by Malcolm X, that they had been very close, until Malcolm X was
kicked out of the Nation of Islam. No matter, I joined the NOI myself
during my college years and became a Muslim (I am not any longer). I
was completely outspoken about freedom, justice, and equality, just like
Malcolm X and Ali. In discovering Malcolm X and discovering Ali the
humanitarian, I was also planting the seeds for my future self.

I especially became fixated on Ali's stand against American racism, and his defiance of the Vietnam War draft. It hand-smacked goose bumps on my flesh the first time I saw footage of Ali saying the Vietnamese people had never called him a "n_____." What kind of Black man, what kind of Black athlete, says and does things like this? I wondered. If Jack Johnson, the first Black heavyweight champion, had represented unforgivable Blackness, then Ali was fearless Blackness. Indeed, Ali was a one-man sports revolution, mind-spraying the golden era of television. Ali took sportscaster Howard Cosell's career to the stratosphere in a way that foreshadowed ESPN. Ali controlled his own image and provided his own self-commentary long before the inventors of Twitter and Facebook were even born. Ali befriended Malcolm X and singer Sam Cooke, and in the process united sports, entertainment, and political leadership. Ali was Nat Turner's slave rebellion remixed with the agitprop comedy of Dick Gregory and Richard Pryor. Ali was Marcus Garvey's Back-to-Africa movement. Ali was Martin Luther King Jr.'s Poor People's Campaign every single time he visited an impoverished community anywhere. Ali was Black Lives Matter before it got downloaded for the twenty-first century. Ali was hip-hop before we called it hip-hop, his hoarse-voiced wordplay the boom-bap and verbal tricks of a dope emcee. Better yet, Ali was Kanye West before Kanye West was Kanye West. Yup, Ali was Cam Newton's dab dance move, Steph Curry's unconscious three-point bombs, and LeBron James's obliteration of physical logic. And Ali did with his sports platform what Malcolm X had done with his splintered wooden platforms on those Harlem street corners: Ali stripped and sanded away centuries of Black fear and Black self-hatred with the very simple but powerful use of his tongue.

MY MOTHER. BARACK OBAMA. DONALD TRUMP.
AND THE LAST STAND OF THE ANGRY WHITE MAN.

167

This blew my mind because I knew, as I digested one Black history book after another, and watched documentaries that included Ali, that the price for a Black man speaking as Ali did could have been death—from a noose hung from a tree, from your home being bombed, from someone pulling out a gun and shooting you, point-blank, for being "uppity." I did not care, cuz Ali had loosened my fears in a way no amount of church and sanctified preachin' ever had. I saw in Ali my freedom song, and a sense of purpose that was undeniable: Be all of who you are and never apologize for any part of yourself ever again.

This is the Ali I followed as he did fewer and fewer interviews and fewer and fewer public appearances once the Parkinson's disease slurred his speech and made parts of his body shake. This is the Ali I watched as he slowly lit that 1996 Olympic torch, even as I sat in an Atlanta hotel room battling a debilitating depression that would consume years of my life. Through decades of his illness, Ali still gave me hope, courage, and a deeper awareness of myself. If Ali did not feel sorry for himself, in the sunset of his life, who was I to feel sorry for myself? This man had sacrificed his life, his body, his brain, his money, his championship title, his freedom, and yes, his voice so that people like me could speak our truths in our times.

Yes, I think of Ali daily as I think of my own crossing, my own life work in service to others. He will never be dead to me. On my living room wall, there is the young and brash Ali in the famous photo standing above a fallen Sonny Liston in their second and final bout. I hear that photo speaking to me right now. Conquer your fears. Conquer your fears. This is why I love Ali, every chapter of his being. I love both the pro-Black Ali and the we-are-all-part-of-the-human-family Ali. I love both the Ali who was about peace and love, and I love the Ali who was clear he was a man of color who had an obligation to challenge oppression and injustice. It was never an either/or for Ali, and it is not an either/or for me. What Ali taught me between those ropes with all eyes on him, in his interviews, with his poems, with the winks and smiles in the years that Parkinson's had silenced his tongue, is that freedom ain't free, and that you cannot separate your freedom from mine, because we are all truly in this boxing ring of life together.

Hamilton, O.J. Simpson, Orlando, Gun Violence, and What the 4th of July, Alton Sterling, Philando Castile, and the Dallas and Baton Rouge Police Shootings Mean to Me

---

I think the first duty of society is justice.

—ALEXANDER HAMILTON

You've gotta give them hope. If a bullet should enter my brain, let that bullet destroy every closet door.

—HARVEY MILK

I'm not Black; I'm O.J.

—O.J. SIMPSON

There's no such thing as hurting someone for their own good. There's only hurting someone for your own good.

—KATE BORNSTEIN

There's no point in saying anything but the truth.

—AMY WINEHOUSE

The world is on its last go-round.

—MY MOTHER

1.

When I was ten years old and in the fourth grade at Public School 38 in my hometown of Jersey City, New Jersey, I was asked to play Thomas Jefferson in a production of the acclaimed Broadway musical *1776*. I was terrified. I was often told to be quiet, by my mother, a loud and strong South Carolina–born Black woman who had survived racism, sexism, and classism in the South, and in the North, from White people, from minimum-wage employers of every stripe, and from my father, a Black man who was never really a presence in my life. Indeed, I felt abandoned by my father, physically, emotionally; and, due to the way my mother constantly yelled at me, I felt emotionally abandoned by her at times, too. Hers was a tough love. Work hard, read and study hard, never never never bring home a bad grade. Be excellent at everything you do. Except for the fact that I was so shook by my mother and her numerous rules that I spoke mad fast or mumbled, or both at the same time, for fear that I only had split seconds to get my words out. Or I, an only child, would say nothing, shoveling ready words and thoughts back inside, keeping them to myself. I simply did not think my voice mattered.

So you can picture my distress when my fourth-grade teacher, Mrs. Coles, asked me to be a part of this *1776* adaptation. Yes, I was an outstanding student. Yes, I did act out in class from time to time like the bad boy my momma often said I was. But I expressed no desire whatsoever to stand in front of an audience. Even when we had the weekly assembly where we grade school kids from different ages came together to sing popular songs of the day, I would pretend I was singing: first, because my high-pitched singing voice was God-awful; second because I had zero confidence in my ability to blend my vocals in with those others.

But I also did not know how to say no to Mrs. Coles. I was raised to do what your authority figures asked you to do. I was to be Thomas Jefferson, and another Black boy, Anthony Washington, would be George Washington. Our school was integrated, with the rainbow children of post–Civil Rights America bumping elbows in ways my mother could not have imagined in the segregated Jim Crow cesspool that produced her. Why no White or Latino or Asian children were asked to play these roles was beyond me. No matter, we were told that Jefferson and Washington were "founding fathers" of America, heroes to be loved and admired and emulated, that there would be no freedom and democracy without their vision and courage and sacrifices, and that we would only be on stage for a short period. I dutifully memorized my lines, had no clue at the time that both Jefferson and Washington, White men of massive power and privilege, had owned slaves Black like me, or that Jefferson had had a long-term Black mistress in the person of a slave named Sally Hemings. I simply knew Jefferson as this remarkable gentleman who could write, speak, lead, build, and create virtually anything he set his mind to—a true Renaissance person, I was told repeatedly, and the principal author of our freedom song, the Declaration of Independence. I wanted to be like Thomas Jefferson, and privately was elated I was going to be him in this school play.

But on the fateful day of the show my mouth was desert dry, I sweated bullets down my face profusely, my heart thumped as if it were going to bottle-rocket from my puny chest, and my knees buckled beneath the weight of great expectations I was not sure I could deliver. Yes, once more I was in a state of paralyzing fear. Meanwhile, Anthony, his kinky hair also white with baby powder like my baby 'fro—to simulate the white wigs of the Revolutionary War period—sat like an old man, stoic, still, ready for his big moment. Other student scenes went before ours. Then we were told to take our places, Anthony and me, for the section we shared. The moth-eaten red curtain went up, and I trembled with trepidation when I saw the full audience populated with students, teachers, administrators, and parents. I could not look at the spectators but for a few seconds. Much of the time I stared above their heads, into space, or at the clock on the back wall. Anthony was dynamic and brilliant: he sang, he danced, he performed some of his lines with humor that drew instant laughter; he projected his voice with the swagger of a Broadway star. His George Washington was a revelation. I, on the other hand, whispered and muffled my lines, and I thought I might piss on myself midway through our scenes. It was a rapid-transit blur, we took our bows, with my eyes still avoiding the audience, and then I ran off stage as quickly as I could. Anthony was congratulated loudly for his portrayal of his namesake George Washington, but barely anyone said anything to me about my performance. When I found my mother she bluntly stated, "I could not hear a word you said, boy!" Like that my acting career was over, and except for the eighth grade when I was salutatorian of my graduating class and had to deliver a short speech, I would not set foot on a stage in any form to use my voice again until I was in my early twenties. I likened the experience to an unbearable torture I had no interest whatsoever in being a part of.

2.

Growing up I never questioned American history or the American value system, or how any of it was communicated to me. Words and phrases like "God bless America," the lyrics to "The Star-Spangled Banner," and the Pledge of Allegiance were committed to memory and became as essential to my knowledge base as knowing my name and my address and my Social Security number. We were taught these things, in school, when we were very young, and we were commanded to say and sing these words repeatedly. My mother had a grade school education and she simply told me, when I was three or four, that I should be a lawyer like Abraham Lincoln, the country's sixteenth president. And that the way to be as great as Lincoln was to do what my teachers told me to do, to be the best pupil at every single thing. Vaguely I knew that Lincoln had something to do with ending slavery. Vaguely we were told that George Washington was the father of this country. Vaguely I learned names like Jefferson and James Madison and John Adams and Alexander Hamilton and Aaron Burr and Patrick Henry. Vaguely I heard that Hamilton was killed in a gun duel with Burr, over one beef or another. No matter, I studied what was given to us in social studies and history classes, eagerly memorized dates and basic facts, and never questioned why the vast majority of historical figures were White men. There was a revolving door of war and violence and bloodshed, but I never thought much of any of it, for that seemed to be the price of the ticket for our freedoms. And their stories entranced me, made me envision myself as them: an explorer of new and foreign lands; a soldier or general in one noble war or another; a defender of our homeland from the Indians; an inventor or discoverer of something that changed America, or the world, for the better; creators of airplanes and spaceships; conquerors of soaring mountains and limitless oceans. These sensational stories made me want to be, well, a White man—confidence, like theirs; hair, like theirs; bravado and fearlessness, like theirs . . .

The only Black people imparted to us, vaguely, kindergarten through the twelfth grade, were Crispus Attucks, who died at the start of the Revolutionary War, but I was never quite sure why, or why he was there in the first place; Rosa Parks, who refused to give up her seat on that Montgomery, Alabama, bus; and Dr. King, who delivered his sterling "I Have a Dream" speech, and a few other sermons that frightened the heck out of me, because his Dirty South preacher-man oratory, dripping with both dignity and doom, always seemed to be lurking mighty close to the death bullet I knew was waiting for him, because they told us so. There were no lessons whatsoever about the Civil Rights Movement, although my integrated schools were the result of the Civil Rights Movement, as we were told, vaguely. There were no discussions whatsoever about slavery, about Africa, about anything Black folks may have contributed, including free labor in the form of human bondage, to the building of the United States. There was nothing about, say, Black music, Black inventions, Black pioneers in professional fields of any kind; no, nothing, like we did not exist, like our history did not matter. And there was virtually nothing mentioned about Native Americans except they were wilderness savages, and pathetically ungrateful; and Latinos and Asians and Arabs and any and all European ethnics (Italian, Irish, Jewish, Polish, and on and on . . .) was missing completely, too. Either you were White, or you simply did not matter in our education either—not in history, not in English, not in math, not in the sciences, not in art, not in woodshop or home economics classes, and not in the many anecdotes we were given to read. And, alas, poor people of all races, and LGBTQ people, and disabled people, with the lone exception of Helen Keller, were completely hidden, too. And the only women ever mentioned were, yup, Helen Keller, Rosa Parks, and Betsy Ross proudly stitching together that first American flag. From any history class I took, even as I got top grades absorbing, wholly, what we had been taught, what little I learned about Black people, about America's racism, came from my mother and her oral history lessons about coming of age in the American South, how White folks treated colored folks down there in the old country. And I got an acutely personal baptism into racism in that same fourth grade year I appeared as Thomas Jefferson, when a gang of Jersey City White boys called the B.O.N.E.S. ("Beat On Niggers Every Second") showed up at Public School 38 and proceeded to hurl rocks and bricks and bottles at us Black and Latino children, solely for being there. But I had no context, historical or otherwise, for understanding why these White boys were doing this to us, why they hated and feared us little children. I was scared, yes, but I quickly kicked it to the curb because I figured it had to be something out of the norm of human behavior in America, our America.

3.

The two places where I could see Black people doing something, anything, were in sports and entertainment. My mother always said that Blacks, better than anyone else, could sing and dance and act a fool naturally. She enthralled me with the repeated saga of her witnessing James Brown live at the Apollo, how it looked like he had wheels at the bottom of his feet, the way he slipped and slid and split magically across that world-famous stage. She and I would watch Jersey City native son Flip Wilson on his landmark comedy show, and we would laugh hysterically at the jokes and antics on Black sitcoms like *Good Times* and *The Jeffersons*.

But it was sports that truly seized my imagination and gave me some hope that something was possible for my otherwise bleak life.

In boxing there were figures like Muhammad Ali, Joe Frazier, George Foreman, and Ken Norton. In baseball there was Reggie Jackson, Joe Morgan, Willie Stargell, Rod Carew, Vida Blue, Doc Ellis, and George Foster. In basketball there was Dr. J and David "Skywalker" Thompson. And in football there was one player who was the epitome of greatness, in spite of the many stars in that constellation: Orenthal James "O.J." Simpson.

I was too young to watch O.J. Simpson on television rush for an extraordinary 2,003 yards for the Buffalo Bills in 1973, breaking the legendary Jim Brown's record. But what I did see were those many Hertz rental car commercials where O.J. was sprinting and leaping through airport after airport, in a full suit and tie, a strikingly handsome Black man with a baritone voice, representing a manner of grace, skill, and progress I had never seen before in any African American male. On the playground of P.S. 38 we played a game called "free-for-all," where we boys, mainly the Black boys, would use a football or tennis ball or sponge ball, or even a stuffed hat or glove, and toss it in the air. Whoever caught it would have to run toward the designated end zone, avoiding the touches and tackles of every other boy on the field. It was our 'hood version of professional football, and time and again we would refer to someone with snaky moves and swift feet as "O.J." or "Juice." This was how much the mythical figure of Simpson loomed over us. To be called by his name or nickname meant that you had elevated your swag as a runner to superhero status. Not just anyone got to be O.J. or the Juice.

Perhaps a year or two later my mother and I sat to watch the blockbuster television mini-series *Roots*, and there was O.J. Simpson in the tip-off episode, mentoring the lead character Kunta Kinte, as played by LeVar Burton. Over time Simpson was everywhere, it seemed, in commercials, on television shows, in movies, even as a sportscaster. Perhaps my one chosen recollection of him is when the Juice carried the Olympic torch leading into the start of the 1984 Summer Olympics in Los Angeles. That moment reminded me of the stories I had read of Simpson as a child: of how he had overcome rickets that rendered him bow-legged and pigeon-toed; how he had survived a childhood of poverty in San Francisco's Potrero Hill neighborhood. How his father, Jimmy Lee Simpson, a janitor, left his mother, Eunice, and him and three siblings when O.J. was only four. How O.J., like many of us ghetto boys, including me, yearned for a father figure and became especially resentful of his dad's absence during his teenage years. How it would be learned that O.J.'s pops was a closeted gay man for several years, and how that was ridiculed, in whispers, in that San Francisco community, as no straight boy wanted to be called a homosexual or have a daddy who was one either. How O.J., determined to make something of his life, was scared straight into understanding his street and gang affiliations were not the paths. How he was a star football player in high school but first had to go to a local community college because his grades were not good enough for the University of Southern California. And how he shined once he got to USC, becoming a national sensation, a Heisman Trophy winner in 1968, and a young husband and father all by age twenty-two. And how he struggled his first few seasons in the National Football League after being drafted by the Buffalo Bills, many dissin' Simpson as a shameful bust. But then the unimaginable happened, he became the first running back ever to generate 2,000 yards in a single season; and the magnetic combination of good looks, an athlete's body, an ah-shucks

Middle America smile, and an ability, no doubt, to mix and mingle with all people, a specific class of White people, made O.J. Simpson the first Black athlete, long before Michael Jordan or Tiger Woods or Steph Curry, to become a cult figure—his popularity rivaling that of the president of the United States. And the Juice's nice-guy-next-door image was the counterpoint to the brash one-man Black revolution that was Muhammad Ali. O.J. was safe and reasonable where Ali was dangerous and wildly unpredictable.

For sure, when I was a youth we would hear time and again about Horatio Alger rags-to-riches stories, of impoverished boys who had overcome great adversity to make something of their lives. Well, in Orenthal James Simpson, American football player-actor-pitch-man-businessman-sportscaster, we had our own Black version, in living color. I paid close attention to what O.J. was doing, right until I got to college, Rutgers University, in the 1980s. During these years my consciousness around my own Blackness changed: I learned the Black history that had been conveniently left out of my schooling K through 12, and I embraced a Black nationalism that made me reexamine O.J. Simpson as someone who did everything in his power not to be, plainly, Black. It was during these years that I gravitated toward race-conscious Black athletes like Jim Brown, like Kareem Abdul-Jabbar, and most assuredly Muhammad Ali. It wasn't so much that I completely rejected O.J. Simpson. What I was rejecting were the parts of him that seemed to discard his total identity, and his Black self-love, because he valued more, so it seemed, the power and privilege he was afforded due to his close proximity to Whiteness and White America. That was not a price I was willing to pay: the trashing of my own soul; and the more I learned about the so-called founding fathers, the genocide that was inflicted on Native Americans, and how African people, my ancestors, had been kidnapped and coerced like cattle to build America, from the ground up—one of the ugliest stains on the history of world civilization—the angrier I became. It was anger in those days that made me hate White America, White people, and, to be mad honest, anything remotely White, like milk or bread or the walls of wherever I was residing. So I thought less to little of O.J. Simpson during these formative years of mine, did not consider him one iota during the latter part of the Reagan years, into the Bush years, as hip-hop and crack cocaine simultaneously exploded, and, soon enough, the city of Los Angeles in the aftermath of the not-guilty verdict for the White cops who mercilessly beat Black motorist Rodney King some eighty times, on videotape—

4.

I remember it like it was yesterday: Friday evening, June 17, 1994. I was watching the New York Knicks play the Houston Rockets in Game 5 of the NBA Finals, on NBC, when news anchor Tom Brokaw broke in and said there was a police pursuit of a white Bronco that contained O.J. Simpson and his close childhood friend Al Cowlings, on the Los Angeles freeway. NBC did not completely take over the telecast, but eerily continued presenting the game while also, in a box in one corner of the screen, showing live the white Bronco as Brokaw narrated. Just as surreal were the people, pre–the explosion of Facebook and Twitter and Instagram, who had found out about this pursuit and were cheering O.J. Simpson on during this sixty-mile chase. I had grown up watching the Juice evade one football tackler after another, become a superstar and celebrity on and off the field, but now the grim reality was setting in that this man, this Black man, may very well have murdered not one but two people—two White people—his wife Nicole Brown Simpson and an acquaintance, Ronald Goldman. I thought for sure that police would shoot O.J. Simpson down along that highway, or when he and Cowlings inched their way back to his Brentwood driveway. Or when O.J., after nightfall, had finally gotten out of the car clutching family photos, collapsing into the arms of local police.

But O.J. was spared, at least on that day. He was caught and tackled in a way he, I, we, could never have fathomed; an American dream had become an American nightmare. And we would come to learn, during what was billed as the trial of the century, that the squeaky-clean image was a fraud, a hustle, that here was a man who had played a ferociously violent sport, and he himself was violent. He beat his second wife, we would learn during the trial, ruthlessly. His rage and mood swings and jealous outbursts were the stuff of domestic violence cases many women could readily identify with. I cringed as I heard detail after detail. I was a staff writer at *Vibe* magazine at the time, covering a range of major hip-hop artists of the day, including Tupac Shakur on several occasions. The same Tupac who himself admitted that he did not show proper concern for a woman in a New York City hotel where he was arrested for sexual assault, that he turned his back and said nothing when his "friends" proceeded to sexually attack, allegedly, that woman (only Tupac was ever brought up on charges and tried in court). And I was also in the midst then, in my twenties, of reassessing what manhood and violence meant to me. I knew I did not want to be a foul-tempered human the rest of my life. I had grown up like a walking time bomb because, I believed, that mentality was spilled over my spirit as a child. Yes, the circumstances of my own journey had scarred me that deeply—the poverty, the verbal and physical outbursts by my mother, the pain of my father's absence, life in an environment where I was constantly looking over my shoulder, wondering when and how I was going to die, because death was such a part of the life cycle for Black boys and Black men. But just like O.J., I had managed to escape, to college, to things I was passionate about, finally: writing, becoming an activist, and being in service to others. But the darkness does not just escape you because you have somehow crossed from one reality to another. Wherever you are from, there you are, staring back at you like your image in the mirror. Yes, I was violent, to men, toward women, toward anyone that I felt, in those days, had violated me. Yes, I was as violent as America, our America. A violence that was—is—a form of mental illness where that violent tendency becomes the chief way we confront any perceived threat or danger, or the chief way we handle turmoil or beef.

So, indeed, I was mightily torn during the trial of O.J. Simpson and heard the loud exclamations of both Black America and White America. For Black people, O.J. became, in spite of himself and his lifelong shuffle away from Blackness, a damaged symbol of what Black America had endured, since slavery and segregation, since the season of lynching and the season of water hoses, attack dogs, and fire bombs: an icon of victimization and resistance both, a Black man who had been pronounced guilty—many of us felt prematurely—by White America, in the same way those lynch mobs had been judge, jury, and hangman as nooses were placed around our necks and we dangled, lifeless, from those mouth-less trees. For none too few White Americans O.J. was the Black beast and the Black boogeyman it had long suspected Black people, particularly Black males, to be. We were dangerous, untrustworthy, violent, immoral, oversexualized, and crazy. And we had to be stopped, put in our place, justice had to be done, with all available tools—

Women and the few legit male allies who existed in the 1990s were correct to say sexism is as much a plague on our earth as racism. O.J. viciously whooped Nicole Brown Simpson several times during their marriage. While I was being hypnotized by Ezra Edelman's gripping new ESPN documentary film, *O.J. Simpson: Made in America*, the hardest parts for me to digest, and to hear, were Nicole's 911 calls for police help, and those still photos of her nearly decapitated head drowning in a river of her red blood. Yes, I have learned in the years since my own backward and destructive behavior, and thanks to years of therapy and spiritual work and being in circles of women and men who view and know women and men as equals, to not see manhood as violence first and last; to acknowledge that O.J. Simpson, like so many of us men—White, Black, Latino, Asian, Native American, Arab, Jewish, Christian, Muslim, Atheist, Agnostic, it don't matter—was a very sick man who, at the very least, did very sick things to Nicole Brown Simpson, in the name of manhood and power and privilege and pride and ego, and an incurable desire to own and control every aspect of her life. When he felt he could not, he abused her, like his own body had been abused for years on that football field. O.J. Simpson was a man who fled the monster that is racism by reinventing himself as something he was not, and in the process, he had become an oppressor and monster himself. And, as the ESPN doc reveals, local police, men, came to the Nicole and O.J. home on several occasions, but no one dared to stop Simpson for good in what was an obvious pattern of domestic violence, physically, mentally, spiritually. Had O.J. Simpson been an everyday Black man terrorizing a White woman like that, he would have been arrested immediately. But here sexism and the glittering lights of celebrity pushed race, at least for one shining moment, to the back burner.

The above said, I foolishly tried to avoid the ESPN O.J. film because I did not think it would shed any new light on what I had already known about him leading to his ultimate demise. It does and then some, yo. That O.J. was born into the same period of segregation as my mother means something. That O.J. came of age during the great Civil Rights protests but deliberately and publicly chose to stay on the sidelines means something. That O.J. became like a Black man in White face, like many a Black American before and after him, eager to please White America, and likewise terrified of the power of White America, to the point that he became an invisible Black man in plain sight. Moreover, I thought about the fact that O.J. played football, our ultra-violent modern-day gladiator sport. We did not know in 1994, in 1995, about this thing called CTE (chronic traumatic encephalopathy), about the catastrophic effects of constant blows to the brain on football players; things like, yes, violent behavior, suicidal thoughts, drastic mood swings, and severe bouts of rage. For sure, the five-part ESPN O.J. doc film is one of the best I have ever seen— ever. It makes your flesh crawl; it makes you think critically; it reminds us in the most painful ways that race and racism are central tenets of the American social fabric and that we cannot, should not, avoid ourselves, our shared history. Yet, still, if there is one singular criticism I have of that otherwise amazing miniseries it is that it does not mention CTE once at all. Two decades later, and given the endless parade of football players—Junior Seau, Mike Webster, Dave Duerson, Frank Gifford—who displayed wild emotional mood swings, you've got to wonder. Football, our beloved American football, is a metaphor for violence and insanity and destructive manhood run amok. Calvin Johnson, recently retired All-Pro wide receiver for the Detroit Lions, said he stopped because of its brutality, because of the toll on his body, and readily admitted that players pretty much get head injuries on every other play or so, if not every play.

That implies we all, regardless of our identity, have been socialized to believe a man is to be aggressive, violent, competitive, hypermasculine, a warrior, a fighter, no matter the cost, even to ourselves. We punch, we kick, we bite, we stab, we shoot, we rape, we threaten, we murder. And we have been socialized that there is one dominant group in America, and on this earth, that has done everything great and noble that we should emulate—the ever-powerful and ever-privileged White man—and so the only way you could possibly be a part of that is to renounce your identity, integrate, assimilate, take on a bootleg definition of White American maleness recycled with whatever parts of you that you dare to hold on to: anything and everything that you feel will help you to survive, and win, at the cost of your own sanity and your own life.

5.

When the Simpson verdict came down, it was decidedly split between Black and White America. Black Americans live in one America, mostly, and White Americans, mostly, live in a different America. Some of us, no question, overlap, cross boundaries, bust down barriers, but the vast majority of us, in spite of integration, Barack Obama, Oprah, hip-hop, a shared love of food and sports and music, actually do not know each other, ourselves, or the history of America beyond the very basics, and even that is a stretch for some of us. Our eyes are different, our ears are different, our sensibilities of what we feel and experience are different. For Black folks, who had witnessed those cops acquitted in Los Angeles for the Rodney King beating—amongst hundreds and hundreds of cases in our lifetimes before and since—it meant cheering and crying as if we were cheering and crying for an O.J. Simpson touchdown. It meant cheering in spite of the fact that some believed, as I did and do, that the Juice did in fact kill Nicole Brown Simpson and Ronald Goldman. This is the disaster of American racism; that a group can be so beat down and wounded by it that we will celebrate as a victory a clueless and violent Black man getting off with double murder, because his great escape was our big payback for centuries of oppression and discrimination and injustice.

I was a guest at MTV studios on that October day in 1995, with anchor Tabitha Soren, and civil rights activists Jesse Jackson and Al Sharpton, when the verdicts were read. There was much talk that Black America would riot everywhere if O.J. was found guilty. As we four sat in that ice-cold MTV studio and listened to the decision come down, I could see the face of Tabitha, a White sister, morph into horror and fear, and her slim body sag in her chair. Reverend Jackson squeezed Tabitha's hand hard, as he had been holding it, and Reverend Sharpton sighed, the kind of sigh one produces when a heavy burden has been lifted from one's shoulders. I had mixed emotions because I was in sheer disbelief. Nothing in American history, like nothing, had prepared me for anything like this. But that majority Black-woman jury had sent a message to White America, one White America was not prepared to receive. Surprise, awe, anger, revulsion, disgust; and, suddenly, the criminal justice system was now broken. Suddenly the jurors were stupid. Suddenly we needed to have reform. That was the twisted irony of America's long sojourn with race and violence. Black America believed, by and large, that had Nicole been Black, no one would have cared. White America believed that because O.J. had money and celebrity status, he got off. Both were right. And both were ignorant in different ways. We as Black folks were ignorant for celebrating the O.J. verdict as if we had somehow won our freedom from slavery. Our emotions got the best of us, four hundred years of indifferent treatment in America had, well, stunted us to our own humanity, and many did not realize as we hailed O.J., we were also hailing the cruel butchering of Nicole and Ronald. For White people their ignorance was rooted in what Malcolm X once notoriously called chickens coming home to roost. When you have been conditioned to believe that your skin color and your value system and everything about you is superior to anyone else, when you have been conditioned to believe that White is right and everything else is wrong, when what you have been taught in school, in your religious institutions, in the mass media culture—here there everywhere—is that your life matters above all others, that you are the foremost figure in any space at any given time and place, then it is extremely difficult to lose anything, to have your power blow up in your face, in any form. That was the O.J. verdict, as uncomfortable as that may sound. O.J. fundamentally was not just his own creation, but also a creation, and a creature, of White America, as the ESPN film suggests, boldly: the good, the bad, and the ugliest. The whole tragic occurrence, one of the most tragic in American history, reeked of a Shakespearean play, ship-loaded with sex, drugs, violence, murders, alibis, deception, dark humor, ill-fitting gloves, botched evidence, and what seemed to be foul play from every angle conceivable.

My mother called me as soon as the verdict came down, her worldview hardened by the racism she recalled from her native South Carolina and her adopted Northern environment of New Jersey. A worldview that included being called every foul name for Black people one can think of, rarely ever being called by her first name, and from the time my mother was eight years old, she worked exclusively for the good White folks in her dirt-road town. Breathing heavily and straight trippin' about the verdict, too, my mother said to me, matter-of-factly, "Kevin, you heard O.J. got off, right?" I responded that of course I knew. Then my mother said to me, with the dread and sorrow and echoes of Black mothers who may have seen their sons lynched for merely looking at a White woman: "I hope O.J. reminds you of this, child: stay far away from White women!"

I was dating Black women, but that was not the issue to my mother. Her point was that any poorly considered relationship with White America could mean the end of me. And her point was that O.J. Simpson was very lucky to not be in jail, or dead, for I believe my mother also felt O.J. was guilty. But Black people, especially Black women, for a variety of reasons, are loyal to Black men even when we are not loyal to them. I thought of this as I watched the ESPN doc and listened to the soundbites of two of the Black women jurors who were steadfast that it was not just O.J. who was on trial, but racism in America. If revenge was ever to be exacted, right or wrong, this was the time to do it. And thus it was so. The conundrum is that in America we have done such a piss-poor job of dealing with the horrid legacy of racism—no real national dialogue, no real reconciliation, like ever, and no real understanding and acceptance of the fact that racism is race plus power and privilege—that this debilitating social disease manufactures, time and time again, dysfunctional and insane behavior, like O.J. and the circus that was that trial of the century—

And equally as tragic has been O.J.'s life post–the trial of the century. I had no idea how far homeboy fell. The drugs, the alcohol, the midlife crisis of living like he was a rap star in his new South Florida encampment, complete with videos, him rapping, and women easily the age or younger of both his daughters. O.J. was not only an alleged murderer, but he had accelerated the pimp lifestyle he was indulging in when married to Nicole Brown Simpson. So without saying it aloud, the ESPN doc is also about sexism, about misogyny, about the demonic definitions of manhood, about destructive addictions to fame and celebrity, drugs, drink, women, sex, and, yes, violence and abuse, too, which have landed O.J., in his senior years, in that Nevada jail.

I winced several times watching the rise and dramatic fall and demolition of Orenthal James Simpson. I doubly recoiled knowing a lot of it was his internalized Black self-hatred and Black self-sabotage, made in America. O.J. truly believed he was not Black, that he was somehow above the law as local police of every race gave him pass after pass before the murders, because he was the Juice. No, he was only the Juice as long as he performed, as a White man in a Black body. The moment he thought he could get away with murder, he was born, again, into what he was created to be in that San Francisco ghetto: n_____ orphan of the American Dream.

6.

Yes, n_____ orphan is what I heard, vaguely, about Alexander Hamilton once I started hanging around grassroots activists. It was in my early days as a community organizer and it was suggested on multiple occasions that Hamilton, one of America's so-called founding fathers, was, partially, a Black man, and that he passed as White; that he had some African blood running through his veins. Did not know if this was fact or fiction, but given how so many things had been left out of my education, like Benjamin Banneker, a colonial America Black man as accomplished and all-purpose as Benjamin Franklin, I speculated periodically about this Hamilton dude. Could it be that Hamilton had been whitewashed, like much of United States history? I pondered this as I read, in college, Hamilton's contributions to *The Federalist Papers*, learned that he, like his contemporary Thomas Jefferson, was the quintessential multitasker: soldier, lawyer, scholar, businessman, writer, newspaper publisher, first Secretary of the Treasury, statesman, revolutionary. And that his life had been blown away by Aaron Burr in a gun duel, due to ego-driven, power-hungry, long-standing disputes. And he was on the $10 bill.

Otherwise Alexander Hamilton was not one of those Revolutionary War–era folks you gave much thought to, nor it seemed, did our collective school system. So I was mad surprised when the very gifted Lin-Manuel Miranda announced he would be writing the book, music, and lyrics for a play about Hamilton. Previously best known for the Broadway hit *In the Heights*, Miranda is one of the most artistic visionaries of our times: he acts, he sings, he spits rhymes, he dances, yes, but, to me, Lin-Manuel's true genius is in his ability to put words to paper. He is a writer, a great writer, a whiz kid with a hip-hop nerd resourcefulness that is the electrifying subway screech and halt of Piri Thomas's *Down These Mean Streets*, the salsa sidewalk poetics of the Nuyorican Poets Café, the old school show tune trick bag of Sissle and Blake, Gershwin, Berlin, Sondheim, and Rodgers and Hammerstein, and the boom bap drum licks of rock and roll and rap. There is abundance in the head of this proud Puerto Rican hombre bred in Nueva York. Probing, I learned that Miranda had stumbled across the eight-hundred-page Ron Chernow biography of Hamilton, and he was hooked. Makes sense, given that Hamilton was born on the island of Nevis in the Caribbean and that Lin-Manuel is a child of island heritage, too. Makes sense as well given that Latinos, frequently forgotten somewhere between Black America and White America and their shared historical dysfunctions, are also often left out of conversations about, well, most things. The way Hamilton was left out of the nation's telling of the founding fathers. Makes sense because both Hamilton and Miranda made names for themselves, against numerous odds, in New York City. Inspired by Miranda's curiosity, I was reminded that Hamilton was born to a Scottish father and a mother whose background still remains puzzling to me, in spite of Ron Chernow's otherwise fine biography awkwardly explaining away "myths" of her alleged mixed background; that Alexander moved to another West Indian island, St. Croix, as a boy; that his parents were never married and he was the result of an adulterous affair (his mother was estranged from an abusive husband); that he was considered an illegitimate child; and that it was wealthy business leaders on St. Croix who made it possible for him to go to the American colonies, to study at King's College, which eventually became Columbia University.

I stopped there because I wanted to see the play and Miranda's interpretation of Alexander Hamilton with my own eyes. I was especially intrigued by two things: Lin-Manuel was using hip-hop, the beats and verses, the culture, the language, the attitude, to remix this story of an ostensibly White founding father into a musical. Second, the playwright boldly decided to cast a majority of Latino/a and Black actresses and actors in these roles documenting Hamilton's life, re-gardless of the fact that people of African descent were predominantly slaves during this period in American history. That blew my mind, made me think back to when I played Thomas Jefferson as a boy in that grade school play, and nothing, like nothing, in my childhood camera phone could have pictured Black and Brown bodies taking on the bodies of White folks, those kinds of White folks, on Broadway, aka "the Great White Way," no less.

Indeed, if the #OscarsSoWhite, then that theater district has histor-ically been #BroadwayBeyondSoWhite. You can pretty much count on both your hands and both feet in the hundred-plus-year history of Broad-way the stars and creators and hit shows where people of color dominated the stage, specifically Latinos and Blacks. . . . Bert Williams . . . *Shuffle Along* . . . *Too Many Girls* . . . Olga San Juan . . . José Ferrer . . . *West Side Story* . . . Rita Moreno . . . Chita Rivera . . . Ben Vereen . . . Miguel Piñero . . . Melba Moore . . . *Dreamgirls* . . . August Wilson . . . George C. Wolfe . . . Savion Glover . . . *Bring In 'da Noise, Bring In 'da Funk* . . . John Leguizamo . . . *Anna in the Tropics* . . . Audra McDonald . . . *In the Heights* . . . Quiara Alegría Hudes . . .

And then there is Lin-Manuel Miranda and *Hamilton*. . . . No one could get a ticket it seemed, for the hottest Broadway show in like for-ever. I begged, I tweeted and posted to Facebook, I called people who called people, I knew people who knew people, and I was turned off, to be mad blunt, by the ticket prices, some north of $1,000; I refused to pay part of my total monthly bills just to see a play, no matter how game-changing. People who did catch *Hamilton* raved about it, add-ing to my angst. It has been a mega-hit, one that forced producers to share in the profits with the majority people of color original cast, a rarity for Broadway. Controversy was stirred when a casting call went out seeking "non-White" actors to replace members of the initial ensemble, presumably. Interesting, yo, considering we've seldom heard the New York White theater elite complain about decade upon decade of exclusion and marginalization of Black, Latino/a, Asian, Arab, or Native American actresses and actors from its stages—

   When my companion and I arrived at the Richard Rodgers Theatre, she and I were struck by the fact that folks had been sleeping outside for several days—food, drink, blankets, sleeping bags, cardboard—in anticipation of tickets, via lottery. I was doubly struck by the massive crowd outside, and the wild energy that was abuzz there in Times Square, and how most of the ticketholders were overwhelmingly White. This was disconcerting to me and reminded my companion and me of the Upper West Side dinner we had left minutes before, where an elderly White wife and husband sitting at the next table chatted us up about *Hamilton*. The wife had seen it, and said, with adolescent innocence, "I did not think I would like a play with rapping. I did not think I would understand it. But I did. I got it." I was intrigued and amused because, well, I am a life-long hip-hop head, literally grew up in the culture, as a dancer, a graffiti writer, a music journalist, a founding staff member of Quincy Jones's *Vibe* magazine, and I coproduced the very first exhibit on the history of hip-hop in America, at the Rock & Roll Hall of Fame. For sure, my next book more than likely is a long-overdue biography of hip-hop's greatest icon, Tupac Shakur. Gravely ironic, given how poorly a Broadway show inspired by his life and music did before *Hamilton* premiered.

Hip-hop, the foundation for *Hamilton*, was created by poor people: poor African Americans, poor Latinos/as, and poor West Indians, in New York City, much of it incubated "Uptown," in The Bronx, in Harlem, before spreading across the five boroughs of our metropolis. These were the same poor people Martin Luther King Jr. warned us at the end of his life not to abandon and forget. That Dr. King who condemned the Vietnam War and said we were sending poor Blacks and poor Whites to fight poor Yellow people in Southeast Asia. That Dr. King, he of the Nobel Peace Prize, global fame, and the moral leader of the Civil Rights Movement. And that Dr. King—eff the awards and accolades—whose final act, before his assassination on the balcony of that Memphis motel, was organizing Black garbage-men there, and a national Poor People's Campaign. Made in America, the birth of the hip-hop nation was more or less Dr. King's vision set to the grits-eggs-and-bacon frying pan rhythms of funkified artists like James Brown. Simple definitions of hip-hop are "winning on our terms" and "making something from nothing." Nothing is right. In its soul, hip-hop is these favorite things: a microphone, two turn-tables, spray paint or Magic Markers, and sneakers and cardboard or linoleum to dance on. These things represent the four key elements of hip-hop: the rapper or emcee, the deejay, dancing, and graffiti art. Hip-hop factually began, in my humble opinion, when a young lad named Clive Campbell—hip-hop alias is Kool Herc—arrived from his native Jamaica in the Caribbean to New York City, in 1967, right in the middle of Dr. King's last year of life. A West Indian immigrant just like Alexander Hamilton, Herc, too, came with a dream, deter-mined to hustle and flow.

I thought about all of this as we made our way into the Richard Rodgers Theatre, especially as I strained my eyes to find, here there anywhere, Black and Latino theatergoers. There were barely any. The few Black and Brown faces I saw were those who worked at the theater, taking our tickets, working security, running concessions, ushering us this and that way. Meanwhile, there were countless White families, undoubtedly rich enough to afford the steep ticket prices, with their children, teenagers, preteens, in tow. I thought about the fact that when I played Thomas Jefferson in the fourth grade, Broadway, although a stone's throw away from my Jersey City birthplace, seemed millions of miles across the universe. The closest I could ever get as a child was that *1776* production I was in, and the commercials of various plays on television. What would my life had been like if I had been blessed to experience Broadway, to be exposed to live theater, as a child, as the White children were doing with *Hamilton* and God only knows how many other plays? I similarly thought of the early to mid-1980s, when as a youth I attended the greatest hip-hop parties in New York City: at places with names like Union Square, the Rooftop, the Roxy, and Roseland. Those same African American, Latino/a, and West Indian youth who created hip-hop begat a second generation, a second wave of hip-hop heads that included kids like me. It was rare, in those days, to see a White person embracing our culture, and if she or he did, if she or he was there, it meant they were also gaining the knowledge, as we said, of not just the music and fashion and language, but also of our lives. Because, frankly, there was no way to access hip-hop without also being forced to confront race, gender, class, poverty, violence, and the many forgotten people and communities of America. As Chuck D, lead rapper of Public Enemy, prophetically said, hip-hop was our CNN.

Once *Hamilton* began, I was mesmerized. Yes, I had seen majority people of color shows on Broadway before (like *Fela!* and *A Raisin in the Sun*, and nearly everything August Wilson had ever done). Yes, I had previously witnessed highly successful Broadway productions with the energy of hip-hop at their core: *Bring In 'da Noise, Bring In 'da Funk* and *Def Poetry Jam*. But nothing, like nothing, prepared me for *Hamilton*. It is a thrilling excursion into the life of an overlooked American hero whose racial identity and immigrant status were questioned more than a few times by his contemporaries. It is one of the best American musicals I've ever seen, in any format. There is music, there is singing, there is rapping, there is dancing, and there are virtuoso performances by the entire cast. I was particularly affected by the majestic talents of Daveed Diggs, who played two characters, Marquis de Lafayette and Thomas Jefferson; and by Leslie Odom Jr., with his stirring and somber interpretation of Aaron Burr. Hamilton's rocky childhood and longing for a whole family made me think of my also being called "illegitimate" because my father and mother were not married either. Likewise, I marveled at how Hamilton made the most of every opportunity, getting his college education paid for, as I did, not finishing undergrad, as I did not either. His passion for writing was mine, too. His dedication to a cause, in this case the American Revolution, the same thirst for answers as we have when we ask, in our times, if Black lives matter. Slavery, immigration, his sex scandal while married, it is all there in *Hamilton*, brought into existence by this worldwide cultural movement we call hip-hop.

But the very same people who created hip-hop cannot, by and large, afford to see a show inspired by what they created. This is the warped rationale of American capitalism. Something becomes hot, "they" raise the prices, be it gentrification in our 'hoods or a Broadway show, they price people out, they make the demand so high it is ridiculous, and they make it something only the exclusive few can experience. And folks downright lucky, like me, who got my two tickets I paid for at a reasonable price, because a very kind man on Facebook connected me to a friend he had who was working for *Hamilton*. Yeah, I got the friend-of-a-friend discount hook-up, miraculously, through genuine human kindness. I was grateful, but I did also wonder, while absorbing *Hamilton*, if this play would have mattered had it been about that Black colonial figure Benjamin Banneker, not Alexander Hamilton. I wondered if the play would have mattered, or even gotten produced, or been the juggernaut it has become, had it been about slavery, about the African people who many of those founding fathers owned, or if it had been about, say, Nat Turner, and the slave rebellion he led, instead of about these power-ful and power-addicted White men, with Hamilton squarely at the center of it all? Some would argue that those are complex questions. And my reply is, no, it is rather simple. Native Americans were here first. The land, theirs, was stolen from them. They were the victims of genocide. African people were stolen from Africa. They were made to work for free as slaves. The genocide was brutal and ugly, and the institution of slavery was brutal and ugly. And in the midst of this White men, White men like Hamilton, fought for their freedom, although their freedom had nothing to do with my freedom. So what makes this play different, unique, and subversive is that Lin-Manuel cuts and scratches, à la a hip-hop deejay, the narrative, and he, a Puerto Rican, is the title character. It is a not-so-subtle way to critique Alexander Hamilton and his founding father homeboys, but also a not-so-subtle critique of the mighty lack of democracy on Broadway, and in America itself.

We were born on the Fourth of July, so they say, our Independence Day, but if you were Black or Latino/a, or a poor White, or disabled, or queer, or Native American, or women of any color or creed, or anyone who was not a wealthy White male businessman or landowner, then freedom and democracy did not really and truly apply to you. That was America then, that is America now. I thought of this as my companion and I were on a short vacation in Connecticut, just chillin', minding our own, for the Fourth of July holiday break. We were sitting on the outdoor patio of a local restaurant when a noisy pick-up truck heaved and hauled up Main Street. There was a large American flag flapping in the slight evening breeze on the left, and there was a large Confederate Flag flapping in that breeze on the right side. My companion and I, both Black, were instantly deflated and defeated, our vacation ruined by a symbol that has everything to do with slavery and denial and hatred and fear and ignorance toward those Black like us. We wanted to end our vacay in that moment, but knew we could not, because we also knew we had as much right as anyone else to be there. But our safe space and our safety were dashed, we felt vulnerable because of who we were in this 99.9 percent White Connecticut town, and, truthfully, felt if a Confederate Flag could be flown so effortlessly then so, too, could someone so effortlessly end our lives for being who we were. Call us paranoid, but anyone who has paid attention to what has been going on in these United States the past few years, one killing of a Black person after another, would be mad paranoid as well. I reckon that is the case, too, if you are, say, a lesbian, bisexual, gay, transgender, or any queer sister or brother or any person simply out at an Orlando, Florida, nightclub, a safe space, so you thought, where someone can walk in, oh so very casually, and proceed to shoot and kill as many of you as he so desires. A safe space the way those prayerful people thought their Charleston, South Carolina, church was a safe space, yes, until a White supremacist young man named Dylann Roof, in their prayer circle praying with them, unloaded his bullets into their God-obeying spirits. Practically one year later in Orlando this man, this American man, this Arab-American man, this Arab-American man who may or may not have been gay himself, and deeply self-hating. This man who was able to get access, yet again so naturally, to guns the way every other shooter or mass shooter has gotten guns as if they were picking fruits or vegetables at a supermarket. Was he or was he not connected to ISIS, a terrorist with foreign ties, or simply someone, like O.J. Simpson and like the many other mostly male mass shooters, made in America, a product of our violent environment?

And then the day after the Confederate Flag sighting, we heard the news of Alton Sterling, a seller of CDs and DVDs in front of a convenience store, being shot and killed by a Baton Rouge, Louisiana, police officer. I watched the video, I watched two police officers tackle and subdue Sterling, I watched one police officer kneel down over Sterling and shoot him, at point-blank range, into his chest. I cried, turned my head away, then looked again and cried some more. Then when the second video angle was released, I cried harder, tears of pain and anguish, because with this new viewpoint one can see that Sterling's empty hands held no gun. Yes, when that cop unloaded his bullets into Sterling's chest, the front of Alton Sterling's shirt became like a field of vivid red roses; and I replayed the part of the video again and again where Sterling's outstretched arms are cutting and scratching the sky, like those deejays who may have inspired Lin-Manuel Miranda; then those arms trembled and shook as I had seen as a boy in church when we poor Black people were begging God, begging anyone, for help. And then Alton Sterling was dead, his casket and graveyard the asphalt streets where he had hustled his CDs and DVDs for years. Dead, even as America was still drunk and blunted with the fireworks and pageantry of the Fourth of July.

Dead the way Alexander Hamilton was that Summer of 1804 day when he and Aaron Burr engaged in a duel, Hamilton's life ended by gunshot, just like that. White-on-White founding father violence, but we don't call it that, now do we? Hamilton was dead, dead like Philando Castile, the very next day after Sterling, the same week, yes, as America's Fourth of July holiday made possible by men like Alexander Hamilton, sitting there in a white tee-shirt in the driver's seat of a car in Minnesota, as his girlfriend Diamond Facebook lives this gruesome and frightening scene of him and her little girl in the backseat, with the just-fired gun of a police officer lipping the edge of the video. Was this real, were these folks acting there in Minnesota, as Miranda and his cast mates were acting on that Broadway stage? Alexander Hamilton had many beefs in his lifetime, with Jefferson, with Adams, with Burr. He spoke about slavery. He did his best to prove himself, worked hard, as hard as Alton Sterling worked selling those CDs and DVDs to feed his family. As hard as Philando Castile worked at that Minnesota Montessori school, in the lunchroom, not only making sure those kids ate, but being a role model of what is possible, as Hamilton was. What is the value of a life, any life, if it can be taken away so easily? What is an act of violence if not a form of mental and spiritual insanity where we feel that hitting, kicking, punching, beating, or shooting and murdering each other is a natural and permanent replacement for peace, for love?

Truth be told, Hamilton's and the founding father's times were as violent as our times now. The play reinforces, start to finish, if one is truly listening and paying attention, that this nation, our nation, was built, brick by brick, on violence, that this violence is a way of life for us. And this nation, our nation, was founded on power, on greed, on hoarding resources for a small minority, at the expense of the rest of us. That sort of thing will drive you crazy, once you begin to become aware of who the founding fathers truly were, it will make you crazy if there were local militias, then, and local police, now, who, excessively militarized, treat regular everyday citizens as threats to the 1 percent who run and dictate everything. It will make you crazy if you served in the American military, in Hamilton's time, in these times, only to see yourself left out of the American Dream. The trauma can be overwhelming, the sadness and anger a deadly rat poison one drinks and vomits into a psychotic rage; and because those same founding fathers ordained your right to bear arms, you just might become Micah Johnson killing police officers in Dallas and Gavin Long killing police officers in Baton Rouge, and seek revenge on local police, especially if you watched, as I did, over and over, those ghastly scenes of Sterling and Castile dying—or Eric Garner, or Tamir Rice, or the uncountable other viral videos of Blacks dying at the hands of White, Black, Latino/a, or Asian police, like it is a spectator sport, a reality television show, a rite of passage to being Black in our America. Not an excuse, not support for anyone who would point and shoot at police, not a call for violence toward anyone—as I do not condone violence in any way—just some context for y'all to consider. And to consider, too, that the police shooters in both Dallas and Baton Rouge were military veterans. War is hell, Marvin Gaye once sang. Well, I am sure, a double hell to return to the US after fighting for freedom for others, as they like to say, but wondering why your people do not have it at home. Call it rage, call it revenge, call it the post-traumatic stress disorder of a post-military life, call it cocking and aiming a gun when you feel like it in America; be it the police killing innocent citizens, or citizens killing innocent police officers, we've come to a severe crossroads in America and you, me, we, have no clue from whence the bullets will come and who they will murder next.

Death is a part of life, my Aunt Cathy always says. Yes, Auntie, fo' sho'. But there is something utterly abnormal about dying, in an Orlando nightclub, outside a convenience store, inside your stopped car, in a duel, on that Memphis motel balcony, at a school, on a college campus, at work, in a church prayer circle, on the streets, in your home, just because we have been so conditioned to believe that we are in a perpetual state of war. Except we have no clue for what or whom we are fighting, except ourselves.

I thought of this when we left Connecticut and my companion—in the aftermath of Diamond's video of her dead boyfriend and her alive little girl in that Minnesota car—said not only was she not comfortable driving and was terrified of the police pulling us over, but that she was more fearful for my driving because I am a Black man in America. I thought of this as we left Connecticut, a state that had slavery, contrary to notions that slavery was just down South, and we headed back into New York City, which at one time was the biggest importer of slaves in America. I thought of this as I saw, in my mind's eyes, Lin-Manuel Miranda, as Hamilton, shouting on the stage of the Tony Awards, the night after the Orlando shooting, "Love is love is love is love is love is love is love, cannot be killed or swept aside. . . ."

Yes, love, I agree, one thousand percent. For it is the most revolutionary act we could ever perform on any stage, to love ourselves, to love each other. What the founding fathers loved was power, was privilege, was property, human and material, and that is why America, our America, remains, limbo-like, in a state of flux, over two hundred years old now, yes, but also forever that infant unable to walk without falling down. America needs to be born, again, but it ain't happening if we do not make it happen. It ain't happening if it is an eye for an eye and a tooth for a tooth. . . . When will this ever end with that sort of mentality, with that sort of revenge and conquer mind-set, from cops, from citizens, from us all? When the Dallas and Baton Rouge snipers shot and killed those police officers, I felt pain, too, for their families, for all of us, our violence, our uniquely American violence, in wars overseas, in the many wars we are fighting against each other on this land, is, maddeningly, torturing and killing us. I am not quite sure what else can be said that has not been said somewhere else. But what I will say is that we've got to make an effort not to be insane, not to be evil, not to be violent, in words, in actions, in our spirits. Because our spirits, right now, are contaminated. When I was in Los Angeles recently I participated in a sit-in with young #BlackLivesMatter activists in front of that community's city hall. The protest, as have been many I have participated in, was peaceful, was civil, was beautiful. #BlackLivesMatter is not a terrorist group, and it is obscene and inhumane for someone to suggest that. They, we, simply want peace, we simply want love, and we simply want the freedom to be all of who we are, no matter who we are. #BlackLivesMatter would not be necessary if all lives truly did matter in America. Case in point is from the moment I posted about that protest, the social media trolls attacked it, and me, violently. But the same kinds of people will say they love America, they will say they love the founding fathers, they will say how much Alexander Hamilton and George Washington and Thomas Jefferson mean to them. But why, beloved, is it OK for you to have your freedom and your heroes and sheroes, but I cannot have mine? Why are my freedom and my very being a threat to yours? And who continues to win when we the masses of people forever fight and hate and fear and kill each other, merely because we refuse to talk with and listen to each other, especially when quite difficult, and merely because we refuse to learn how to love each other?

Prodigy and the America
That Raised Him

I wanna go home not sing this song
but I'm forced to perform speech napalm
—Prodigy, "Genesis"

To be a Black man in America is to be under a constant state of
enormous pressure, stress, and danger, from outside, from within.
From outside there is the ruthless reality of racism, jabbing and stab-
bing at you from every angle, in the mass media culture, at school with
textbooks that forever omit you, with those police encounters that put
your soul on trial even if a simple traffic stop, from individual meetings
with those who view you as dangerous, immoral, aggressive, violent,
whether you've demonstrated any such behavior or not. And then if
you are me or the late Prodigy of the rap duo Mobb Deep, and happen
to hail from one of America's ghettoes, your end could also easily come
at the hands of people who look like you, too. Because not only is the
racism mad real, but so is the internalized racism and toxic manhood
we've digested so well, have taught each other, have gifted from generation to generation like family heirlooms for the boys in the 'hood.

This is what crossed my mind when I learned of Prodigy's tragically sudden death at forty-two years old. Another Black man dead who, like me, was probably happy—and surprised, to some degree— to make it to eighteen, to twenty-one, to twenty-five, to thirty, to forty, knowing that those markers of age and time defeated are, for sure, no small miracle. Add to that Prodigy's battle since birth with sickle cell anemia, and it is little wonder his short and tumultuous life was weighted, at different stages, with alcohol, marijuana, other drugs, anything to numb the trauma and pain of an existence that feels like life matter-of-factly awaiting death.

This, to me, is why so many are taking Prodigy's passing at such a young age so hard. For he truly was one of us, the way Tupac was one of us, the way Phife Dawg of A Tribe Called Quest was one of us. Every generation has its spokespersons, its truth tellers, its artists there to show us what we do not want to see, or hear, and Prodigy was undoubtedly that. It is like he had no other choice. Born Albert Johnson, his grandfather Budd Johnson was a jazz saxophonist who was there right at the tip-off of that uprising they called bebop. His mother sang for a spell with one of the great "girl groups," the Crystals. Yet somewhere between being born out on Long Island, New York, in that hardscrabble suburban village of Hempstead, and teaming up, as a teenager, with a fellow rapper and producer nicknamed Havoc, something burned inside of Albert, and he made his way to Queensbridge Houses, the biggest low-income housing projects in North America, and one of the great incubators of hip-hop genius— like Marley Marl, like Roxanne Shanté, like MC Shan, like Nas.

It was there as a precocious teenager Prodigy willed himself into Lord-T (The Golden Child), which is not surprising given the Golden

Era of hip-hop we were immersed in during the late 1980s into the early 1990s. The dominant thread of Black nationalism and the influences of Afrocentricity, the Nation of Islam, and the Five Percent Nation of Gods and Earths were everywhere. But so was the utter destructiveness of the Reagan years on urban America, including the wholesale attacks on Civil Rights Movement victories, the deadly crack epidemic, and the explosion of gun violence. New York City was the epicenter of this, and also the homeland of hip-hop, and it was just a matter of time before rap would begin to reflect, explicitly, what we were grinding through daily. You look at an early photo of Prodigy and Havoc and realize the original tag of the group was Poetical Prophets, complete with the Kid 'n Play flattops most of us sported in those days. But as the Reagan years became the age of Bill and Hillary there was no turning back from what was inside of us: hardness, cynicism, rage, an incredible need to spit truths, as Billie Holiday had done with "Strange Fruit," as Bob Dylan had done with "Blowin' in the Wind." They called it "gangsta rap." We called it reality. Prodigy, Havoc, Mobb Deep, presented us with rhymes straight outta the blacked-out hallways of an American nightmare reeking of dried piss, cheap, loose cigarettes, skunk weed, and Olde English malt liquor.

The first time I truly heard Prodigy's voice, and Mobb Deep, was the now classic single "Shook Ones, Part II." Spare, raw, rugged, this song on that second album that broke through for them—and much of their music since, including Prodigy's solo efforts—was unapologetically about the people we do not want to see: the single mothers, the baby daddies, the hustlers, the petty criminals, the drug dealers, the strippers, the addicts, the murderers, the men and boys doing time in prisons, the boys on the block watching life pass them by, the poor people desperately trying to make a way out of no way. Prodigy's work was Norman Rockwell's America rebooted with the bullets and blood of a wretched street corner. His poetry was that of Truman Capote scratching, furiously, the dead skin from America's bloated belly. Indeed, Prodigy's verbal theatrics were like that of an impatient spoken-word poet at an open mic, but he was also an indie filmmaker, his stream of consciousness his camera, his subway-jarring descriptions of his New York as mean and rich and unflinching as anything Martin Scorsese has ever conjured.

Where there was shine and glamour to the tales spun by Ice-T, Ice Cube, Snoop Dogg, and The Notorious B.I.G., I think of Prodigy as a different kind of working-class hero. He could care less about being a superstar. If Tupac was Carole King, then Prodigy was Laura Nyro. Those who knew, knew. And like Laura Nyro, another great but under-the-radar songwriter for the people, Prodigy had great highs with gold and platinum albums, and there were the lows of three and a half years in prison and ugly public beefs with rap rivals. But he was also a husband, a father, a step-grandfather, and he was a man battling a debilitating disease with which most folks are not expected to live past forty or fifty.

Perhaps this is why many of us, including me, have said that hip-hop saved our lives. Though Prodigy is gone now, I believe that it saved and extended his, too, especially when he was at his lowest points, with his disease, while in jail, when he and Havoc had broken up for a time. In a world where countless Black males like Prodigy do not have much to look forward to, hip-hop has been our Civil Rights Movement, our self-made twenty-four-hour news channel, our counterculture revolution to win, to make something of ourselves, on our own terms, even if it makes sense to no one except us.

Yes, much has changed since Prodigy began as a fresh-faced youth in the 1990s, but the violence and poverty and hopelessness in America's inner cities remain the same. Those same poor people Dr. King warned us not to forget, those same poor people who created hip-hop, those same poor people Prodigy dedicated his voice and his life to, may have lost a street soldier with his death, but they forever have an asphalt angel because of the music he has left behind.

Re-defining Manhood: Harvey Weinstein and how his toxic manhood is our toxic manhood, too

A s I've watched the Harvey Weinstein saga unfold these past few weeks, and the stunning roll call of accusations of rape, sexual assault, and sexual harassment pile up, from Hollywood royalty, from actresses who never achieved fame, from women and men both, I cannot help but think of my mother, for two reasons. First, when I was a little boy my mom, ever-honest, real, raw, told me that when she migrated from the American South to New Jersey, where I was born and raised, she, like many working-class women of color who'd made the same trek North, worked as the help in the home of a wealthy White family, across the Hudson River in Westchester County. One day, when all other members of that family were gone, the husband appeared before her clad only in a bathrobe. Suddenly, in the sickening manner that Harvey Weinstein has now made infamous, he sat down in the living room across from her, with his private parts dangling in full view. Why my mother told me this tale at such a young age, I do not know. What I do know is she repeated it often yet never went beyond that ugly moment in her storyline. To this day I do not know how she managed to escape that man.

I also know my mother, now seventy-four years old, forever carries the ugly trauma and scars of my father, the only man she ever fell
in love with. He was eleven or twelve years older than her; she worshiped him, and he lusted after her. My Aunt Birdie later told me that
my mother was terrified when she became pregnant with me. My father's wildly unpredictable role in their relationship meant that, when
my twenty-two-year-old mother was about to birth me, she had to call
a cab to take herself to the hospital.

This reckless and callous distance was to be permanent. I saw my
father only two or three times in the first eight years of my life. He
never bothered to make good on the promise of marrying her, and
my mother, with her limited formal education, was forced to raise
me in poverty on government assistance for much of my childhood
and youth. My main memory of him was one rainy day when I was
eight years old: my mother grabbed me by the hand and took me to
the local drugstore to call my father, because we were too poor to
afford a phone in our tenement apartment. On this day—the last day
I would ever hear from my father—he told my mother, as I stood
there, that she had lied to him, that I was not his son, and that he
would never give her another nickel for me. He then hung up on her.
My mother lifted herself slowly from that phone booth, her plump,
short frame trembling: she was devastated, angry, humiliated, and
she would come to say these words over and over, in her very pronounced Southern accent, words that echo loudly in my ears as I
have thought about Harvey Weinstein, film director James Toback,
former Amazon Studios chief Roy Price, R&B superstar R. Kelly,
disgraced and ousted Fox News host Bill O'Reilly, and all of us men
like them: "Men ain't no good." And she would rush to underline that

sentiment, whenever the image or name of my father struck her heart like a hammer, "Do not be like your father."

Here I was a boy child being raised by a single mother, with no male figure to be found anywhere—not a stepfather, not a role model, not a mentor in sight. But what I did have—what we all have, whether we have fathers or not—is the intensively male-dominated tone of our common culture: television, film, books, magazines, comic books, religious institutions, music, sports, the mass media. And these forums all, in turn, reflect back the messaging we learn in school, within our families, within our communities. We are outraged, and rightfully so, by the heaviness and sordidness of the allegations lodged against a Harvey Weinstein, a Bill Cosby, a Woody Allen, an O.J. Simpson, a Roman Polanski, a Mark Halperin—and against the many men whose names we will never know who engage in similarly toxic behavior daily, across the globe.

The offenses of destructive men align along a gigantic spectrum of dysfunction, from pressuring a woman to a hotel room to committing acts of domestic violence, from police brutality and racial profiling to suicide bombings and mass shootings. (Indeed, it's very rare for the perpetrators of mass shootings not to have at least been rooted in a past pattern of domestic violence.) But we have got to also understand that none of this behavior is new. That was the enduring lesson of the incident involving my mother, way back in the 1960s. The hard and fast fact is that across much of the world, we men have been taught from boyhood onward that we are superior—and, as a consequence, that women and girls are inferior, are second-class citizens, or worse yet, not worthy of being viewed as anything other than sexual objects, punching bags, or caretakers to us and our needs.

This is an incredibly toxic definition of manhood, spread across centuries, continents, civilizations, races, cultures, religions, politics, communities, and families. This beast-mode model of male experience has erupted time and again, like a deadly disease, in all those spaces and places so organically, so rapidly, that it's a virtual rite of passage. Indeed, when I was reading about the many instances of Weinstein showing his penis to women, or clutching at women, I immediately thought back to my youth, as a boy, when I was merely ten or eleven, and how I and all the other boys my age would prowl the halls of our school and summarily grab at the buttocks or budding breasts of our girl classmates. We laughed off any protests from the girls—we just did it.

And we were never stopped from doing it—not by teachers, principals, parents, or any other adult. Nor were we taught any differently even on the rare occasions that our behavior might rank a passing scolding from our elders. Why and when we began to do this, I don't know. We just did it, because it was what so-called boys did. And should we fail to follow this standard boys' script, a certain kind of male policing kicked in, with peers and male adults physically or verbally abusing us in viciously emasculating and homophobic terms. If any of us were to seek to stop the behavior (which none of us dared to do), we'd be instantly expelled from this boys' club we so desperately wanted to be a part of. To be a boy, to be a man, was to fight, was to grab, was to shove and push, was to one up each other every chance we got, was to brag about our material things, our status, was to harp on our sexual conquests (incorporating both truth and lies), was to declare war in every form imaginable: on each other, on those we despised. Manhood certainly never involved viewing women and girls, not even our own mothers, as our equals. Women and girls were simply there to cater to us, to support us, to do what we pleased, even (and in some cases, especially) if doing our bidding meant hurting or destroying those women and girls. Because manhood for us, ultimately, was about power, and that taste of power was totally intoxicating.

This real-life modeling of male privilege shaped our identity throughout our developmental years. Our schools rarely bothered to include women as equals in terms of intellectual achievement or career aspiration—which meant that many of us, from generation to generation, from Harvey Weinstein to me, came of age thinking that the only lives that have mattered in history, literature, math, science, religion, and any other sphere of endeavor or influence have been the lives of men—unless someone intervened and told us differently. Ask the average man of any background even today to name ten or twenty women in the history of his community or country or culture who have done amazing things, in any fields, and he would be hard-pressed to reach five. I know this to be true, because I have done this simple exercise in many places throughout the country and the globe. Not only are we grossly mis-educated on what it is to be a man, but we are also severely mis-educated on who women are. To find out why we men and boys traffic in these egregious attitudes and behavior toward women and girls, look closely at how we've been taught and socialized from the moment we were able to speak as little children. We pass this toxic manhood among each other as if we are kicking a soccer ball or tossing a football. And like in any sports setting, the tribal rites of toxic manhood present themselves as a sort of second nature—as the rules of the game. The simple equation of manhood with boundless freedom is acutely embedded in who we are, and who we think we are; it is the background faith behind the supernatural belief in our invincibility and superiority as men and boys, with the world, including women and girls, as our play area for pleasure and power and privilege.

This is why when we men get to college or jobs or careers, we have indiscriminate and emotionless sex, only view women from the neck down, and change partners the way we change our pants or shoes. This is why we men, unchecked, have sex with women who are drunk or drugged, and do not consider it rape. This is why we men will ignore a woman saying no or saying nothing as she suffers sexual assault at our hands—because we've got no clue what the word *consent* means. This is why we men, steeped in the ritual of violence as a form of power and control, hit women, slap women, belittle women, rape women. It's why we feel entitled to push a woman into a bathroom door, as I did to a girlfriend when I was a very young man back in July of 1991. And this is why we men, like Harvey Weinstein, like the many men in Hollywood and media and politics and corporate America now, find ourselves terrified that we will be outed for harassment or sexual assault: because we know what we have done, and what some of us still say and do to women, every single day of our lives. Or, just as bad, we use our privilege to continue our own complicity—when we hear and see our male peers say and do cruel and inhuman things, we remain silent. We thus fail to see that even if we do not directly engage in evil acts of shameless sexism, our deafening silence means we are in agreement, and with that silence we are just as guilty.

What began the turn away from unthinking male privilege was that episode in the early 1990s when I'd pushed my girlfriend into that bathroom door. She and I were in the middle of an argument—about what I no longer recall. But what I do remember is that the more she was winning the verbal scrum, the more my temper boiled, until it exploded with my shoving her, hard, into our bathroom door. She screamed and ran, barefoot, from our Brooklyn apartment, and I stood there, shaking and sweaty. The recognition of what I had done then dropped me, like a dead weight, to the floor with shame and guilt. She eventually came back, and she and I continued to live together for perhaps a month longer, but the damage had been done, and our New York circle of fellow writers and artists and activists knew. Once I had moved out, I saw her on a street in Manhattan a week or so later, and I cursed her badly because she tried to avoid me. Here again the classic script of toxic manhood had seized the day, making it appear that my woefully underdeveloped male ego was more important than this woman's trauma.

She eventually filed a restraining order to keep me away from her—a legal proceeding that made the totality of what I had done, what I had become, daunting indeed. Women friends challenged me to seek therapy, to get help, and I did. A few men who were allies to women and girls said the same. I was told, point-blank, that I was a hypocrite, as a "woke" writer and activist, for talking about social justice issues while engaging in sexist behavior that was harmful to half the world's population. I was told it was clear I knew little to nothing about women and girls. Undeniably, after I had looked back on my stint in college and I was forced to concede that I had never read more than a couple of books written by a woman. I had no clue who bell hooks or Gloria Steinem or other legendary women thinkers were; nor did I have a single notion about what the feminist movement was. I had become, essentially, what my mother had told me not to be; I was, like my father, and like many men, "no good."

I was challenged to take ownership of my actions; my friends and allies-in-the-making assured me that apologies were empty without growth, without deeds. So eventually I wrote about it, all of it, in a short essay for *Essence* magazine entitled "The Sexist in Me," a very public confession, in September of 1992. The responses to that piece were startling, because women wrote me directly—either (mostly) to thank me or to share their own tales of violence and abuse at the hands of men or boys. I had no clue. I had been asleep all my life until that point, never grasping what my mother had been saying to me all along. That realization, and the support of those women who could have easily given up on me as just another no-good man, sparked something in me, and I began to study women's history, women's literature, and women's political movements. In those beginning stages of my own feminist odyssey, I was uncomfortable, and terrified. Most of all, I was unsure of myself as a young man being told, in no uncertain terms, that the very definitions of manhood that had shaped my experience in the most powerful and intimate ways were toxic to me, to women and girls, to men and boys. I couldn't initially bring myself to accept that I was fundamentally living a lie.

It is not easy to evolve or to change as a man in this world, because there really are not many examples of it. What I realized, as I was going to therapy for my anger and my violent behavior, was how little I knew about myself, as a man, and how I really had no definition of manhood that had anything to do with being healthy and sane. I'd been traumatized by the very definitions of manhood that had been passed down to me, and I was confused about which way to go. I also began to realize, then, that my definitions of manhood were also tangled up in my family history—the actions of my father, the trials of my mother, the pain (literal and metaphoric) that she felt from his treatment of her, and how much of that hurt had been taken out on me. My mother did what she

knew and acted on what she felt for the very simple reason that there
were no safe spaces, no healing spaces, for women like her—no outlets
whatsoever. She raised me the best she could, and I am quite clear,
today, that I would not be who I am without her. Without her being
familiar with the terms or any movements my mother was, for sure, the
very first feminist, the very first womanist, I ever met, I know now. In
rejecting the ways of my father and men like him she was saying to me
"You've got to go a different way."

But even with her voice there, challenging me, I did what boys did:
I played sports, I played video games, I lusted after girls, and I sup-
pressed the side of me that loved reading, that loved the arts, that was
highly sensitive and prone to crying because, well, that was not what
boys or men did. I thought of these things and more as I went to those
therapy sessions. They also came back to me, powerfully, as I sat and
listened, often with tears in my eyes, to one female friend after another
acknowledge having been raped or sexually assaulted in some form,
or hit or beaten by one man or another in their lives, in several cases a
male relative. I thought of these things as I began to reassess, way back
in the 1990s, my relationship to male-centered art forms like hip-hop
and rock music, and our awful treatment of women. And I thought of
these things as women confronted me then, as they confront and challenge me now, to be an ally, to be a voice urging us all to take a different
path, one that knows and regards women as equals.

But most of us never get there, never even start, as clearly evidenced
by thirty years of accusations against Harvey Weinstein. Change demands tough, fearless searches for the man in that mirror, self-criticism,
and owning of all the things that toxic manhood sets out furiously to
deny: our imperfections, our vulnerabilities, our easy lapses into male

privilege. And meanwhile, that privilege, and the power that comes with it, is deeply tantalizing and addictive. In addition, our definitions of manhood are tightly knotted to violence and hate and division and war and domination, while a genuine spirit of feminist equality rests just as inextricably on the practice of peace and equality and love. And in the deeper reaches of our brains, so many of us men feel so incredibly inadequate in our own lives, so weak and powerless, no matter how wealthy or poor we are, that we have come, without apology, to view the abuse and control of women as central to propping up our puny egos and our punier sense of self-worth. To be a different kind of man means that we would have to give up any form of "power" that hurts us, other men, women and girls, the human family—that we would have to become honest, and vulnerable, and emotionally naked in a way that forces us to confront ourselves as we have never done before. This is what I had to do, what I do now, because I do not want to be in a box, in a toxic male prison, for the rest of my life.

This is the real tragedy of Harvey Weinstein, and of all of us. These many years since that day and that incident with my girlfriend, I have become deeply versed in women's history, and think long and hard about various issues around gender and women and girl empowerment. I have never relapsed into putting my hands on a woman in that violent way, and I never will again, I am sure of this. I've given countless speeches, and organized a wide array of workshops, blogs, forums, conferences on the connections between sexism and how we define manhood. I have done several years of self-healing work—therapy, yoga, meditation, my spiritual practices, conversations with circles of men who also grapple with the question "What is a man?"— and I still continue to wrestle with the spiritual and emotional legacies of my sexist past. I have, I would like to think, been a good and consistent ally. But I also know that I am still very much a man, a highly insecure and painfully sensitive man struggling to navigate a universe that does not reward men for being honest, or for seeing and treating women as equals. And I am still very much a man who grapples with how to relate to women, who thinks, more than ever, of each word and each action, because I must. Because, if I am brutally honest, and I am, I know countless men, myself included, have at some point in our lives, exposed our penises, said sexually provocative words to women we have worked with, offered a woman a hotel room, or one of the laundry list of things women are now coming forth with about Harvey Weinstein, about other men. So, I'm still learning—and struggling to remind myself in real time—when to listen, when to speak, when to be an ally, and when to say if something hurts or bothers me for fear of being called sexist or unsupportive. I think about this daily with my wife, with my mother, with my assistant, with all women I encounter. Do I hear them consistently, see them consistently, respect and honor them consistently? And when I do not, do I own that? Do I check my own self, and hold myself accountable as a man? And I challenge other men, hard, as I challenge myself, hard.

And I think long and hard, given that I am recently married to a woman who is a feminist and creator of a choreoplay called *SHE*, about myself daily in new and strangely awkward ways—particularly since I'm collaborating with her as the producer of this work of art. I sit there quietly listening to my wife tell stories about herself, about women who've reached out to her for help, for support, who are survivors of violence and abuse. I sit there quietly after *SHE* performances and hear the many women and girls share, in this safe healing space, what they have endured. I think often, too, of the many women and girls in my journey from boy to man that I have hurt or wounded in some way, of the few I have been able to apologize to, to the ones who do not want anything to do with me ever again due to past behavior or indiscretions. I did apologize to that girlfriend I pushed into that bathroom door years later, and she did accept. And it's my humble hope that my work, now, these many years later, can serve as a sort of life-long apology for myself, for other men who have violated women and girls in some way.

And this, finally, is where I believe real change must start, with me, with Harvey Weinstein, with all men: a willingness to listen to the voices of women and girls, and a willingness to take ownership of our behavior, to say we are sorry, that we want to learn, that we want to heal and do better and be better. Only at that point can we set about redefining manhood in a way that does not wound women and girls, and that does not wound men and boys, either.

As I read the accounts of the many Harvey Weinstein accusers, I cringed, because I have heard some variations of these stories so many times about so many different types of men in so many different types of industries—starting with my mother when I was a boy. And I was forced to recall the many ways in which we men choose to ignore the plague of our own spiritual and emotional corruption—how we always protect each other and remain disgustingly mute when we witness these things. Here, too, I was among the chief offenders: One day in college I heard someone savagely beating his girlfriend behind our student organization building, and I never said anything, never confronted him. Many years later, I'd known of one close friend having an extramarital affair in plain sight, with his wife ultimately finding out and being shattered by it; I'd once again chosen the path of least resistance and failed to check this friend as he proudly boasted of his escapades. These are but two disheartening examples from my own past of the way that so many of us carry this so-called locker room talk into every arena of power, up to and including a White House currently occupied by an admitted sexual predator. In Donald Trump's America, despite the fallout from the Weinstein scandal, many of us men still feel supremely entitled to keep instinctively replaying the rites of toxic manhood because we couldn't care less about the interests of anyone except ourselves.

This is why I think if any good has come of the whole Harvey Weinstein affair it is the resurrection of the #MeToo campaign, begun by an African American woman named Tarana Burke in New York City long before social media launched it into prominence. I sit quietly on Twitter and Facebook and digest one account after another, of celebrities and working-class women both, and it has been jarring—as jarring as anything in my wife's choreoplay, as jarring as anything I've heard at women's shelters, on college campuses, in the many messages I still receive to this day from women and girl survivors of male violence and abuse. Through the years of doing this work as an ally, I've been surprised whenever I meet a woman who has not been sexually assaulted—that's how pervasive, and wretchedly normalized this behavior is.

I also don't know how any man with any sense of humanity could read these #MeToo posts and not begin to wonder what he can do to stop it. We keep shifting the burden to women and girls. We keep talking about how a victim of sexual violence dresses, or why she was in this place or that place at a dangerous time of night. We keep saying violence against women and girls. But what we need to be saying, to really begin to move the needle, is that we have to teach men and boys, worldwide, that we cannot and must not objectify, rape, hit, beat, hurt, and murder women and girls. We need to keep insisting, over and over, that manhood does not equal violence.

Harvey Weinstein may never understand this, because when you have been steeped in that kind of power and privilege for so long, and when the consequences of your own destructive behavior have been for so long unchecked and covered up, it would take a monumental shift in your soul to become a very different kind of man. I do not know if that is possible for him, or for any other men whose souls and minds are similarly lost to the debilitating addictions of power and privilege. But what I do know is that this toxic manhood we men and boys willingly participate in is a mental and spiritual kind of torture that has been damaging the whole world for far too long, and that it must end. And we men and boys have no other choice but to help make it end.

My Mother. Barack Obama. Donald Trump. And the Last Stand of the Angry White Man.

Nobody knows my name, nobody knows what I've done

—Bessie Smith

This is what it sounds like

When doves cry

—Prince

PART 1

My mother is sick, and she has been in much pain for nearly two years now. There is no easy way to say this other than to say it directly. She is distressed, and I am distressed, extremely, by this situation. I cannot say that it was not expected, my mother becoming ill, but, nevertheless, I cry regularly—merely by thinking about it. My mother's illness began in November of 2016, the same month Donald Trump defeated Hillary Clinton to become the forty-fifth president of the United States. My ma, forever a very proud and very self-sufficient woman, has mostly kept things to herself throughout my life. For example, I still do not know the uncut version of how my mother and father met, how he courted

her, under what conditions she became pregnant with me, or why, completely, my father was not there when I was born, or why I only saw him
two to three times the first eight years of my life, before he told her he
was done, that she had lied to him, that I was not his son. Nor do I know,
wholly, the backstory of my mother's childhood in the racist, segregated
America of the 1940s and 1950s and early 1960s of which she was born,
and raised, and socialized to be who she has been ever since. Oh, yes, she
has given me plenty of unsolicited testimonies, several of those tales I
have heard repeatedly, but when your mother is sick and your heart feels
like it is going to fracture the way the earth does, abruptly, during an
earthquake, you, an only child, cannot imagine your existence without
the one person who has been there for you constantly, from the moment
you drew your first breath; and you begin to hear and see and feel your
mother's stories in a radically different way.

My mother has long had diabetes and high blood pressure and acute
arthritis, has long taken prescription drugs for these ailments. And when
my mother dutifully retired, at age sixty-two, after twenty-five years as
a home health care worker to senior citizens, just as she was becoming
a senior citizen herself, I noticed in that very moment her walking with
a dramatic limp, that she was wobbling instead of moving upright, and
wobbling with tremendous discomfort. It was as if her mind had texted
a message to her body that the backbreaking work begun when she was
a little girl, picking cotton in the sun-fried fields of the American South,
was over, at long last, and that her short, plump frame was instantly to
pay the price for it: the years of twisting and bending and stretching
and lifting and carrying; the years of being the help to others, to their
families, while also raising her own child, alone; the years of walking
and bussing it to work, through rain and high winds, through snow and

dangerous ice, through the humbling heat of Summer and the callous cold of Winter; up the stairs she walked and down the stairs she walked, those twenty-five years of caring for the elderly, of washing and bathing those not able to wash and bathe themselves; those twenty-five years of picking up those aging bodies who sagged in her arms like a heavy load, including the ones who died as she was nurturing them in some way; everything had finally taken its ugly toll on my mother. In those first years of her retirement I only half-heartedly and guiltily tried to get my ma to seek real medical attention, not more prescription drugs. Her response to me, each time I tried, is what she has been saying to me endlessly: "Boy, you don't know nothin'. I'm an independent woman. I'ma be alright."

But my ma is not alright, this much is clear to me now. When she finally broke down and told me, on that November day, that she had been having awful dizzy spells, that her hands and ankles were badly swollen, that she could barely use her fingers, that she felt electrified whips of torture, on the regular, shoot across her back, her arms, her legs, I knew that my mother was in a terrible place. It made me think back to maybe a half decade before when my mother called me in a panic and told me she needed to go to the hospital immediately. I was in Brooklyn, New York, where I have lived for over half my life at this point, and my mother was there in my hometown of Jersey City, New Jersey. I frantically phoned an old high school friend, Leonardo, to get to her since I knew it would take me a while to make it across the Brooklyn Bridge and through the Holland Tunnel. He did, and when I reached the hospital there was my mother lying belly up on a metal table, in a hospital gown, with multiple tubes protruding from her body. I was shocked to see how much weight my mother had gained, how much her stomach had ballooned since her retirement. It was almost as if I had been so consumed with my own life, with my work of being a writer and an activist and a public speaker, with, truthfully, my own trials and tribulations, that I did not know my mother, did not know the troubles she had seen. In that hospital room, I sat with my ma as a battery of tests were run, and during one especially somber lull I stood up with my back to her and sobbed uncontrollably, with my hand muffling my mouth, at the dreadful thought of losing her. "No, Ma, not now, please. . . ."

The hospital doctor was blunt. My mother had to lose weight, she had to lessen her sugar intake, she had to stop cooking and eating the over-the-edge cholesterol-loaded stuff. My mother agreed to do what was told to her, to stay the course with her prescription drugs, too, but she straightaway returned to the diet given to her at birth, the only diet she knew, one that filled her up, that gave her great satisfaction and joy: soul food. So, I became the ever-convenient punching bag for her feelings of being dispossessed of her identity: my mother mocked me whenever I broached the idea of changing her diet, ridiculed me for being "a vegan," and maintained that I was the one who was going to get sick because I "only ate lettuce." She did not understand that part of the reason why I had become a vegan was because I had watched her and other family members, and many folks around me, get preventable diseases because of what they ate and drank. I just did not want to knowingly go down that path. I especially thought of this when my mother told me, from that metal table, that she had not been a patient at a hospital since she'd given birth to me in the late 1960s. A stunning revelation that my mother, like so many of our self-sacrificing mothers, had gone her entire life ignoring one symptom after another until it had halted her in her wobbly footsteps. It was then and there that I could see the stark-naked fear in my mother's eyes, but she dared not express it to me aloud. She did not want to talk about anything other than my getting her away from that hospital as fast as possible.

But this second health scare has been different. It was almost as if in the years between that hospital visit and November of 2016 my mother's body just kept going in a downward spiral on the inside, until her hands and arms and back and legs and feet decided to give up and become one huge and debilitating torment. I will be honest and say I did not know what to do at first, how to best support or help my mother. I'd heard stories from friends who had become their parent's or parents' caretaker. I had seen social media posts through the years of a parent falling gravely ill, then slowly dying, and the devastation it brought to the child or children. I had had people in my life, close friends, who had been through a similar rite of passage, where the child suddenly becomes the parent and the parent suddenly becomes the child. But nothing—*nothing*—prepares you for this role, this responsibility, when it is automatically and ruthlessly you who is that person taking care of that parent. You sit and listen to your mother download what she is feeling in the various parts of her body. You hear her even as you are scanning the redness of her tired eyes, the budding wrinkles you never saw before across the smooth chocolate plane of her face, the layers of loose flesh that dangle, like mushy wet clay, about her chin and neck. Your ears digest her words as your eyes make their way across her shoulders, down her back, to her arms and hands, where you see, clearly, that they have swollen as if someone had blown air into each of her fingers and the palms of her hands. You jump-cut to her ankles and feet and, yes, someone had air-pumped those, too. Your mother speaks of the years of soreness, of the many falls while working, that she has hidden from you until now. You seek help, ask advice, because as that only child you have no sister or brother to turn to, this is all on you—

I know my mother's eating habits are atrocious. I know my mother, especially since her retirement, has neither walked much nor exercised in any form, that she spends uncounted time in her favorite living room chair, a recliner, inhaling hours upon hours of television—the news, the talk shows of personalities like Steve Harvey and Ellen, anything, I imagine, that makes her feel good. After consulting with a wide range of people online and offline, one bit of advice stuck with me: just be there for her. How, I did not know at first, because my mother is not very sociable, does not like to go out much, except to church and the grocery store and errands to pay her utility bills. My mother, who I love dearly, can be mean, rude, perpetually enraged, if I am going to be transparent about it all. That alone built the sky-high mental wall that separated us since I was a little boy. And I am so clear that if not for two-plus decades of therapy, nearly a decade of yoga practice, and having my art, writing, as an outlet since I was a teenager, there is really no way I would be able to be in the presence of my mother in any way possible. I know far too many who have absorbed equally abusive behavior from their parent or parents—verbally, physically, emotionally, all of the above—who keep great distance from them and, in some cases, have cut them off and out entirely. I simply cannot do that to my ma, because, well, I love her, because I would not be who I am without her, and because I know what she has survived. It ain't been no crystal stair. So here she is, in her seventies now, in the golden years of her life, just trying to be happy and comfortable. My mother rises early in the mornings and goes to sleep early at night, oftentimes falling asleep while watching television right on that recliner. So, in the first moments of those November 2016 days, I decided to ask my mother, rather than tell her, how I could be of service. Her response: "Take me grocery shopping every week, so I do not have to walk there."

And that is exactly what I began to do. Grocery shopping with my mother. Something I had not done since I was a kid. There in Jersey City, a community I had escaped at age eighteen for college, that had both shaped and wounded me in unthinkable ways, to the point that it has left a permanent and disfigured scar on my mind, a love-hate relationship that I am certain I will take with me to my grave. But I had to help my mother, which meant I had to suck up any negative feelings I had lingering about her, about my hometown, about being there physically, more than I'd been in years. And there I have been, week after week and month after month, with my mother, at her local market, the one she prefers, outside picking out the shopping cart for her to make sure the wheels move exactly right. There inside, always grabbing five or six plastic bags for her fruits and vegetables. In the first weeks of grocery shopping with her I challenged my mother on her food selections, especially after we had visited my holistic doctor in Brooklyn. I should have known better. The moment we left my doctor's office my mother said to me, point-blank, "I do not give a f___ what he said. F___ that mother_____. Ain't nobody gonna tell me what to do!" And these were some of the nicer words spoken by this Christian woman who is so verbally fluid she can pivot from random Bible scriptures to the crudest foul language so spontaneously that even Dave Chappelle or Chris Rock would blush. But I took to heart what my holistic doctor said to my mother: that far too many medical professionals only try to control the sickness, very few ever talk about healing. Thus, I pray to myself daily, as my doctor's words ring in my head whenever I grocery shop with my ma, that she will soften her stance, that she will heed his words in spite of her intense resistance, and come to understand the gravity of what my doctor said to her, of what she must do: change her diet over time, begin to do some kind of exercise, slowly wean herself off prescription drugs, and stop seeing sugar and fast foods as her two best friends. Yet as we go up and down aisle after aisle in this grocery store my mother grabs the worst possible things to eat, and I am deflated, defeated, and find myself arguing with her about her food choices, and her arguing back with me, cursing me, and matter-of-factly saying to me, on several of these trips, "You are trying to take away what makes me happy!"

It was on one of those occasions when my mother said that to me, after a few months of these weekly grocery trips, that I let it go, I stopped questioning her food choices aloud, and just did what she told me to do: to push the cart for her when it became too heavy; to "notice my pocketbook" whenever she quick-stepped away from the store shopping cart to grab one item or another; to quietly move her cart out of the way given her habit of always halting abruptly in the middle of one aisle or another and leaving it there to block others; to learn exactly when to offer assistance in the store, when to reach for an item she needed, when and how to unpack and put away her groceries once home, and where, precisely, to put her personal shopping cart every week in her bedroom, by her mirrored dresser. It has been because of these trips, over time, and as I have withstood with my mother all kinds of weather, all kinds of obstacles to my work schedule to be there for her, and all kinds of insults and toxic words and put-downs from my ma, that I finally began to see the whole woman that she is, and how she came to be, in ways I had never fully grasped before. . . .

How she was born and raised in the Low Country of South Carolina; Ridgeland, South Carolina, Jasper County, in a two-room wooden shack; how she shared that cramped shack with her mother and father—the only grandparents I have ever known—and three sisters and a brother. How they were so poor that they would sometimes only have syrup to pass around in bowls as their meals. How they were so poor that modern conveniences like a bathroom with a working toilet or electricity, even, was not an option. There was a lightless and dingy outhouse in the yard that they had to enter to go to the bathroom. There were kerosene lamps to see in the pitch-black night. Yes, they were so poor that the girls sometimes had to take turns going to school because there was only one decent dress to wear, and thank goodness, the four of them were relatively close in age. They were so poor that my mother began picking cotton, at age eight, in the fields owned by local White folks—my mother out there as a little girl with people old enough to be her parents or grandparents, each of them equally trying to make a way out of no way. There were also stories of what America was like during those days. My mother would say to me often, when I was a boy, that I had no idea what they experienced in the American South, that we were poor, yes, but that I could not imagine how poor they were. What I gathered, as a child, as a man listening to my mother today, is that poverty is economic violence against human beings and it is a nonstop assault on your mind, on your soul, on your body, and it damages you, permanently, even if you are able to escape it, and that it was passed by my mother's parents to her to me as if we were earnestly passing a collection plate in one of our churches.

And then there was the very serious divide between Black people and White people, that it seemed that White folks hated Black folks mainly for being Black, but it would not be until many years later, when I was in college and began to study American and African American history, in a very serious and critical way, that I finally comprehended, fully, the breadth of what my mother and her family and families like theirs endured in that old country, in that old America. I mean, imagine your life, if you are my mother, a very beautiful and intelligent little Black girl, with very dark skin, being told practically from the time you could understand words and images, that you were ugly, that you were not equal to Whites, that your life was doomed to be the servant, in some form, for White America, but never completely a life for yourself. I have wondered, as I have made my way up and down the aisles of that grocery store with my mother, what she might have wanted to be when she grew up, or if she even had any dreams at all. On a few of those grocery trips I tried to ask my ma but got rebuffed each time. Because, I have learned, Black people in America, with a few exceptions, often do not want to talk in detail about the past, not the dangerous parts of it anyhow, not the parts they miraculously survived. We just keep going, as my mother keeps going, wobbling from aisle to aisle in that grocery store, pushing her cart with a deep sense of focus and determination, as she pushed her life, as she has pushed me my entire life. Yet I have also wondered about her explosive anger, her fire-hot temper, the one that was passed to me, like how the super-rich pass family inheritances, where she might have gotten it from, what made her so terribly full of rage as a little girl. So uncontrollably angry, my Aunt Birdie once told me, that the tip of my mother's nose would become pockmarked with beads of sweat. I think of my mother's father, Pearly Powell, my grandfather, a very short and thickly built jetblack man, who, I heard from the time I was a kid, had an equally volcanic temper, how my mother and her three sisters and brother and his wife, my grandmother, lived in day-to-day terror of his outbursts. He who wore blue overalls as Southern Black folks did in those days. He who hated White people, because of how much they hated him, because of how they treated Black men like him; and, also quite frankly, because of how some of the White men had savagely murdered his father, and then stole the majority of my great-grandfather's land from my great-grandmother. Yes, my grandfather was a mean man who knew how to fish and hunt and raise vegetables and fruits, who knew how to toil in the earth, and to steer, effortlessly, the mule-led wagon that got him around, because there was no money for a car. Yes, my grandfather was a mean old man who was taught, by the White world, by America, by his family, that violence was the solution for all problems, and, without hesitation or shame, did to my mother and her siblings and his wife what my mother did to me as a child: beat them ferociously. Beat them the way Black slaves were beaten ferociously by White masters and White overseers on those plantations. Beat them ferociously the way Indians were beaten by those who lusted for this American land at all costs. Beat them ferociously the way women have been beaten by men since the beginning of time. Beat them ferociously the way people of all backgrounds have beaten each other bloody in that thing we call war. Beat them down, ferociously, the way the severe poverty beat down my grandfather and grandmother and my mother and her sisters and brother, to the point where they were painfully frightened of people, of the world, I have been told by other relatives.

And beat them down the way my grandfather and grandmother were beaten down by Whites of all ages, who called them "Uncle" and "Aunt" instead of Mr. and Mrs. Powell, because there was basically no respect for Black people, not even if you were a White youth or child. "Uncle" like "Uncle Ben" and "Aunt" like "Aunt Jemima," names given to Black people in America to sideline us, to marginalize us, to make us feel like, yes, we are still slaves, forever the mammies and nannies and sharecroppers to that part of White America that refuses to call us by our rightful names, refuses to see us as whole and complex human beings. The way, my mother told me, the White kids would call the Black kids where she grew up "nigger" and "coon" and "spear chucker" and "darkie" and "spade" and "jungle bunny" and "jigaboo" and every other name one can think of, names that made their way into American popular entertainment that lasted over a century, from the 1800s to the 1900s, via minstrel shows and minstrel songs, entertainment that, yeah, amused and drew much laughter from Whites in America while simultaneously making Black girls like my mother feel like they were worthless, unattractive, nothing, with no possibility whatsoever of any sort of a future, unless they worked for it until their bodies fell apart, quite literally. And even that would never be enough.

And, yes, I think of what my ancestors must have felt when, while there in Africa, European invaders came with guns and the Bible, co-opting and manipulating local Africans to assist them in kidnapping and enslaving people Black like me, to bring them, forcibly, to haunted ships that would cross the Atlantic Ocean; how they made their way—those that did not die or commit suicide—to places like New York City, like Charleston, South Carolina, like various parts of Latin America and the Caribbean, to become, as captured human beings, the first global economy in this new world. A world they did not create, a world that transformed them into something—some *thing*—new, different, foreign, completely, from who they had been. African people turned into human property. The mental and physical and spiritual terrorism of that experience, for a couple of centuries, stripped of their names, their spiritual belief systems, their goddesses and gods, their music, their culture, their identities, their very beings. Made to do what the slave masters and those plantation overseers told them they had to do. Told, perpetually, that they were inferior, stupid, not worthy of being treated as human beings. Made to work the fields, to work in the big house, to be baby makers and baby breeders, to be the master's mistress by the only word that fits: rape. To be property sold at will, on a whim, whenever the mood struck. Families here today but torn asunder tomorrow: a family member liable to be sold at any given moment. Marriages not honored and respected consistently. Children ripped away from parents. Mental and physical violence as an everyday reality, torture and brutality as an everyday reality, who cared if their hands were up, defenseless, who cared if they said they could not breathe? The utter insanity of it all, enough to make a people wonder what they had done, indeed, to be so black and blue. Yet in the midst of that they still created music—field hollers, spirituals, what would become the blues, jazz, rock and roll, soul, reggae, calypso, merengue, salsa, and, yes, hip-hop. You can slice or chop out their tongues, you can emasculate them, you can tar and feather and burn them and then hang them from trees, you can kill them and steal their land as you did to my great-grandfather Benjamin Powell, but you cannot stop them from singing, you cannot stop them from pushing, you cannot stop them from dreaming.

That is why I am so very clear that the dreamers of my immediate family were my mother and her two sisters, Catherine and Birdie, who dared to see another world outside of the backwoods Southern

village they had been born into. These three sisters, led by my Aunt
Birdie and my mother, plotted their escape, first to Miami, to work in
the homes of wealthy White folks, to save enough money to then move
North, to Jersey City, where a cousin they were close to had settled.
After less than a year in Miami my mother and Aunt Birdie scooped
up the youngest girl, Catherine, back home in South Carolina, and
brought her "up the road" with them. When they landed in Jersey
City, they first shared a bed, the three of them, in a one-room rental,
but no matter, as they were determined not to return to the old country
they had fled. There was no therapy, there was no yoga, there were no
healing spaces or sister circles or meditation groups or #MeToo and
#TimesUp for my mother and her two sisters. There has been no path
to ever resolve the decades-long arguments between my mother and
Aunt Birdie. There has been no exit for my Aunt Cathy to bolt from the
decades-long bullying of my mother, her closest relative. They simply
have had each other, they simply have had whatever they had brought
with them from the South to the North, and they simply have had to
figure out, for themselves, how to win, how not to die or commit slow
suicide in this foreign place, in this new land.

We talk much about America being built by immigrants, but that
is only partially true. No, America was a sacred ground that Indians
occupied first, and that the ancestors of people like my mother built, for
free. It is also a place where people like my mother have been assaulted
and molested and abused and injured, by systems of oppression, systems of discrimination, systems of hate, their entire lives. Women like
my mother do not know a world where the triple evils of racism and
sexism and classism have not done a war dance on their psyches, a half-
step forward, dozens of steps backwards, just to make it to tomorrow.

For those reasons, I can only imagine the ecstasy my mother must have felt when, as a young woman, she met my father, she in her early twenties, he a man in his early thirties. I do believe that my mother fell in love with my father, fell in love with the idea of being swept off her feet, as has been depicted forever in American movies. And I do believe that my father, equally as damaged and broken as my mother, did what he had been socialized to do, as a man: he stole her virginity, he stole her heart, he got her pregnant, with me, he left my mother to travel to that hospital, alone, to give birth to me, and he abandoned my mother to raise me by herself, on welfare, food stamps, government cheese, and the sort of poverty and desperation and hopelessness I would not wish on anyone. As I have journeyed with my mother through her illness, through the aisles of that grocery store, in those quiet moments in her apartment when we just sit and stare at the television, I have wondered often if my mother ever allowed a man to touch her again. I have wondered often why my mother spoke for years, when I was a child, of getting married, to my father, to anyone, then at some point just stopped saying it, giving up completely on the possibilities of love for herself. I have wondered often if anyone ever hugged or kissed my mother, if anyone ever told her that they loved her, that she was loved, that she is love. I thought of this one day in my mother's living room when she slipped off the plastic-covered recliner and landed on the floor, unable to get up. Frightened, I leapt to the floor to help her, but my mother's weight is more than mine, so I struggled tremendously at first. As I held my mother in my arms I looked into her eyes and I saw the little Black girl who was never told that she was beautiful, who was never told that she could be somebody, at any point in her life. I saw the little Black girl who, like the Black woman she would become, had to put on the protective armor of anger, of defiance, of single-minded determination, merely to exist and survive in an American ghetto. I saw the Black woman who would come to challenge crooked landlords and stingy employers and no-good men and supremely judgmental school officials who would try, on several occasions, to either kick her bad-tempered boy child from school or put him in special education. I tugged and lifted my mother up, as she had done with her patients as a home health care worker for many years, both smiling and crying as I did so, because I was embarrassed to be so close to her, the closest, physically, we had been since I was a little boy in her arms, holding tightly to her for love and protection. Back in her recliner, my mother sighed heavily, and I sat on the sofa, dabbing the dripping sweat from my forehead. Ours has been an incredibly rough relationship. I have carried resentments against my mother since I was a child. As a boy, I blamed her for our poverty, for my father's abandonment, for everything. I hated her, then, every single time she called me "dummy" or "stupid" or a "mental case," a term she had picked up somewhere, God only knows where. I was absolutely terrified of my mother, the violence and abuse she heaped upon me as a child, the times she asked me "Are you gonna be good?" as she beat me with a belt or a thin, stinging tree branch, or her bare hands, leaving welts every single occasion on my arms and legs; the times she confused me so, in one breath saying, "Do not be like your father!" yet in another "You are just like that no-good father of yours!" I have hungered with outstretched hands, sobbing like a baby, as a boy, as a teenager, as a man, through the fogs and clouds and storms of my life, to be told by my mother, that she loved me, for her to hug and kiss me, but those things simply never happened. So, as I held my mother in my arms for what felt like my entire lifetime I prayed with my eyes wide open and I said to myself, I forgive you, Ma. I forgive you for the mean words. I forgive you for the violence, for the beatings. I forgive you for hiding major parts of your life story from me, I forgive you for it all. I really have no other choice. I do not want to be that child, like some of my friends, who, even though their parent is dead and gone, they still resent or hate that parent, as if they are mentally chained to that trauma and that hurt no matter what. I do not want to be that person, I do not want to be trapped, I want to be free, and I know in forgiving my mother, as I have come to be her caretaker, I am also forgiving myself, too, at last.

Then I looked around my mother's apartment as I always did, and saw what had always been there with fresh eyes: the certificate from her former labor union about her years of service; the photo of a Black preacher I did not know holding a Bible with his head cocked just so; the ghostly image of the White Jesus at the Last Supper; the clock to tell my mother time as she has always wanted to be on time, even in retirement; and above the sofa, above my head, a framed picture of Barack Obama, his wife, Michelle, and their two daughters, Sasha and Malia. When I was a youth, I remember going to the homes of many Black people, relatives and non-relatives both, and how virtually every single apartment or house had the photos of Martin Luther King Jr. and John Kennedy and Bobby Kennedy together. Back then I was perplexed as to why, but I gathered they meant something to Black folks in America, these three men who all were killed when they were young. Years later I would come to understand that in a nation where people who are not White and privileged are treated as outsiders, as undesirables, as interlopers, we look for sheroes and heroes we can connect to, who speak to us, who speak for us, who can be and are what we will never be in our own lifetimes. We need and look for what they call in the Black Pentecostal church "supernatural miracles." Except for one Black preacher or another my mother had never had images of Black people on her walls before, not even Dr. King. But in Barack and Michelle, I am sure, my mother saw the supernatural miracle of their marriage and a love she will never have for herself, and she saw a Black man as president through the eyes of that little Black girl in South Carolina who could have never imagined such a reality, not in her lifetime, not in a million lifetimes.

PART 2

The first time I ever heard the name Barack Obama was in the late Winter of 2004 when my friend asha bandele, then a writer and editor for *Essence* magazine, told me she was writing a short article about a relatively young Black man from Chicago, already an Illinois state senator, who was running for the United States Senate. I did not think anything particularly odd about his name as I had been "a Black Movement child" for two decades at that point, so it was not unusual to me for Black folks to have African- or Islamic-sounding names. Some of us, like Obama, were born with those names, while some had taken such names as an act of rebellion against what we label our "slave names," given to our ancestors by White slave masters, and as a way to reclaim some shred of our history and culture long ago lost to us. Anyhow, I registered his name in my mind, then it slipped away, until asha hit me up again, after the piece appeared in her publication, asking if I would be interested in attending a New York City fund-raiser for Barack, as there was a strong possibility that he could actually win that US Senate seat in Illinois. I was not able to go, but I was a bit intrigued as a political animal myself: I had studied political science in college; I was mesmerized, as a college student, by the two presidential campaigns of the Reverend Jesse Jackson in the 1980s; as a young activist I did extensive voter education and voter registration work, in the North, in the South; and because 2004 was also a national election year, I was especially interested in seeing President George W. Bush lose, given how horrific I felt his first term had been.

In that Summer of 2004 I was assigned to cover the Democratic National Convention in Boston by Black Entertainment Television, in partnership with CBS, so I found myself roaming through that city's Fleet Center wondering if John Kerry, the party's nominee for president, could actually defeat Bush and the Republican Party's uncanny ability to make him seem like a woefully unqualified and unpatriotic candidate. This was not my first rodeo. I had reported on the 2000 Republican National Convention in Philadelphia, so I knew these would be long days and long nights of policy and platform discussions, meet-ups with media and political pals, and as many parties as I could cram into a sleepless schedule. I cannot recall if there was a buzz about Barack Obama giving the keynote speech for the convention. What I do recall is that I was sitting up close on the night of Tuesday, July 27th, and was surprised to see a striking and tall Black woman introduced as Michelle Obama step to the podium to speak. It doubly blew my mind when she referred to the man she was up there to present, her husband Barack Obama, as "my baby's daddy." There was something remarkably refreshing about the fact that this woman would dare use Black talk, hip-hop speak, at an American political convention. There was something refreshing about the fact that she, like my mother, was a dark-complexioned Black woman in a space where you rarely saw women who looked like her. Then Barack came out, and as is the case normally with political conventions, there were already OBAMA signs up that had been given out for folks to wave as he spoke.

I was struck by how baby-faced he was, how polished Barack was as a speaker—what folks call charisma—and by the fact that he was very clear about his message: there is only one America, that the divides were senseless. I also took note of the fact his words were not remarkably new, that he had gotten "hope" from Jesse Jackson's two presidential campaigns in the 1980s ("keep hope alive!"), that he was essentially retooling the quintessential American Dream to fit his own journey of being the son of an interracial relationship between an African immigrant man and a Kansas-born White woman. Yes, I had heard some variation of this rags-to-riches tale since I was a little boy in grammar school. But because George W. Bush and his administration had wreaked havoc on the American people in that first term, folks were mad thirsty for something, for someone, for anything, that would offer them an alternative to what we felt, to be blunt, was evil and sheer stupidity in the White House. Barack Obama embodied that. He was dynamic, handsome, had pushed his way up from a working-class life to become a Harvard-trained lawyer, he had been a community organizer, and the very fact that he was half-White and half-Black meant that right in his blood was the ability to speak to a range of people, to be a unifier, as manifested in this, his first national speech. I also believe, because of the nature of racism in America, and because of our shared obsession with skin color, with colorism, that it did not hurt that Barack Obama was a light-skinned Black man, either. I seriously doubt had he been the complexion of his wife, or my mother, he would have been embraced in the same way, not as a mainstream politician with whispers of a future presidency practically from the moment he left the stage that night.

Later that evening I found myself at an after-party that celebrated Obama's speech. It was packed with people, particularly Black people, ooh-ing and ah-ing and fawning over him. Similarly, I had seen this before, too. I saw it with Jesse Jackson. I saw it with Sister Souljah when she and I were in college together and Souljah was one of the major youth activists of her day. I saw it with President Bill Clinton and General Colin Powell. I saw it with Tupac Shakur and Snoop Dogg and other hugely popular rap stars I have written about. And I had felt elements of it in my own life, after appearing on the first season of MTV's *The Real World*, and after becoming a writer for Quincy Jones's *Vibe* magazine. In our society we have been taught, virtually from the time we are born, to seek out sheroes and heroes, to become obsessed with celebrity, with the rich, or some combination of all, to find value in the lives and stories of others on television, on the radio, in movies, oftentimes while not seeing any value in ourselves. People who are Hollywood celebs, or prominent athletes, or talk show hosts, or religious leaders, or reality TV stars, or political figures, or even dead famous people from history are bumped up in our imaginations to represent that which we often feel we cannot be ourselves. For example, I have thought continually about how the Reverend Doctor Martin Luther King Jr. has been put on such a pedestal, since he was killed in 1968. He has gone from being a very human human being in his lifetime—someone who not only was a great leader and organizer and strategist, but also a man who had cheated on his wife, regularly smoked cigarettes, and had self-esteem issues because of the darkness of his skin and the shortness of his height—to being hailed as a saint, a mythical figure, a man who has become humanly untouchable, the way we were taught, as children and beyond, that George Washington or Thomas Jefferson or Abraham Lincoln were similarly saint-like and untouchable giants of history. It creates a condition in this nation, amongst its people, passed from era to era, generation to generation, century to century, of far too many of us looking outside ourselves for something, for someone, to empower us, to give us freedom and justice and equality. When we know, if we really examine, say, the Civil Rights Movement, that it is a fallacy to even faintly suggest that Dr. King did the bulk of that work by himself, or that he was the singular leader of it, something he would reject himself, which we'd know if we ever took the time to actually study his life work and his sermons and his writings. There were countless women and men, countless girls and boys, countless leaders with names like Ella Baker and Fannie Lou Hamer and Malcolm X and Coretta Scott King who were there, too. There were countless organizations with names like King's Southern Christian Leadership Conference, like the Nation of Islam, like the Congress of Racial Equality, like the National Urban League, like the National Association for the Advancement of Colored People, like the Student Nonviolent Coordinating Committee, and like the Black Panther Party. But someone somewhere decided that American history would not be taught holistically, if at all, not in our textbooks and certainly not in the media or mainstream pop culture, so what we wound up getting is the thumbnail sketch largely focused on Rosa Parks refusing to give up her seat to spark the Montgomery Bus Boycott, and Dr. King having a dream.

So that was my fear, immediately, with Barack Obama. I did not doubt his sincerity, or his intelligence, or his intentions. What I was concerned about were the forces around him, who were primed to market him, as if he were a hot new brand from the music industry or the movies or an ad agency, into our next great national leader. And as we moved beyond that July 2004 speech, to Barack getting elected to the United States Senate and George W. getting re-elected to the presidency, to the human tragedy of Hurricane Katrina, to the various wars in various places, to the nasty rifts that continued amongst Americans, to a persistent and loud rumor that Barack would indeed run for president, you could almost feel the desperation in the air for that to happen, for him to save us. And when the day did occur in February of 2007, in the same Springfield, Illinois, where Abe Lincoln had begun his political career, I knew, in my gut, that we were about to experience something like a phenomenon we had not experienced in decades, in the United States. And sure enough, we did.

There were, magically, Obama tee-shirts and hats and posters everywhere. There were fund-raising groups and fund-raising parties for Obama wherever I traveled to do my own speeches and activism work throughout the country. There were people of all backgrounds, younger, older, but especially younger, suddenly obsessed with the person of Barack Obama. Somewhere in the midst of all of this, touchstone phrases of his 2008 presidential campaign would emerge: "Hope" and "Change" and "Yes we can." People were comparing Barack to Abraham Lincoln, to Dr. King, to both John and Bobby Kennedy, to Gandhi, even to Jesus. I found it curious that Malcolm X's name was rarely evoked, even though Barack had said very publicly in his memoir that it was the reading of *The Autobiography of Malcolm X*, as was the case for me and innumerable Black males, that had changed his life. No matter, people loved that Barack was cool, that he had a cool wife, that

he was still young enough to play basketball, to use cool words from
the culture of hip-hop. "Martin walked so Barack could run" became
one of the many things I saw on tee-shirts and posters and heard people
say. The power of this was so mesmerizing that an army of Generation
X and Millennials began to openly think about running for political
office ourselves, including me, and indeed I wound up doing so both in
2008 and 2010, for the United States Congress in Brooklyn, New York,
my adopted hometown. Multitudes registered to vote for the first time
in their lives, because they finally believed they had someone to vote
for in Barack Obama. And I would say just as many ignored the fact
that voting in presidential elections mean nothing if you do not also
consistently vote in your local elections, too. And I would say just as
many ignored the fact that voting by itself is not power, nor empowerment, if you, if we, are also not active and organizing and building
and creating in our local communities on a regular basis, too. Those
things notwithstanding, I had not felt such a pull like this to politics
since the Summer of 1984, when I was a pre-first-year college student
at Rutgers University in New Jersey and sat with other eighteen-year-
olds and listened to the tantalizing Democratic National Convention
speeches of Jesse Jackson and Mario Cuomo. I do not know if I truly
believed that Jesse could be the first Black president of the United
States. But I had never before seen a man, a Black man, able to verbal-
ize for me what I had felt and carried around my entire life, even within
my subconscious. And it seemed, two decades later, Barack Obama
was doing the very same thing for Americans of every stripe in 2008.
The "rainbow coalition" that Jesse had often spoken about, which
had been borrowed from the community organizing of Illinois Black
Panther leader Fred Hampton—yes, Hampton had coined the term

as he worked to unite multiethnic street gangs in Chicago who were fighting each other. Obama's base of support, White, Black, Latinx, Asian, Native American, Arab, Jewish, Muslim, Christian, straight, queer, able-bodied, disabled, young, old, poor, and the super-wealthy, essentially became the rainbow coalition that Hampton and Jackson had envisioned, and it also resembled the beloved community that Dr. King spoke of, marching Barack Obama straight to the 2008 Democratic Party nomination over a highly surprised Hillary Clinton and the Clinton machine. What I also remember is how a lot of Black leaders, specifically Black elected officials and Black Christian ministers, were over-the-moon suspicious of Obama, did not want to support him, had been supporting Mrs. Clinton, even as their followers were flocking or defecting to Barack in record numbers. Some parts of Black America can be terribly conservative in that way. I believe part of this has to do with how much we have been through in American history, how it makes many of us fearful or distrustful of change, of anything new or different, of anything that we cannot control ourselves. Obama did not come up the traditional ranks of Black leadership: he was not a spin-off from the Civil Rights Movement, he did not hail from activist or political parents, he was not made in the Black church, he did not come from any Black nationalist traditions. In a sense, he was a product of post-integration America, the safest aspects of it: he was refined, polite, Ivy League–educated, and relatable to multicultural America, the liberal and progressive and centrist parts of it, and even some staunch Republicans, like Pat Buchanan, gushed over Barack Obama. He was neither Malcolm X nor Dr. King, in point of fact, but more like Booker T. Washington. Obama, like Booker T., spoke in a way that made White America feel comfortable while also challenging Black America

to take responsibility for ourselves, as if we did not, while simultaneously being a symbol of great success for Black America. And like
Booker T., Barack would never talk too much about race or racism.
That mixture of messiah figure and social conservativism, masked because of his brown skin, was all but ignored by Black folks. I heard
few critical conversations about his platform or vision for America,
but quite a few Blacks said, "I'm voting for him because he is Black."
Barack's race was the criteria, the platform, the vision. Meanwhile, I
noted a lot of White Americans who flocked to him constantly used
words like "articulate" as if Black people could not, before Barack,
construct more than a couple of sentences at a time. Not all White
folks, but I heard that enough to make me cringe at the racism of the
commentary each time. And it was said over and over that Barack was
proof that anyone could be president of the United States. Absolutely
not true. You had to be a certain kind of Black person, as Barack was.
What was not lost on me either was that his bloodlines did not even
have any ties to American slavery, given his Black father was an African immigrant and his mother was White. In a way, Barack was a
very atypical African American, he was portrayed as exotic, even, the
outsider Black man in the United States running for president.

And his was a presidential run for the ages. As I campaigned for
Congress in my beloved Brooklyn in the Summer of 2008, a strenuous
uphill battle against an old-school Black incumbent who had been in
the seat for thirty years, I kept thinking to myself that I had to get to
Denver, to the Democratic National Convention, to watch, live and direct, that historic moment when Obama would accept the nomination
of his party. I had been, a few months before, at a fund-raiser and pep
rally for Barack at the Brooklyn Downtown Marriott, in the ballroom.

It was packed, with much of Brooklyn's political leadership present. When Obama showed up it reminded me of the time when I was in San Antonio in 1996 for the National Basketball Association's annual All-Star game. I was there to write a piece on the second Olympic basketball team, Dream Team Two. It was a mundane practice until it was over and, unexpectedly, what felt like hundreds of media converged on Michael Jordan, some with their own ladders, so that they could hold their cameras or audio recorders high above the scrum. I remember thinking to myself, "Wow, they are acting like MJ is God." Well, the same thing crossed my mind when Obama entered that Brooklyn ballroom. Grown adults were as giddy as children, people nearly trampled each other to get as close to him as possible. Cameras flashed here there everywhere. I cannot even recall if he made a speech or not. I just remember his face in the sea of faces and hands and arms reaching for him as if they were reaching for freedom, or power, or Jesus.

It was the same exact energy, on an overdose of steroids, when I persuaded my campaign team to allow me to go to the 2008 Democratic National Convention in Denver, for all of twenty-four hours. It was a haze, interrupting my campaign to get there: the airport was jam-packed, the streets were jam-packed, there was an electrical surge in the high altitude of Colorado, powered by the masses of people who had descended on Denver. I imagine that this must have been what it felt like when the March on Washington happened in 1963, where Dr. King gave his famous "I Have a Dream" speech. I imagine this is what it must have felt like when the Beatles, one year later, arrived in America, to mass hysteria. And I imagine that this must be what it feels like, anywhere on this Earth, when the Olympics, and the whole world, descend upon a particular city. It was a circus-like atmosphere I had never witnessed before in my own life, not even with Jesse Jackson's presidential bids, and those were exciting.

I do not recall how I did it, but I managed to get one ticket for myself to sit very close to the main stage where Barack Obama would accept his party's nomination. Even though I was there, I still had mixed feelings about the whole thing, about him, because it bothered me that he was elevated so much, that it practically, with the snap of some fingers, made other leaders, including other Black leaders, seem like they no longer mattered. Everything and everyone was matter-of-factly being compared to Barack Obama. It was unavoidable, me included. I pondered this as a lengthy video presentation about his life, and his now famously familiar roots and life story, was screened. And then Barack got up to speak, with that decidedly Black male swagger of his. I do not remember his words, but I do remember it lacked the power of, say, his rare but classic speech on race in America earlier that year in Philadelphia. It did not matter to the thousands there and the millions watching on planet Earth. There was this feeling that the election of Barack Hussein Obama would somehow rejuvenate America, and the world, that it would show, in a flash, how far this nation had come since the days of lynching and attack dogs and water hoses and dehumanizing racial segregation. I knew it was every inch a mirage, a lie, in my bones, because I knew America too well. I felt that Barack Obama, no matter how noble his campaign, was being propped up to mask the searing racism and economic injustices of our country, as if one single person, made to be a kind of superhuman superman, a savior, could, like an animated Disney character, hypnotically evaporate what far too many Americans had long experienced, physically, emotionally, spiritually, economically. Moreover, many of us Black folks bought into it because, well, when you have been down for so long, been hated and hated on for so long, been discriminated against for so long, you look for symbols and victories wherever you can find them. In Barack Obama, and in his wife Michelle Obama, too, we had, for once, a political family, political leadership, that not only was mad real, like us, Black, like us, but in our minds represented the best of who we were, and what we could be. The best like Joe Louis, or Marian Anderson, or Michael Jackson, or Serena Williams, or Viola Davis, or the *Black Panther* movie global juggernaut—their victories our victories, their awards our awards, their overcoming our overcoming. This is and has not been a small task in a society that has often put us down, belittled us, referred to us as lazy, seekers of handouts, hustlers of government assistance, and on and on. You want to see our excellence, then here are Michelle and Barack and their two daughters. Watch how they finesse through the hate and fear and ignorance and emotional and verbal violence of those who still view Black folks in America as, well, niggers. Watch how they handle the rabid human attack dogs, the casual and the not-so-casual racism. Watch how they bring people together, how he goes from state to state, city to city, small town to small town, winning over people who have barely spent time with Black people or other people of color at any point in their lives. Yes, into the Fall of 2008 it was astonishing to see people who I could not imagine would have supported a national Black leader in the past rallying around the sensation of Barack Obama. Even with my doubts I, too, like many, hosted an election night watch party—Tuesday, November 4, 2008—at a nightclub in New York City's Greenwich Village called Element; and the rainbow coalition of people there cheered as each state's electoral college votes came in, and those who were complete strangers reached across race and gender and sexual orientation and class and religion and no religion and ability and disability to hug each other as it was announced that Barack had won! People openly wept, some convulsed in total shock and had to sit down, on a chair, on the dance floor, particularly when now President-elect Barack Obama came out on the stage in that frosty Chicago air and declared, "Change has come to America. . . ."

I remember our watch party turntablist, England-born DJ Misbehaviour, playing Sam Cooke's "A Change Is Gonna Come," my favorite song ever, at some point after Barack won, and I remember that I stood there staring into space. I did not cry, I did not rejoice, I just soaked in the moment of what this momentous victory meant to so many, like my mother. He had accomplished something extraordinary, something otherworldly, something Bobby Kennedy had outrageously predicted in the 1960s, something Richard Pryor comically spoofed in the 1970s, something we never fully believed Jesse Jackson could really ever do in the 1980s: Barack Obama had become president of these United States. I cannot stress enough the massive psychological effect Obama's presidential victory had on this country. For Whites, it was an opportunity to say they had participated in the impossible, getting this Black, this biracial, this multicultural man, into the White House, that it proved there were White Americans who did view the others, at least others like Barack, as equal. For Black people and other people of color, like my mother, it validated their lifetimes of hardship and abuse and neglect by this country, even as we have been as patriotic or more patriotic than our White sisters and brothers. It meant that elusive American Dream had come one giant leap forward. It meant, for the first time, that when children of color went to school, they would no longer see images solely of White male presidents of the United States, but now someone who could be them, and they, him. This is why there was euphoria in America, this is why there was euphoria globally. Yes, again, people who have been down and out need small victories and large victories, regardless of how fleeting and symbolic those victories may be.

But not maybe a week later, the jarring perception of this Black man as Superman was thrown in my face like a pot of scorching water. A group of us university-educated Black males were invited to speak at Morehouse College in Atlanta, the historically Black school for men. We talked about Obama's achievement, about the state of Black males in America, about our own personal journeys. It was sponsored in part by Teach for America, and it was startling when its founder, Wendy Kopp, a well-meaning liberal White woman, came up to me after the discussion and said, with much enthusiasm and no malice whatsoever, that she did not know there were Black men out there as well-spoken and intelligent as Barack Obama, in reference to those of us who had just participated in the panel discussion. This was particularly hurtful given that Ms. Kopp was the head of an organization that sends teachers into poor communities around the nation to work with, among others, Black boys. It made me wonder, one, was she that devoid of Black folks in her life, except for those kids in those Teach for America schools? And, second, was White America once again treating a Black person, in this case Barack Obama, as "the special Negro," as if he were some primitive creature, an exception, not the norm, that no others like him could possibly exist? I knew the answer to that question already, because I myself have experienced it, and quite a few of us have, who are Black, who have been able to navigate our way beyond the Black community, into spaces where White Americans, liberals or conservatives, it does not truly matter, are often ill-prepared, historically, emotionally, spiritually, to relate to Black people as full human beings, and thus fall, unwittingly, into inconvenient untruths we call stereotypes. I knew this was a setup for Barack, that within a year of his administration, if that amount of time, people would start to dis and doubt him. This election, and the massive inauguration that came in January 2009, were as good as it would ever be for him, just like Dr. King was never as popular again as he was on the day of the March on Washington. I skipped the inauguration for a couple of reasons. One, I was torn between being there in DC and at a college in Ohio doing a paid speaking engagement for money I needed. Two, the Obama-mania had reached such a fever pitch that I was, yes, originally planning on going, and even was a part of one of the many social events there, until one of my so-called friends cut me from the host committee. I also lost another friend, who I hooked up with a live painting gig at a different big inaugural affair, when he yelled at me, via cell phone, because he was not paid on the spot by the organizers. People were losing their minds, I thought, fighting each other and fighting to be a part of this gargantuan status symbol known as Barack Obama. It became a status symbol to show your photo with Barack on your facebook page. It became a status symbol to say you worked on his campaign, or in his administration, or knew someone who did. And it became a status symbol, during the course of the eight years that he and Michelle occupied the White House, to say that you had been there. I never went, although I did timidly inquire a few times and, I suppose, I could have, if I really wanted to.

But I just lived during those eight years of the Obama administration. I would run for Congress, regrettably, twice as I said, and
lose on both occasions, draining me, draining my finances, and suck-
ing my soul dry (politics truly is a blood sport). I would return to
the most dysfunctional relationship of my life shortly after my second campaign, and by July of 2011, would have my heart broken in a
way I could have not fathomed: she left me when it was clear I had no
idea where my life was heading next, and because I had no money. I
would watch the unconditional love for Barack Obama slowly begin
to disappear, beginning with the battle over health care for all Americans—"Obamacare"—and observe the indisputable sound and fury
of White people, including angry White men in the United States Congress, declare war on the president. I would notice that Obama, over
time, would get more death threats than any president in US history;
that he had been billed as a unifier when he was running for office, yet
was just as swiftly turned into a polarizing figure, hated by certain kinds
of Whites, revered by most Black folks even as a growing chorus wondered, aloud, what he was doing for us. During his years in the White
House I would suffer through a nightmarish bicycle crash, dislocating
my right shoulder, and I would experience the worst kinds of betrayals
from friends, fraternity brothers, also some family members, including
my mother when she refused to help me any further on a bad condo
mortgage situation we had gotten into together. I declared bankruptcy
during the Obama years, and spent many days alone, love-less, my
self-esteem somewhere between being OK and being very much in the
gutter. I would sit and watch the news during his eight years, counting
the number of Black people who were being gunned down or other-

wise killed by the police. I paid identical attention to the Americans who would get their hands on a gun, or multiple guns, and blast bullets at schools, churches, shopping malls, workplaces—here there everywhere. I would grimace every single time President Obama talked of killing terrorists, of the many bombs—"drones"—that were dropped on people, including innocent women and children, after he had been given the Nobel Peace Prize, clearly very prematurely, during the first months of his presidency. I think President Obama started with the best of intentions, did some good things given the mess he was handed from George W., as it pertained to relief for college students and relief for stressed homeowners; there was also his diverse judge appointments and the most inclusive presidential cabinet in history; there was his protection of public lands in the spirit of Teddy Roosevelt; and there was his pinpointing historical landmarks that mattered to people of color, to LGBTQ people, like the Harriet Tubman Underground Railroad monument in Maryland and the Stonewall Inn in New York. But this is the same president who also deported record numbers of immigrants during his years in the White House (before Trump emerged with his fiery "build a wall" rhetoric); who did a very unexceptional job with public school education reform; who failed terribly around the Dakota Pipeline access; who gathered millions of email addresses during his 2008 campaign, with the lofty promise of being an activist presidency, but who never turned all those emails and people into a sustained movement for change and reform; who passed along various financial breaks to corporate America; and who never created a vibrant financial vision for lower- or middle-class America in his eight years.

The above said, I would likewise grimace at the two extreme reactions to him from Black America: the ones who did not want to hear any criticisms of him or his presidency whatsoever, for Barack could do no wrong, even as it became clear to me that he mostly avoided any conversations on race and racism for the duration of his time in the White House. I also grimaced at those who said, repeatedly, that he was not doing anything for Black America, as if he had been elected to be president of Black folks only. I grimaced because Obamacare did indeed help African Americans like my mother, some of the mortgage relief certainly helped Black people, and God knows that Barack granted clemency to more inmates in prison than any president in history and was actually the first sitting American president to visit a prison. So, while there was no way he could just openly shout "Black Power" at White House press conferences, or from Air Force One, it was obvious that he and his team were trying to help Black people, all people, they were trying to be inclusive, in a way we had never seen before.

Yet the sad reality on this tenth anniversary year of Barack Obama's historic election is not much has genuinely changed for the vast majority of Americans. It is not actually his fault, because the president of the United States is fundamentally a mouthpiece or a figurehead position for the power structure of this country. A power structure, many have learned, because of things like the Occupy Wall Street Movement, that is woefully slanted toward the richest 1 percent of our population. Barack did what he could with what he had to use, but the truth is that this is not about the president of the United States at the end of the day. It is about power and privilege, who has it, and who does not. There is nothing inherently wrong with being wealthy. That is not my issue and, heck, I would love to be wealthy myself, as long as my wealth is not earned by stepping on or over my fellow human beings. The issue is we do not, and have never, been a democracy. All people in this land have never been treated equally. Like never. We know what happened to Native Americans, to Africans who were turned into slaves. But we also know that poor Whites have not been treated equally either, or poor people of any background. Nor have we treated women of any race as equals. If we did, if we do, then there would be no need for #MeToo and #TimesUp in the twenty-first century, over two hundred years since the American Revolution. And along the way we have also disparaged Native Americans and the Irish and Jewish and Italian and Polish and German and Japanese and Chinese and Puerto Rican and Mexican people, among many others. We have hated on Arabs, Muslims, the disabled, and we certainly have hated on lesbians, gays, bisexual, transgender, queer people. We have been equal opportunity with our hate, equal opportunity in our reckless disregard for full democracy, with each new era, each new generation, identifying someone new to hate. At the core of what is America is Whiteness, or, rather, heterosexual White maleness. The straight White man, in the main, as the doer of all that is great and noble and good and heroic. This is what we were taught when we were children as we were given the stories of Christopher Columbus discovering America, of George Washington never telling a lie, of Abe Lincoln freeing the slaves, of Woodrow Wilson being the great protector of American democracy during the years that marked World War I. What is conveniently left out, because it would upset the entire narrative of White male power, of White supremacy, is that Columbus and "explorers" like him committed genocide against Indians, that Washington was a slave master who, like other founding father slave masters, hypocritically fought for his independence from the British while denying it to his Black slaves, White women, and any White man who was not wealthy and powerful and privileged like him. And we know that Abraham Lincoln flipped back and forth around the issue of slavery, of freeing Black folks, and finally did so, in some parts of the United States only, when it became politically and militarily clear that he had to. And it is well documented, in his own words, that Lincoln never viewed Black people as the equals of White folks. Meanwhile, Woodrow Wilson, a Southern gentleman, a scholar, the president of Princeton University before being elected to the highest office in the land, was an unapologetic racist who, practically from the moment he got into the White House, worked to re-segregate federal agencies, and would screen the supremely racist film *The Birth of a Nation* in said White House, and was proud of the fact that he was quoted a few times in the movie. This was one hundred years ago, long before Donald Trump became president of the United States. White manhood is mad fragile in our nation, has always been, and by and large has always been defined, at least partially, by its oppression and domination of others. Racism is both the crutch and the weapon of those White men in America who are highly insecure and utterly mediocre, and who fear the power and genius of the others. This is not a fairy tale. This is not a mirage. This is the autobiography of America—

So, as I heard the shock of folks when Trump defeated Hillary Clinton in that November 2016 presidential election, I wondered what history they had read, or not read, which America they had been living in their entire lives. For the rise of Donald Trump and the last stand of angry White men—of angry White people—are not new; for this racism is not new, not even remotely. Nor is this belief system called White supremacy new, either, and nor is it solely confined to people, back then, or now, who are defined as conservatives, as racists, as not believing in the equality of us all. Whenever there have been victories of any kind for Black people, for other people of color, in our America, there is almost an insanely immediate reaction of great discomfort and great backlash. It happened with the Civil Rights Movement, it happened with Barack Obama. It is a sick need to prove superiority, to restore the so-called natural way of things in America, which means White people at the top and the rest of us scrambling at the bottom, evermore. Indeed, what set the table for Donald Trump was the racist backlash to Barack Obama, were those Congressional members who vowed to block anything he did, those Whites in power who fanned the flames of fear by placing blame on immigrants, on movements like Black Lives Matter, who made it seem as if they were more patriotic, as a matter of fact, than any other group in America. For sure it is problematically ironic that Black Lives Matter was birthed during the two terms of the nation's first Black president. For sure I do believe that even the explosion of police and civilian murders of Black bodies was likewise a backlash to the Obama years, be it George Zimmerman gunning down Black teenager Trayvon Martin, or Dylann Roof blowing away Black folks in a prayer circle he had joined in that Charleston, South Carolina, church. These are acts of racial terrorism, designed to create fear, paranoia, a sense of doom. And the Republicans, as toxic as they wanna be, were hellbent on stopping everything President Obama tried to do, even if it meant hurting economically their own White working-class and White middle-class base, because they could simply blame the struggles of those White sisters and brothers on Obama, Obamacare, Mexicans, immigrants, Black people, Muslims, anyone and anything that was—and is—an easy target. Their anger at Obama, at the others, was manufactured, in a sense, and it also was—and is—real. That is why this is, without question, an American tragedy, the presidency of Donald Trump, the leadership of both him and his vice president, Mike Pence, and what all of this has wrought. Quite clearly it was White Americans, rich ones and poor ones, White women and White men, Whites with college educations and Whites with not much schooling at all, who elected Trump. It was his direct and subtle embraces of race and racism and White supremacy—lying through its yellowed teeth that it was patriotism—that made Donald Trump a populist candidate, with his shaming and blaming of the others with the bullets in his perpetually cocked and loaded verbal gun. "Make America Great Again." But the question for us others, always: Make America great again, for whom, precisely, and how? For here is a man who had no prior political experience, no military background, who had declared bankruptcy around his businesses at least a half-dozen times, who is an unabashed racist, an unabashed sexist, and an admitted assaulter of women. But none of this is truth in Trump's America, and they believe they are the victims, these angry White Americans, that someone is trying to take something away from them. Or, put another way, the same angry White conservatives in this nation who attacked President Barack Obama without pause for eight years, even as Barack and Michelle had to be perfect with their public behavior, hypocritically and consistently make excuses and alibis for the toxic words and toxic deeds of Donald Trump. I mean, they called Barack stupid, incompetent, lazy, a liar, a fake US citizen, the "food stamp" president, and, to boot, the worst president ever; and they called Michelle ugly, a gorilla, an ape, and made fun, continually, of the size of her backside, while tossing in, for good measure, thinly veiled references to Michelle actually being a man. But at least we know where they stand, however twisted their logic, however absent their integrity, and however empty their souls.

I say this because I think about what my mother has said to me her entire life, she a product of the American South before the Civil Rights Movement happened, she who has experienced the ugliest kind of racism in both the American South and the American North: "I will take Southern White people any day over Northern White people. At least in the South you know what you are getting." What my mother has been saying, since I was a boy, is that there is not much difference, to her, between a White conservative and a White liberal. That far too many liberals pretend to be progressive, pretend to be about the equality of the human family, then treat you as badly as or worse than White conservatives do. The big difference: White conservatives are brutally honest about it. They talk about building walls to keep out people from "shithole countries"; they call Black women like my mother who are single moms "welfare queens"; they label things like Affirmative Action "quotas"; the coded language for the prison-industrial complex is "law and order." But, again, none of this is new. This has always been the case in America, a battle between different White men for power, this explorer or that explorer, this party or that party, this strip of land or that strip of land, this mogul or that mogul, this ideology or that ideology. When Donald Trump won, I already knew that he would, in spite of his ugly, sexist comments about grabbing women by their _____, and in spite of his crude and vicious attacks on Mexicans, Blacks, Hillary Clinton, and so many others. He comes from the same racism that makes me paranoid, every single day of my life, whenever I leave my home, so paranoid that I may never come back alive, that I retreat to grab my wallet, or at least my driver's license, so that I can be properly identified if something should happen to me at the hands of the police or some White racist, specifically, simply for being a Black male in America. Trump's bravado and racism and sexism may have shaken the very foundation of legions of White liberals, but it was not a surprise to any of us, me, my mother, people like us, who have had to survive this sort of political and emotional and spiritual molestation our entire lives.

Additionally, Barry Goldwater spit this very same kind of racism and hate and fearmongering when he was the Republican nominee for president way back in 1964. Back then he was called an extremist. But a mere four years later the Republican Richard Nixon was elected president speaking a slightly modified version of Goldwater's vocabulary. Indeed, it was in 1968, when Bobby Kennedy was running for president, as a Democrat, that you saw a White male leader, in the form of Bobby, able to speak to and link the struggles of Black and White and Latinx and other communities, which was revolutionary, and transcendent. I do believe if Bobby had lived, he could have stopped the rush of White Southerners—"Dixiecrats"—from the Democratic Party to the Republican Party, that visionary leaders like him could have prevented the Reagan Revolution, the Tea Party, the alt-right. And we know that the Reagan Revolution effectively drew a line in the sand between Democrats and Republicans, that with Reagan's campaign and his eight years in office there were wholesale attacks on the Civil Rights Movement, on voting rights, on the rights of women to control their own bodies, a movement so powerful that it has literally gone on from Reagan to Trump, and in between affected the way Democratic presidents Bill Clinton and Barack Obama both campaigned and governed: squarely from the center, and more often than not reacting

to the Republican conservative crusade rather than laying out a clear
and proactive Democratic agenda. That is also because both parties
are largely now controlled by money and power and privilege, not by
the American people. What we have had all these many years since
Dr. King and Bobby Kennedy is this back-and-forth dance between
Democrats and Republicans with the American citizens caught in the
middle and pitted against each other. To quote my friend Antonio Tijerino, head of the Hispanic Heritage Foundation, "One party is mean,
and the other party is weak." We know this to be fact, because we see
and feel it every single day. I know this to be fact because I have traveled this country extensively, all fifty states, big cities and small towns,
huge highways and lonely backroads, speaking, organizing, writing,
interviewing people. I see and hear and feel the many subcultures and
dialects and attitudes. I see and hear and feel people who are just like
my mother, even if she is Black and they are not: they work hard, they
want what is best for their families, their children, and many, like my
mother, have various kinds of prejudices born of an educational system
and mass media culture that reduces learning and critical thinking to
soundbites, and a few basic "facts," and not much else. And there goes
the direction of the American political system, too. This is why, when
I have studied closely the speeches and press conferences of Ronald
Reagan, George H. W. Bush, Bill Clinton, George W. Bush, Barack
Obama, and, yes, Donald Trump, I find many of the same words and
phrases, remixed only slightly depending on if that particular president
was a Democrat or a Republican. Because this is not really about the
American people, this is really about a system that is built to protect
a few at the expense of the rest of us. A system that often pits races
and cultures and identities against each other, that has taught many

to be racist, or sexist, or classist, or homophobic and transphobic, or religiously hateful, or anti-immigrant, or just plain disrespectful and dismissive of the disabled. Even my ma has echoed such language when she has said, throughout my life, very foul and ugly things about Latinx, or immigrants, or queer people. That they are coming to get us. That they are taking our jobs. That they are living in sin and going to hell. That it is us against them. . . .

I submit that those White men drunk with power and privilege in America have always been angry, have always been violent, have always created one form of us versus them when necessary, to keep people at each other's throats, to keep themselves in power. I submit that when the others have challenged these types of White men, that we are the ones who have been labeled the problem, crazy, angry, because people with power rooted in hate and fear and violence and ignorance and division have always got to mark their spaces, have always got to tell you who you are, in the vilest manner possible. I think what makes Donald Trump a shock to at least half of America is that he is so raw and so uncensored and so self-centered that he appears to be an aberration when he truly is not. When I think of Donald Trump, I think of that White male principal my mother met with at that Jersey City grade school, he who clearly detested the Black and Latinx and Asian children who were integrating his building in the 1970s, and told her, because he did not understand me, and did not want to understand me, that I would end up on the streets "with the rest of them." I think of the White male gym teacher just a couple of years later, at that same grade school, who felt the need to inform me, a twelve-year-old Black boy, that I had a chip on my shoulder because I dared to walk around the school with my head up, dared to know, as my mother had taught me, that I was smart, that someone needed to knock that chip off my shoulder henceforth, inferring that it would be him. I think of the White male Jersey City police officer, on that unlucky Winter day when I was fifteen, who came with his partner onto that Bergen Avenue bus, to break up the fight between myself and a Puerto Rican boy named Richie, and who carefully placed the White-skinned Richie in the front seat of the squad car, un-handcuffed, while I was thrown, hands cuffed behind me, into the backseat; how when I complained and refused to be quiet when the White officer barked for me to shut my mouth and he, all two hundred–plus pounds of him, balled his beefy fist and smashed me in the face, bloodying my nose and the entire front of my body. Yes, I think of Donald Trump's father, who might have participated at a Ku Klux Klan recruitment rally in the 1920s, in Queens, New York, where The Donald was born, and who was for sure sued for racism and housing discrimination in the 1970s. I think of the Donald Trump I remember seeing over and over again on television in the 1980s and the 1990s, forever bragging about his wealth, his many women, his children, his kiss-the-sky constructions in New York City. Oh yes, I recall the Donald Trump who spectacularly made himself into judge, jury, and executioner of the Central Park Five, teenage Black and Latinx boys falsely accused of raping a White woman jogger, who then each spent time in jail, until the real rapist admitted it was him, and they were released, years later; and how to this day Trump has never apologized for publicly destroying these young men's lives. But, again, this sort of White male behavior is not new, nor is it restricted to a catastrophic president like Trump.

As I have watched the solemn yet brave march of women in Hollywood, the media, politics, the arts, in academia, in the sports world, and corporate America stepping forward to proclaim #MeToo, what has not been lost on me is the number of liberal or progressive White men they are accusing, very powerful White men, who have raped and molested and harassed and discriminated against or alienated so many of these women. I honestly never thought I would ever witness something like this, where White men in power would be challenged in this way. What is also not lost on me is that #MeToo was created by a Black woman, Tarana Burke, a decade or so before this began, or that Anita Hill, another Black woman, long ago pioneered challenging sexism publicly, when she dared to speak out against then–Supreme Court nominee Clarence Thomas, a Black man, in 1991. But it seems that sexism does not matter to some unless it is White women speaking out against it, as if Black women and other women of color, like my mother, have not experienced these attacks on their persons their entire lives. This is not to take away from the very real and tragic stories I have read and heard about, including from women I know, like my friend Annabella Sciorra, the actress, who alleges she was raped by Harvey Weinstein and had her career methodically undermined in the aftermath. I cannot even imagine what it is like to be a woman of any race, now that I am fully aware of my own journey as a man, to have to do battle with sexism every single day of your life, in some form. The way Black people feel like we have to brace ourselves, every single day of our lives, for some sort of racist assault on our humanity, be it big or small—an assault is an assault. Donald Trump and his election, ironically, may be the best thing that has happened to America, to American women, because in the wake of his words, "grab them by their _____," we have had Women's Marches across the country and worldwide, and the explosion of #MeToo and its follow-up #TimesUp, and more women than ever looking to run for political office.

Yet still there are two things I think about as all of this unfolds. First, what about women, women of color, like my mother, who are working-class, who do not have the privilege and the platform to speak out and against oppression, what happens to them, who will speak for and honor and celebrate them, not just in these accelerated public moments, but when they are in their senior buildings, in their beauty salons, at their fast-food restaurants, working in the homes of the wealthy, as they push well-to-do White children around in strollers in the Brooklyns of America? And will these White women who are speaking out so boldly also be willing to look at their own privilege, their race privilege and their class privilege, will they rethink, as they challenge these men, how they view people of color, how they view poor people, how they view women like my mother, how they treat the nannies who care for their children, the housekeepers who clean their homes, the many women, the many working-class women, who make them go as they live these super-charged lives in Hollywood, in politics, in corporate America, in sports, in the media, in the arts? I am asking, as they fight for their own equality, do they really view women of color like my mother, like my Aunt Cathy, like my Aunt Birdie, like my late Aunt Pearlie Mae, like my dear and departed Grandma Lottie, as their equals, even though these women will never travel in the same spaces and places as them? I recall, a few years ago, participating in a march and rally on New York City's affluent Upper East Side, organized by the great Taiwanese American activist, Ai-jen Poo, and the group she founded, the National Domestic Workers Alliance. The protest was about the rights of these mostly women of color workers to receive basic job benefits and fair wages. The march started off peacefully enough, but before you knew it White women in allegedly liberal New York City were yelling and cursing at these women, at all of us protesters, as we walked through their neighborhood. It was not a good look. The same kind of White women, I am sure, who are now saying #MeToo and #TimesUp as loud as they possibly can. Take care of our children, take care of our homes, but do not ask us to take care of you—

Or, second, I have wondered, as we have seen men halted in their tracks upon accusations of sexual violence in some form, why has this not happened with systemic racism in the four hundred years that Black folks have been in America, given how much nonstop violence and harassment we have faced? Why has there never, like never, been the same massive reaction, the same challenges where the guilty or the accused have been forced to come clean, to resign, to leave careers behind, in the wake of their racist abuse of us? Is it because White women, no matter how at odds they may be with White men today because of this new movement, are still viewed, by and large, as pure, as sacred, as more valuable and beautiful than any other group in America? White women, and the very fragile manhood of White men, we know from history, were the reason why a Black boy, fourteen-year-old Emmett Till, was ripped from a bed in the dead of night while visiting his kinfolk in Mississippi, by White men beyond angry that he allegedly whistled or said something inappropriate to a White woman in that Mississippi town he was visiting; therefore, they had to teach him a lesson: they beat him so savagely his face was destroyed, one of his eyes was dislodged from its socket, his head an unshapely and lumpy water balloon, a fan tied about his neck with barbed wire, and there he lay, dead, in a river, with a bullet hole in his head, for good measure. Because that White woman's words were more valuable than Emmett Till's life.

Thus, until people who are outraged by the injustices done to them feel equally the injustices done to others, nothing will ever be permanently transformed in our America. The system will remain as it is, there will be some changes, just as there have been changes since that day—August 28, 1963—when my mother celebrated her twentieth birthday in that wooden shack in South Carolina as Dr. King was giving his majestic "I Have a Dream" speech. I can certainly see and feel the progress from my grandparents to my mother to me. This, for me, is not even about being a Democrat or a Republican, or a liberal or conservative. I care about what kind of human being I am, what kind of human being you are. I care about and love who I am as a Black person, as an African person, yes, and I care about and love who I am as a member of the human family, too. It is not an either/or, for me, it is both. I have the right to claim all my identities, and so do you. But I also know I have a deep responsibility, rooted in the chaos of this nation from the very beginning, to know who I am, to honor who I am, and to also be unafraid to get to know you, too, if you happen to be different from me. A great and longtime friend of mine, Lauren Summers, challenged me many years back, by asking if I wanted to be a bridge builder or a bridge destroyer. I was stumped by the audacity of the question, but she was saying to me, very bluntly, that I could not be both. Either I was going to walk this earth with peace and love, or I was going to walk this earth with violence and hate. It took me a long while to understand her question, the depths of it, but I do, I really do, more than ever. I think, for example, if the many White sisters who are stepping up to say #MeToo really are serious about ending oppression, then they must also be serious about listening to voices and stories of women like my mother, too. They must also be serious about following the leadership of Black women, of women of color, since these women's very lives—as Gloria Steinem has proclaimed—are the origins of American feminism. That is what democracy looks like, equals, yes, but also having the humility and dignity to listen to those who have been victimized by whatever power and privilege you might have. I no longer want to debate White people of any background or identity about racism. In America, you benefit because of your skin color simply because you are White. You have both historical and present-day benefits. So, the questions: What are you going to do, to challenge that, in your White communities, within your White families? What are you doing to educate or re-educate yourself not to be racist, not to be so fragile, as a White person regardless of your gender or gender identity, so that you do not get bent out of shape any time a person of color says anything that challenges the very real White supremacy that permeates every corner of America, and this world? Or do you actually believe, sister, brother, fellow human being, that White supremacy is only something that is owned by racist right wingers who show up in places like Berkeley, California, or Charlottesville, Virginia, to spread violence and fear and hate? No, it is a mind-set that we are speaking of, just like sexism is a mind-set, like classism is a mind-set, and I wonder, my gosh, how my dear mother is even still standing, having lived through all of this? Or, better yet, it makes sense why she has been sick, because this all breaks you down eventually, if there is no movement to examine and understand, to practice self-care, to heal. And why would my mother not be angry, why would she not be mean, why would she not be defensive and defiant, and why would she not regard her one-bedroom apartment as her own little government, as her one safe space in the world, as Michelle and Barack and that White Jesus look at her and protect her from all of this?

At the end of the day, I simply cannot erase my skin color even as I am clear I have to challenge sexism and classism and homophobia and transphobia and all forms of hate and oppression, always, within myself. What I am saying is that even within our different marginalized groups, there remains, still, a very real skin-color hierarchy. And while that goes on, that tiny minority that controls everything continues to hoard its power and its privilege, and it continues to dictate to the rest of us what we can and cannot do, who we can and cannot be. Because, again, this is so much bigger than who is president of the United States. Because this is so much bigger than the Democratic Party or the Republican Party. This is so much bigger than Donald Trump ever getting impeached and us winding up with the equally problematic Mike Pence. This is about the very soul of America, which way forward, or do we remain stuck, or do we continue to drift backward?

In other words, it should be basic for any human being to know that that love is better than hate, peace is better than violence, knowledge is better than ignorance, courage and compassion are better than fear, and a healthy respect for difference is always better than just tolerating people. If nothing else Barack Obama's presidential run in 2008 re-

vealed, if just for the months of that historic campaign, what we could
be when the best of who we are come together for a common purpose.
When there is love and compassion and kindness and nonviolence and
peace and a vision for the human family, when we are coming together,
not fighting or destroying each other. This is what both Martin Luther King Jr. and Bobby Kennedy were talking about fifty long years
ago. For Martin, it was called The Poor People's Campaign, because
he understood what Americans had in common, and MLK also understood that if we did not help people economically, then their lives
would continue to be torn asunder, and they would continue to be divided from others because of race, because of geography, because of
the political manipulations of those with power. Indeed, those very
same poor and struggling middle-class White Americans who voted
for Donald Trump are the very same poor and struggling middle-class
White Americans who were listening to Bobby Kennedy in the last
years of his life, including his ill-fated crusade for president in 1968.
Like Trump, Bobby was a wealthy White man, he had a father who
was super-wealthy, he came from privilege. And like Trump, Bobby
had been contaminated, in his early years, with a lust for power, driven
by ego and, yes, anger. But when his brother, President John F. Kennedy, was assassinated on national television in 1963, a mere three
months after Dr. King's "I Have a Dream" speech, something shifted
dramatically and spiritually for Bobby. For the first time in his life,
he could empathize with the trauma and pain of the others, in the far
reaches of his soul. Bobby found the compassion and kindness and
love that Dr. King and the Civil Rights Movement had been putting
forth all along. Both Martin and Bobby, by 1968, sought a progres-

sive, multicultural, multigenerational movement, one rooted in love, yes, one rooted in we the people, yes, the people's movement. But tragically, when King was killed in April 1968 and Kennedy in June of that year, those lower- and middle-class people were either abandoned or forgotten. If they were Black and other people of color, they became what has been called a permanent underclass, locked in America's most neglected communities; if they were White, and regardless of where they lived, they were scooped up and transformed into right-wing Republicans by the Reagan Revolution, the revolution that has led us straight to Donald Trump; if any race, they have witnessed factories closing across America, jobs and opportunities drying up, while the rich continue to get richer; if any race, like my mother, they have spent their entire lives surviving paycheck to paycheck, then Social Security check to Social Security check, life reduced to bills, failing health, and holding tightly to any beliefs and any values that provide a glimmer of hope for a better tomorrow.

This is why Barack Obama touched many in 2008. This is why both Bernie Sanders and Donald Trump touched many in 2016. Yes, I am putting their three names together because whether we like it or not, what they have in common, besides being men in an America that sorely needs a major infusion of women's leadership more than ever, is the fact that they made it plain, as Malcolm X said, in the way they related to people while campaigning. They said what people felt, they said what people needed to hear. This is why, even with their many shortcomings, it suggests a different path for American leaders. This is why, I believe, people in America rejected both the Bush and Clinton political dynasties in 2016. People are tired of business as usual, the same recycled political speak, the same names and faces, no matter how well-intentioned. Polar opposites, yes, but Bernie Sanders and Donald Trump represent truth-telling to their followers. My issue with both Sanders and Trump is that their followers by and large neither include nor mirror people like my mother and me. Moreover, that truth-telling has got to be rooted in what is best for all people, not just some people. That truth-telling has got to be about healing people, not hurting people. That truth-telling cannot be limited to when politicians are campaigning, nor is it just American politics that needs to be transformed. Most importantly, we need a new kind of American and global leadership, whether someone holds a political office or not. For sure, it cannot just be an endless line of people running for political office—women, people of color, LGBTQ people, disabled Americans, others. No. There is a reason why countless people detest and do not trust politicians. There has to be that radical revolution of values Dr. King spoke of in this nation, where people come first, not power and privilege; where there is opportunity for all people, not career moves and relationships that only benefit a few; where people matter more than things, where people matter more than sporting events, where we do not continue to prop up symbols that do not translate into justice for all. We know that Donald Trump and people like him do not truly care about everyday people, about everyday Americans. What they care about is power, money, control, the blame game, bullying, and classic divide-and-conquer politics. Thus, these beautiful but angry people that I have encountered in places like Texas and Kansas and upstate New York, that I have even encountered in allegedly liberal places like Los Angeles and New York City, have allowed the hate and fear to fester so much inside of them—blaming the others—that they vote against their own economic interest time and time again. I do know that there are reasons why folks like these do not trust Hillary and Bill Clinton; I do know that there are reasons why folks like these were up in arms when Hillary Clinton referred to them as "deplorables"; there are reasons why they will never abandon Donald Trump or angry White men like him: it is because they are being spoken to in a way that matters to them, and because how they are being spoken to reaffirms what they have been taught their entire lives about race, about gender, about what is America, about what America is not. Like my mother, they know no other way, see no other world. And, like my mother, they hold dear to their values, to their Christian values, and, like her, they believe in and fear God, and they are certain America is a Christian nation, and has always been. But I do not believe that the God my mother worships is the same God that these angry White Americans worship. My mother's God does not support the hate of any people, does not deny people the right to vote, does not openly embrace hate and White supremacy, nor does my mother's God tell women what they can and cannot do with their bodies. What these angry White Americans do have in common with people like my mother is fear, without question. As courageous as my mother has been my entire life, there is also no denying the terror she feels every single day she watches the news, the terror she has felt her entire life, simply because of who she is. But the huge difference is that my mother does not go out and try to destroy people, with practice, with laws and policy, with hate, with violence, with ugly, hostile marches and rallies, with domestic terrorism in one form or another. My mother sits in her senior citizen apartment, she waits dutifully each month for her Social Security check, she pays the few bills that she has on time, she never misses voting in elections of any kind, and I do believe that my mother feels in her heart that America is the best place for her, and I do believe my mother will forever love and dream America, in spite of how our nation has treated her, and people like her.

That said, the final point is that in half an American century we've gone from the Kennedys and Dr. King to Barack Obama and Donald Trump and all the president's strangely diabolical men and women, and it doesn't feel good, it makes my mother uncomfortable, makes her wonder what is next after all she has seen. She talks regularly about the shortness of life, she reminds me constantly, much to my discomfort, that she will not be here forever, that she is tired, but likewise my mother urges me to keep my life together. Ma knows life ain't easy for no one, especially no one who comes from where we come from, who are people like us, the others, seemingly banished to the invisible corners of the American Dream. I hear my mother loud and clear because the past few years have been some of the harshest of my life. In spite of regular exercise, as much sleep as I can get, and being super health conscious and a vegan with my diet, I have felt an exhaustion, these past few years, like I have never felt before. The weight of it has worn me down, physically, mentally, spiritually. I have had great highs with my work and opportunities, and I have had great disappointments in my interactions with people of various backgrounds, in person, online, via cell phone. Sometimes it was the other person, sometimes it was me. Honestly, in the midst of this Trump era I have thought long and hard about my old hurts, any of my negative feelings about people, why this person or that person and I no longer talk, what could possibly be so bad that people are divided from each other, given the monumental task now before us in America, to help save a people, a nation, that ostensibly has no clue how to do so.

But there are clues, and I do have hope no matter what, and those clues and that hope rest with elders like my mother, and they rest with the multicultural army of young people, those young people here today and those young people not yet born. I see that hope with youth like Emma Gonzalez, David Hogg, Jaclyn Corin, Sarah Chadwick, Cameron Kasky, Alex Wind, and Alfonso Calderon of Florida declaring loudly, boldly, fearlessly "never again" and organizing monumental resistance to gun violence and the NRA and mass shootings and shootings of all kinds in a way we have not witnessed young people leading and organizing since I was a youth myself in the 1980s and participated in the American and global anti-apartheid movement and New York City street protests against police brutality. I see that hope with the mostly White youth I was with in North Carolina at Charlotte Country Day School, just a day or two after Donald Trump was elected. There was a joy, a longing, a feeling, a shining in their eyes, amongst these young people born in the 2000s, that there can be a different sort of world, that there must be a different sort of world. I see that hope with the young men of color I was with in Washington State days before Donald Trump was elected—African American, Latinx, Asian, Native American, Arab—as they shared their dreams, their sorrow songs, their stresses, their anxieties, and, yes, their fears. There was a joy, a longing, a feeling, a shining in their eyes, too. And these Washington State boys, like those girls and boys in North Carolina, as they talked with me, as they asked me the hard questions, as they sought a safe space to be themselves, to be free, whatever that means for them, are holding on to something they may not even see in many of us adults, that they can barely see in themselves sometimes due to the clutter of tech gadgets and social media and messages and symbols bombarding them from every direction. It is what my mother had in her when she was that young Black girl playing in her skinless front yard of rural South Carolina a lifetime ago, as sweat beads peppered her nose and the sun's greasy hands tamed and twisted and braided her hair, that somehow and some way, she, we, the rainbow children, gonna make a way out of no way, that we did not come this far just to give up now—

Acknowledgments

Thank you to Rakesh Satyal, Loan Le, Suzanne Donahue, Peter Borland, Judith Curr, Kitt Reckord-Mabicka, Albert Tang, and Atria Books/Simon & Schuster for the support of this project. That boost truly means a lot to me. Also, I must thank the very brilliant Michael Cohen and Katerina Nunez for adding your keen editorial eyes to this particular book journey. A salute as well to the collective genius of Michael Scott Jones (book cover photographer), Sarah Elaz (book cover model), and Kerry DeBruce (book cover designer) for making the vision in a dream of mine a reality—all of you are rock stars.

I also want to acknowledge the following media outlets where versions of these pieces were first published: "Letter to a Young Man" (originally published in *Utne Reader*, June 2016); "Will Racism Ever End? Will I Ever Stop Being a Nigger?" (originally published in *Utne Reader*, March 2016); "The Day Our Prince Died" (originally published in *HuffPost*, April 2016); "A Letter to Tupac Shakur" (originally published in *Biography.com*, June 2017); "Why Is Baltimore Burning?" (originally published in *HuffPost*, June 2015); "Cam Newton, and the Killing of a Mockingbird" (originally published in *HuffPost* in 2 parts, January 2017); "The Liner Notes for the A Tribe Called Quest Greatest Hits Album That Never Happened" (originally published in *Complex*, November 2016); "JAY-Z and the Remaking of His Manhood. Or, The Crumpled and Forgotten Freedom Papers of Mr. Shawn Carter." (originally published in *Biography.com*, September 2017); "Me and Muhammad Ali" (originally published in ESPN's *The Undefeated* as "Ali: hero to a young black boy," June 2016); "Hamilton, O.J. Simpson, Orlando, Gun Violence, and What the 4th of July, Alton Sterling, Philando Castile, and the Dallas and Baton Rouge Police Shootings Mean to Me" (originally published in *Utne Reader*, July 2016); "Prodigy and the America That Raised Him" (originally published on National Public Radio (NPR), June 2017); "Re-defining Manhood: Harvey Weinstein and how his toxic manhood is our toxic manhood, too" (originally published in *The Baffler*, October 2017).

Bio

A writer, activist, and public speaker, Kevin Powell is the author of thirteen books, including his critically acclaimed autobiography, *The Education of Kevin Powell: A Boy's Journey into Manhood*. That autobiography is currently being adapted for the screen. Kevin's next book will be a long-awaited biography of Tupac Shakur, the global hip-hop and pop culture icon. As a journalist, essayist, political and cultural critic, and blogger, Kevin's work has appeared in a range of publications, including *British GQ*, *Utne Reader*, *Medium*, *HuffPost*, the *New York Times*, the *Washington Post*, *Esquire*, *Newsweek*, *The Baffler*, *Ebony*, *Essence*, *Vibe*, the *Guardian* (in London, England), *The Sunday Times Magazine* (in London, England), *CNN*, *Complex*, and *ESPN*. He is also the host of a podcast, *One on One with Kevin Powell*. As an activist and humanitarian, he is cofounder of BK Nation, an American organization focused on civil and human rights and opportunity for all people. And as a speaker, Kevin has lectured widely, at colleges, corporations, and various kinds of institutions and governments, in America, Asia, Africa, and Europe. You can follow him on Twitter, @kevin_powell, or email him, kevin@kevinpowell.net.